JUDGING
SCHOOL DISCIPLINE

The Crisis of
Moral Authority

Richard Arum

HARVARD UNIVERSITY PRESS

Cambridge, Massachusetts

London, England · 2003

Library of Congress Cataloging-in-Publication Data

Arum, Richard.
Judging school discipline : the crisis of moral authority / Richard Arum.
p. cm.
Includes bibliographical references and index.
ISBN 0-674-01179-1 (alk.paper)
1. Moral education—United States.
2. School discipline—Law and legislation—United States.
3. Education—Social aspects—United States.   I. Title.

LC311.A78 2003
370.11′4—dc21   2003050864

JUDGING SCHOOL DISCIPLINE

Contents

Preface

On October 31, 1991, in my fourth year of teaching English at Castlemont High School in Oakland, California, one of my students was shot three times at lunch in the courtyard next to my classroom. The student survived the assault, but the incident, which would have been viewed as a tragic aberration in some suburban schools, at Castlemont was greeted with neither surprise nor disbelief, only dismay. In the Fall semester of that year, students had already fired guns on at least three other occasions in nearby Oakland public schools. Castlemont High School was particularly plagued with disorder, with teachers and students physically threatened and classroom instruction often interrupted. As an educator and building representative for the teachers' union, I felt deeply troubled and pedagogically and politically responsible for the unacceptable educational environment at that institution. Despite much well-intentioned student, teacher, administrator, and community attention to school problems, we were not able collectively to identify and implement solutions that would improve the school's climate. While the school community discussed the merits of metal detectors, increased uniformed police presence on campus, and a plan to build an impenetrable wall around the school, even proponents of these authoritarian measures acknowledged the undesirability and inadequacies of the proposed remedies.

During that year of endemic violence and disorder at Castlemont High School, many teachers at the site were equally concerned with a more fundamental institutional shortcoming. The school was doing a poor job of educating and socializing youth. Few students were trained to enter the labor market (traditional vocational education programs had been decimated in California during the fiscal crises of the 1980s, and only a handful of new vocational-academic programs existed at the school to compensate for their loss); and at best, just a dozen students in each graduating class went on to attend four-year colleges. The extent of the problem was documented in government data collected by the National Center for Educational Statistics for the 1991–92 academic year: Castlemont High had 511 ninth graders, 448 tenth graders, 276 eleventh graders, and 195 twelfth graders. Some of the students lost between ninth and twelfth grade may have transferred and completed high school elsewhere, but many more simply dropped out of school and were thus at high risk for lives characterized by unemployment, incarceration, and poverty.

The school's failure was not just a matter of educational achievement, but also of its inability to foster moral development and successfully socialize youth in its charge. The high school, for example, received renewed attention two years after the shooting, when students on a field trip to a screening of *Schindler's List* got thrown out of the theater for "laughing raucously at depictions of Nazis murdering Jews" (*San Francisco Examiner;* January 25, 1994). The ensuing controversy inappropriately focused national attention on students' inadequate historical knowledge of the Holocaust and anti-Semitism, rather than on the more pertinent matter of the school's failure to promote moral development and socialization. To be sure, some students remained immune to the flaws of this educational setting. Thuy Thi Nguyen, for example, went on to complete an undergraduate degree at Yale, received a law school degree at the University of California Los Angeles, and is now successfully working in public interest educational law in the Bay Area. But these anomalous successes simply suggest the extent to which the school settings emphasized in this book are clearly not the sole determinant of individual educational outcomes. Nevertheless, many other students predictably fared less well than Nguyen.

In recent years, the life-course trajectory of one of my best students has been the most troubling outcome I have grappled with in thinking about the consequences of inadequate school-based socialization. Andrew was originally one of the school's rare success stories. In high school I worked closely with him, sponsoring a club devoted to promoting citizenship (the Junior Statesmen of America), in which both Thuy Thi Nguyen and he served as active participants and leaders. We read together in English class works with strong moral themes by writers such as Bertolt Brecht, Langston Hughes, Zora Neale Hurston, Toni Morrison, Jean Paul Sartre, Alice Walker, August Wilson, Richard Wright, and others. Andrew always stood out as one of the most sensitive, articulate, and insightful in address-ing these works. He finished high school with a 3.67 grade point average and was named Most Likely to Succeed in the high school yearbook; he then enrolled in the University of California, Davis.

Two years after finishing high school, Andrew was spending an evening with his pregnant sister's boyfriend, who had been previously convicted of shooting an individual during an armed robbery in Oakland in 1990. The events have been well chronicled in Andy Furillo's insightful piece, "From Mean Streets to Student Whiz—then Murder?" (*The Sacramento Bee;* July 9, 1995). Although Andrew had no prior criminal record, he willingly joined his sister's boyfriend in an armed robbery spree that culminated in the murder of an unarmed 29-year-old Sacramento resident. Andrew's sis-ter and her boyfriend later used the victim's credit card at a Longs Drugs Store (Andrew's workplace) to buy two hundred dollars worth of pots, pans, deodorant, disposable diapers, baby wipes, spatulas, a spoon, a blow-dryer, an iron, and a receiving blanket; purchases which led to their subse-quent arrest. From prison, Andrew later wrote the following note:

> Dear Family of Slain Victim,
>
> Late Thursday night, me and my partner approached James (I only know his first name/not meaning any disrespect). A terrible crime was committed moments later. Although I was not the one to pull the trigger, nor have any idea that it would happen, I am still to blame also. I just want you to know I would never kill anyone. I have had loved ones taken from me and I wouldn't want anyone to go through that type of pain. However, it has al-ready happened. I had no idea. I'm sorry. I just want you to know I feel hor-rible. Most likely more so than the person that actually did it.
>
> Sorry,
> Andrew

When the reporter, Andy Furillo, asked in a jailhouse interview whether Andrew had thoughts about the outcome of his criminal case, he replied: "I've asked God for forgiveness. I feel he's forgiven me. It doesn't matter what the outcome is, as long as God has forgiven me."

In the state of California, pleading guilty to involvement in an armed robbery where a murder occurred is not likely to produce a good outcome. Despite his exceptional academic promise and regardless of having no prior criminal record, Andrew is currently serving a life-term sentence without possibility of parole at California State Prison Corcoran for his participation in the events. Some people may view Andrew's situation primarily as an indictment of recent changes in California laws that have imposed stiff penalties and limited judicial discretion in sentencing; I have struggled with more personal questions. How did I as an educator fail this gifted student? What is wrong with our schools, when the "best and brightest" students have failed to be socialized to know better than to participate, even indirectly, in the activities that transpired that night?

Given the tragic potential consequences of our failure to socialize youth properly for conventional societal roles—a task for which the schools must nowadays assume the lion's share of the burden—we must have the courage as citizens and scholars to put aside ideological predispositions and recognize that a crisis in the legitimacy of school discipline and related problems in youth socialization are the central issues facing American public schools today. *Judging School Discipline* makes such a case.

I began teaching in the Oakland public schools in 1988, after a history of political activism in college (a history that at one point—following a protest of CIA recruitment on campus during the Contra War—subjected me and several of my peers to an administrative hearing threatening campus expulsion), and worked there through 1993. Why Oakland in particular? Although I had grown up in a privileged East Coast family and suburban environment, I had also had personal contact with Muhammad Ali in the years following his resistance to the Vietnam War draft, and thus had early exposure to and developed admiration for African-American struggles for civil rights.

In the academic year 1990–91, Castlemont High School in East Oakland, California, was 99.5 percent nonwhite, enrolling 1,233 African-American students, 139 Hispanic students, 51 Asian-American students and 7 white students (National Center for Educational Statistics, 1996). According to the 1990 Population Census, the census tract where the school was located had 29.8 percent of individuals living below poverty level; 37.6 percent of individuals over age 18 had not graduated from high school, and only 4.2 percent of individuals over age 18 held a bachelor's degree or higher.

I ask questions about school discipline, moral authority, and socialization in my research today, because as a teacher I learned that these were the core problems facing American public education. Following my teaching experience in Oakland, I entered a graduate program in Sociology at the University of California at Berkeley to develop expertise in empirical analysis in order to address these issues. In my first semester I surveyed students at Castlemont High School on their attitudes toward school discipline, and continued to ruminate about these matters over the following years. At Berkeley, my sociological imagination in general and ideas for this project in particular developed primarily through the generous intellectual mentorship provided by Neil Fligstein and Mike Hout.

I began formally developing the project after arriving at the University of Arizona in 1996. Initial seed money for the project came from the University of Arizona's Social and Behavioral Sciences Research Institute, directed by Woody Powell. The research for this project was subsequently funded externally through the National Science Foundation's Program in Social and Behavioral Sciences (SBR-9807450) and the National Academy of Education—Spencer Foundation's Post-doctoral Fellowship Program. This external support allowed me to work full time in the 1998–99 academic year on the research, as well as to attach a team of talented graduate students to the project. Their work was essential, given the scale and scope of the empirical research undertaken—including reading 6,277 court cases, coding them by content, as well as examining and combining multiple data sets on students, teachers, administrators, schools, and states. The graduate students working with me were also involved in writing initial drafts of the empirical chapters. Irenee Beattie's involvement, in particular, was critical, as she co-authored two of the empirical chapters. While I take full responsibility for the research design and conceptual framework for the project as a whole, Beattie was mainly responsible for writing Chapters 2 and 3, and contributed important intellectual insights to the conceptualizations. Chapter 4 combined Richard Pitt's work on corporal punishment and Jennifer Thompson's research on student, teacher, and administrator reports of school discipline. Chapter 5 benefited from the research efforts of Sandra Way.

At the University of Arizona's Sociology Department, I enjoyed talking about this project with Woody Powell and Paula England as well as many other colleagues there at the time. Sherry Enderle provided essential expertise in the financial administration of the grants. The research benefited from comments from faculty audiences at Stanford University School of Education; New York University's School of Education and Department of Sociology; University of California at Los Angeles Department of Sociology; Duke University Department of Sociology; University of Arizona

School of Law; Ohio State University Department of Sociology, and meetings organized by the National Academy of Education.

As the project developed, colleagues from other universities provided helpful formal or informal comments guiding the research. John Meyer in particular was influential. Nella Van Dyke made useful suggestions, contributions, and support for the writing of Chapters 2 and 3. Peter McCabe at the United States Department of Education Office of Civil Rights provided access to archival records; Aurora D'Amico provided assistance in securing access to restricted Department of Education data.

The work for this project was completed at New York University, after my arrival in Fall 2000. Here I am particularly indebted to Doug Guthrie for continuing conversations—begun in graduate school—on the project and the discipline of sociology more generally. Dalton Conley, Marc Scott, Jon Zimmerman, and graduate students participating in a seminar on the Sociology of Educational Law also made helpful comments and insights that improved final iterations of the work. At New York University, administrative support was given by Lucy Frazier as well as Lisa Bernhard, Ann Gannon, and Tom Lynch; Lizzie Anderson and Patricia Chow provided editorial and research assistance. At Harvard University Press I am grateful to Elizabeth Knoll for her faith in the project and her useful editorial suggestions for the manuscript, as well as to Anita Safran for her careful attention to my prose.

Most of all, in completing this project, I am indebted to Kelly McGehee, who by example taught me how to embrace beauty and truth in the act of creative production. My children, Eero and Zora, have served as inspirations throughout; my parents and siblings, as well as the family of public educators I joined through marriage, have been steadfast in their support and encouragement.

—R.A.

JUDGING SCHOOL DISCIPLINE

1

Questioning
School Authority

The aim of education is, precisely, the socialization of the human
being; the process of education, therefore, gives us in a nutshell
the historical fashion in which the social being is constituted. The
unremitting pressure to which the child is subjected is the very
pressure of the social milieu which tends to fashion him in its own
image, and of which parents and teachers are merely the representatives and intermediaries.

—EMILE DURKHEIM, *RULES OF SOCIOLOGICAL
METHOD* (1895)

The current focus of educational research on improving cognitive development, measured often narrowly by standardized test score performance,
has distracted attention away from other critical problems associated with
contemporary schooling in this country. While educational achievement
in many public schools certainly leaves ample room for improvement,
discipline and student socialization also have often been ineffective and
clearly are a cause of widespread public anxiety. Our research focuses on
these issues and examines in detail the extent to which judicial court decisions have been one factor that has affected public school discipline.

In recent years, there has been academic debate over the extent to which
low educational achievement in public schools should be qualified as a crisis. The optimists have noted that in the past two decades more students
were likely to finish high school and develop basic literacy and mathematic
skills. Whereas in the 1950s only 60 percent of students finished high
school, by the end of the twentieth century close to 90 percent of students
finished secondary school.[1] At century's end, we had come closer to providing basic educational training for all than ever before in the country's
history. Hence educational researchers David Berliner and Bruce Biddle

concluded that public schools suffered more from inflated expectations and distorted perceptions of their performance than from any fundamental pedagogical problems.[2]

We are skeptical of Berliner and Biddle's claim that no serious problems face American public schooling and that a crisis has simply been manufactured by political interests hostile to public education. If there is a crisis in American schooling, however, its components include the erosion of moral authority and associated ineffectiveness of school discipline as well as low educational achievement. Certainly there is little evidence supporting the contention that the level of disorder and violence in public schools has reached pandemic proportions. Yet such is indeed the case in certain urban public schools, where institutional factors related to court climates—the primary focus of this book—have combined with other social factors to create school environments that are particularly chaotic, if not themselves crime-producing. While the situation in general thus does not qualify as a crisis in a pedagogical or criminological sense, it might accurately be considered one in broader political and organizational terms.[3] Problems of moral authority in public schools—recognized as such by widespread public opinion—have prevented many public schools from socializing youth effectively. More critically, these problems have undermined public school legitimacy, eroded popular support necessary for maintenance and expansion of these institutions, stimulated political challenges and the growth of competitive organizations, and thus have come to threaten public school organizational survival in many state and local settings.

Public concern over ineffective discipline in schools is long-standing in the United States and clearly predates more recent legal challenges to these practices. For example, in the 1950s Gallup public opinion polls, nearly two-thirds of respondents felt that school discipline was not "strict" or "severe" enough.[4] This generalized cultural dissatisfaction has arguably become more acute in recent decades, as school disorder now not only distracts from classroom instruction, but often takes a particularly violent turn. Recent national data from the U.S. Department of Education and the *School Crime and Safety* report by the Department of Justice provide a sense of the empirical dimensions of the current problem. At the end of the last century, approximately thirty students per year died of homicides committed on school grounds; 10 percent of all public school teachers were threatened with injury by students; and 4 percent of teachers were physically attacked in the course of the year. In urban public schools the rate was even higher, with 14 percent of teachers threatened with injury and 6 percent attacked. More than 10 percent of high school males reported carrying a weapon on school property over the past month, while 34 percent of urban high school seniors reported that street gangs were present in their schools.[5] Although many of these threats and actual incidents of student and teacher victimization were relatively minor, they created an atmosphere of disorder that disrupted the educational process, particularly in urban settings where poverty was rife.[6] Disorder in schools coupled with much publicized shootings also undermined individuals' sense of school safety. Following the Columbine school shooting, for example, 45 percent of parents with children in elementary and secondary schools reported that they feared for their children's physical safety in schools.[7] In addition, as incarceration rates have tripled in recent decades, schools have been held partly responsible for these trends, with 73 percent of adults believing that "poor quality of schools" has been either a "critical" or "very important" cause of crime.[8]

Problems of moral authority strike at the core of public education, because primary and secondary schooling is as much about the socialization of youth as it is about teaching rudimentary cognitive skills. Emile Durkheim, one of the founders of modern sociology, argued that "the nature and function of school discipline . . . is not a simple device for securing superficial peace in the classroom—a device allowing the work to roll on tranquilly." Schools, instead, are often the first social institution outside the family responsible for contributing to the process of molding youths for productive adult roles in society. Discipline, according to Durkheim, "is essentially an instrument—difficult to duplicate—of moral education."[9] From this perspective, public schools are as much about shaping individuals' attitudes and dispositions as about imparting specific sets of cognitive skills. High school students in particular often confront school authority as well as school adolescent peer cultures when they struggle with serious developmental questions: Who am I? Am I a good student or a bad student? Am I moral or immoral? Do I respect school and parental authority or reject the influence of such adults?[10] When Americans think about what is wrong with contemporary public schooling, survey responses suggest that they are often struck by the failure of public schools to provide institutional encouragement for the proper socialization of youth.[11] When middle-class parents remove their kids from public schools and place them in private schools, are they as much concerned with how public schools fail to provide school climates conducive to socialization as they are troubled by how little learning takes place? The two concerns are of course not unrelated: if schools fail to exercise moral authority over their students, they are unable to socialize students adequately and become chaotic places where teaching and learning fall by the wayside.

To be sure, other educational researchers in the past have thought about these problems, yet our work is novel and path-breaking for a number of reasons. First and foremost, we do not assume that an erosion of moral authority in schools was inevitable or that it simply reflects broader changes in political and popular culture—similar cultural changes in European countries, for example, did not result in the institutional changes that occurred in U.S. schools. Instead, we attempt to identify the specific institutional mechanisms that undermined the moral authority of schools. Rather than assume that problems of school discipline were associated with the general, culturally defined attitudes of students, parents, teachers, and administrators (which would indeed be quite difficult to change), we look for evidence that it was the institutional environment around schools that changed the parameters within which disciplinary practices emerged and were constituted. Specifically, we focus attention on the involvement of U.S. courts. Their rulings overturning school discipline had a significant role in contributing to the decline in moral authority and the erosion of effective disciplinary practices in American public schools. The role of judicial oversight and the level of court interference in school decisions concerning discipline is unique to the United States and not found in most other developed countries. U.S. court decisions have varied over time and across jurisdictions, however; some have tended to favor students, some school authorities. We provide evidence that this variation in the direction of court decisions was partly responsible for the difficulties schools encountered when they attempted to implement disciplinary practices that fostered both learning and effective socialization. While our account emphasizes the role of court decisions in structuring disciplinary practices related to the emergence of student peer climates, we do so because of the overlooked importance of this influence. Clearly, a myriad of other individual, school, and societal influences are also implicated in affecting school discipline and youth socialization.

The research presented in this book is quite novel in its methodology.[12] New technology now allows social scientists to examine court decisions systematically and thoroughly, whereas previously such an approach would have been technically impossible. Specifically, we were able to search a modern computerized legal archive that includes records of all contemporary state and federal appellate cases. We identified *every* court case that made its way to the state and federal appellate courts and involved contestation of school discipline.[13] Rather than simply examining important relevant Supreme Court cases (such as the *Goss v. Lopez* decision), we examined 6,277 legal cases from 1946–1992 and conducted detailed analysis on more than 1,200 relevant cases to identify patterns of systematic variation in judicial decisions. In the last two decades, great improvements have also occurred in the systematic collection of data on students, teachers, and administrators. We were thus able to combine four separate nationally representative data sets with detailed information on tens of thousands of students, teachers, and schools to identify how variation in court decisions was related to changes in school disciplinary practices and how school discipline affected student learning and socialization. We chose 1992 as an end date for our analysis, as that was the last year when detailed data on individual student perceptions and outcomes were available.

The significance of our research findings convinced us of the need to write a book accessible to the widest possible audience. We have relegated all discussion of technical analysis and detailed statistical findings to endnotes and appendix. When we discuss results in the text, we do so with the aid of maps, easily understood charts, and qualitative descriptions of the relevant processes. We believe that by writing for a larger audience we can stimulate the public discussion of these critical issues that is essential for improving American public schools.

Challenges to Legitimacy

To understand why the moral authority of school discipline has recently been eroded requires one to consider how the expansion of individual rights has come into conflict with the schools' prerogative to control student misbehavior. Social scientists have referred to the growth of "adversarial legalism" and litigation in recent decades. Educational litigation increased dramatically during the late 1960s and early 1970s, a period we will term the *student rights contestation period*.[14] While the volume of litigation has subsequently stabilized or moderately declined, both the threat of legal challenges to school authority and the effects of litigation on school practices remain. Today's schools inherit from that period a historical legacy with two prominent features. First, students have developed a sense of legal entitlement that—although not firmly grounded in accurate understanding of case and statutory law—has produced skepticism about the legitimacy of school disciplinary practices as well as a general familiarity with resorting to legal avenues to contest such practices. Second, contestation of student rights has left an organizational legacy that has been institutionalized in school forms, practices, and culture—including widespread normative taken-for-granted assumptions about the necessity of organizing school discipline in particular ways.

Educational litigation increased dramatically in the late 1960s and early 1970s for complex political, cultural, and institutional reasons. The political and cultural aspects have been generally well understood, while the institutional determinants have been less well appreciated. Identification of the latter is particularly important for making the argument that changes in public school discipline in the United States were unusual, distinctive, and far from historically inevitable. The extent to which challenging school authority in the late 1960s and early 1970s was related to the general political and cultural context of the times has been clearly recognized in prior scholarship.[15] Many American citizens, particularly among racial minorities and students, had become politicized and mobilized to fight racism and poverty at home and U.S. military involvement abroad. The students in this social movement (many of middle-class origins) often explicitly celebrated the questioning of authority. School authority thus inevitably came into direct contact with this generalized youth rebellion, which resulted in conflict and challenges over school practices.[16]

That the judicial system became a principal arena for challenges to school authority and that these challenges would produce profound changes in school practices requires further explanation. Youth advocates in the late 1960s and early 1970s embraced a political-legal strategy that had been successfully developed by the Civil Rights Movement. Specifically, organizations interested in advancing the well-being of youth—particularly disadvantaged youth—began to utilize court challenges to advance the social interests of children. In a 1973 article in *The Harvard Educational Review*, for example, a young idealistic lawyer who later served as president of the Legal Services Corporation explicitly advocated this position:

Although the introduction of the adversarial system into juvenile court proceedings is deplored by many, lawyers representing children should ensure three critical prerequisites for fairness. First, they can articulate and argue the child's position . . . Second, they can require that the law be strictly followed. And third, they can make new law in the area by appealing cases and lobbying for statutory changes. Independent counsel for children should not be restricted to children accused of delinquency, but should be required in any case where a child's interests are being adjudicated. The courts must become more sensitive to such cases.[17]

The idea that advocacy groups could "make new law in the area by appealing cases" was a political strategy that had gained adherents with the successes of the National Association for the Advancement of Colored People's Legal Defense and Education Fund, Inc. (NAACP Fund).[18] The NAACP Fund was founded in 1939 to coordinate litigation to challenge racial segregation and discrimination. By the time of the *Brown v. Board of Education* decision in 1954, the organization had won thirty-four of the thirty-eight cases its attorneys argued before the Supreme Court.[19] Success for public interest law reformers continued to increase with the frequent sympathetic decisions from the Warren Supreme Court (1953 to 1969). These decisions led to a dramatic expansion of the applicability of the Bill of Rights to individuals challenging state and local institutions, including public schools, and advanced "a view of democracy as one in which individuals can effectively claim rights against the state."[20] As importantly, decisions by the Warren Court inspired the law profession to embrace the notion that "most of the 'flaws' in American society could and would be corrected through legal means."[21]

With the successes during the Warren Court of the NAACP Fund and other early public interest law advocacy groups, such as the American Civil Liberties Union (ACLU), social reformers with legal backgrounds turned to creating appellate case law precedent to promote social change. In the early 1970s new public interest law firms were established, usually with financial support from large private and corporate foundations, and often with an explicit interest in litigating issues related to youth and schooling. The Ford Foundation and other similar organizations (including the Carnegie Corporation, the Field Foundation, the Stern Family Fund, the Edna McConnell Clark Foundation, and the Rockefeller Brothers Fund) were particularly prominent in the establishment of this legal sector.[22] Law and society scholars Joel Handler, Ellen Jane Hollingsworth, and Howard Erlanger found that 17.6 percent of docket entries for a sample of public interest law firms in 1973 had education as their focus, the most frequent response category identified.[23] Yet these law firms, while important, were only one feature of the institutional context during the period of student rights contestation. In 1975, the 72 public interest law firms that comprised the core of this legal sector employed only 478 lawyers (an average of seven per firm).[24]

While the student rights contestation period can be partially understood as emerging in general from a period of political youth rebellion that coincided with the rise of public interest litigation and the Warren Court's increasing willingness to apply the Bill of Rights to individuals challenging local government institutions, an important and somewhat ironic piece of this institutional context has yet to be clearly identified in our historical account. Much of the institutional impetus that supported and instigated challenges to school disciplinary practices in U.S. courts emerged neither spontaneously from private citizens nor indirectly through the efforts of nonprofit public interest law firms, such as the Children's Defense Fund. Instead, legal challenges to local public school disciplinary practices occurred in large part because of federal funding and support for legal activism during this period. Specifically, the major institutional actor advancing legal challenges to public school disciplinary practices was the Legal Services Program established by the Office of Economic Opportunity (OEO). The OEO was established in 1965 with a mandate that was interpreted to include promoting law reform as part of the War on Poverty under President Johnson. While about forty percent of initial OEO legal funding went to support existing local legal service organizations that provided basic legal services for the poor, more than half of federal funding went toward creating new legal service organizations that stressed law reform. In 1966 Clinton Bamberger, the first national director of OEO legal services, stressed the law reform goals of this new organization: "Lawyers must uncover the legal causes of poverty, remodel the systems which generate the cycle of poverty and design new social, legal and political tools and vehicles to move poor people from deprivation, depression, and despair to opportunity, hope and ambition."[25] Earl Johnson Jr., the director of legal services in 1967, shared this commitment and asserted that "the primary goal of legal services in the near future should be law reform."[26] While subsequent OEO leaders, such as Nixon appointee Donald Rumsfeld, clearly did not always share much enthusiasm for this legal activism, political and administrative opposition to the program was generally unsuccessful in altering the activist orientation of OEO-funded legal service organizations until at least 1975, when federal legislation set up the Legal Service Corporation to reorganize the units in the previously named Legal Services Program and "cut down on law reform litigation."[27]

Legal Services organized its law reform efforts through coordinating local offices with "back-up centers" specializing in particular areas of law. The former director of the Legal Services Program, Earl Johnson Jr., boasted that eight percent of federal resources were devoted to "back-up" and "regional advocacy" centers, which specialized in "high-impact legal work" (such as appellate litigation), and one-fourth of local legal service organizations had created "'appellate units' composed of attorneys devoting full time to appellate litigation and other high-impact work."[28] The Center for Law and Education was established at Harvard University as a "back-up center" to provide support for change in statutory law and appellate litigation in the area of education that would "protect and advance the interest of the poor."[29] From 1967 to 1972, the Legal Services Program expanded even when many other anti-poverty programs organized in the Office of Economic Opportunity were in decline. In 1967, the OEO Legal Services Program received $27 million in federal funding and employed nearly 1,200 lawyers; by 1972, the program received $71.5 million and employed over 2,000 lawyers.[30] In addition, during this period, OEO law reform work increasingly focused on challenging local public school practices—OEO law offices more than doubled the proportion of time spent on challenging educational practices (from 3.7 to 7.7 percent).[31]

Legal Services was remarkably effective at deflecting legislative pressures for accountability and outcome assessment, which plagued other Office of Economic Opportunity programs.[32] In the words of Earl Johnson Jr.,

> The Legal Services presents a many-fold more complex evaluation task than "Head Start," Job Corps, and most other OEO programs . . . At this point in time, it is not necessarily stretching the facts to argue that because of *Serrano v. Priest*, its desegregation cases and other actions influencing educational policy, Legal Services constituted a better investment in *education* than Head Start which absorbed most of OEO's "education" budget.[33]

In similar fashion, New York City Legal Services Program Director Lester Evans suggested in 1972 that the program could "measure our success by the amount of attacks on us."[34] The Legal Services Program also historically enjoyed not just powerful opponents (such as Ronald Reagan), but

influential political allies, including prominent members of the legal establishment and Republicans and Democrats in Congress—many of whom
had law degrees.[35] Legal Services lawyers were explicitly encouraged by federal legislators to focus attention on expanding student rights. For example, Walter Mondale in 1970 delivered his "Justice for Children" address to
the U.S. Senate, promoting the expansion of "rights of children vis-à-vis
institutions—rights of children in school to engage in free expression and
not to be subjected to discipline without due process, rights of children in
court not to be subject to being disposed of without adequate counsel or
real rules of law."[36] With legislative support, OEO "back-up centers" like
the Center for Law and Education continued to receive 99 percent of their
funding from federal sources between 1972 and 1975.[37] It is worth emphasizing that during the period we have termed the student rights contestation period, OEO funding supported the maximum level of federally sponsored legal activism designed to promote educational reform; OEO lawyers
were also responsible for key court decisions during this time—including
the *Goss v. Lopez* decision—that dramatically expanded student rights in
public schools. In addition, corporate and private foundations provided
significant support to establish and maintain public interest law firms that
focused on educational litigation during this period.

The phenomenon of local schools being subjected to coercive federally
sponsored litigation can only be understood with reference to the unique
political institutional character of the U.S. system of government. Prior to
Brown v. Board of Education and the War on Poverty, the federal government played almost no role in either providing support to or structuring
the character of public education in the United States.[38] Johnson's War on
Poverty program had two important elements relevant to our study: 1) additional federal attention and support was focused on improving public
education; and 2) appellate case law was appreciated as a vehicle capable
of promoting liberal reform. Federal spending on public elementary and
secondary education in the 1963–64 academic year amounted to only
4.4 percent of school revenues; by 1967–68, federal support had doubled
and accounted for 8.8 percent.[39] As John Meyer and his colleagues have
pointed out,

> The U.S. constitutional pattern—differing greatly from that obtained in
> many other modern states—has also heavily influenced the evolution of
> federal funding and authority in education in recent decades. Rather than

expanding direct national controls in the management of education, reform efforts during the 1960s and 1970s took the form of categorical or
special-purpose programs. No programs were created for the general
support and management of education, and none defined or attempted
to assist its primary goals or core processes. Rather, special purposes were
defined and furthered with specially organized funding in a highly frag-
mented system.[40]

While Meyer and his colleagues were correct in their observations, they ne-
glected to emphasize the role of federally sponsored litigation that was
increasingly used to create compliance and conformity in shaping local
school practices.[41]

At the time when the War on Poverty was launched, educational reformers were relatively united in their advocacy of an increased government
role in supporting and controlling public education. Leading sociologists,
of course, were no exception in this regard. James Coleman's expertise was
fully engaged in conducting and drafting the seminal *Equality of Educational Opportunity Report* mandated by the Civil Rights Act of 1964; and
Christopher Jencks—who later with a group of distinguished colleagues
would suggest that "living in the right school district seems to make relatively little difference to an individual's educational attainment . . . the average effect of any given school is . . . small"—wrote in 1965 that "the scientific revolution has made the localism of America's schools and colleges
intellectually ineffectual and socially obstructionist" and that an increased
federal role was inevitable and generally desirable.[42]

Since educational reformers working through the federal government
had only a limited capacity to affect local public school policies, efforts to
exercise influence were often structured indirectly, through meager financial incentives provided by federally supported categorical programs or
through the use of federally sponsored litigation. The latter instrument,
of course, was not only indirect, but also imprecise: by definition, regulations emerged not from professional educators and policy makers carefully
considering pedagogical issues, but rather, haphazardly and with inherent
contradictions and ambiguities, through the actions of legal professionals
(lawyers and judges) who advanced and considered arguments based primarily on legal precedents and personal judgment.

While reformers who pursued their aim through legal interventions
were clearly motivated by the best of intentions and were responding to

real inadequacies and inequalities in schooling, their own professional and institutional orientations were likely to affect their work significantly. Social scientists, noting the elite background of many of these lawyers, have commented on the extent to which at the time "the legal profession's image of itself" included a belief that "lawyers were by training and work experience particularly suited to grapple with complex social problems." Legal Services was able to attract ambitious and idealistic law school graduates— often by granting them prestigious fellowships—and they sought to "manage or reorder society" by making precedent setting appellate case law.[43] The high caliber of these individuals as well as the institutional backing of a large federal agency had a profound impact on the law. While prior to 1965 Legal Aid lawyers had never appealed a case to the Supreme Court, between 1965 and 1974 OEO Legal Services brought 164 cases to the high court and found much success there: a 63 percent success rate overall. OEO cases challenging state government practices, as most school litigation did, had a 67 percent success rate.[44] The model of reform embraced by these adversarial lawyers was a conception of legal liberalism wherein social progress was equated with an expansion of individual rights. As legal historian Laura Kalman has suggested, "The (Warren) Court made liberals happy for it dodged the tension between liberty and equality . . . by using liberalism's language of individual rights and freedom to help children, the disenfranchised, non-Christians, suspected criminals, minorities and the poor."[45] Critics of this brand of liberalism included conservatives who joined legal realists in objecting to the creative judicial rationales used to support court decisions; communitarian advocates, who saw expansion of individual rights as entailing costs to community interests and the common good; and neo-Marxist and other critics on the left, who interpreted these rights as "bourgeois liberties" that would detract attention from political mobilization designed more fundamentally to alter social structures and inequality.

While the Legal Services Program thus had some features of a "social movement" designed to advance a particular form of liberalism—albeit one comprised of bourgeois foot soldiers with significant elite sponsorship—it also must be recognized as "a government bureaucracy" that "drew lawyers from a variety of backgrounds who joined for a variety of reasons."[46] Legal Services and similar groups thus could be characterized as involving, at an individual level, lawyers motivated by a liberal missionary zeal and a sense of self-righteous assurance to correct injustices found in individual cases as well as inequalities found in society. At a more mundane institutional level, they were bureaucratic entities involved in efforts to discover and exploit organizational weaknesses so as to foster institutional expansion, increased resource allocations, and greater organizational influence.[47] The increased focus on educational litigation from these law reform organizations from the late 1960s to the early 1970s likely involved both sorts of motivations. When public school educators were confronted with institutional adversaries who were willing to assert that court challenges were more effective than preschool programs in improving educational opportunities for the poor, it is not surprising that public schools as organizations would creatively adapt to these external legal challenges in unanticipated ways that produced unintended negative consequences affecting the quality of schooling for all students.

In the case of school discipline, we believe these unintended consequences have been quite pronounced. The reason that "adversarial legalism" has been so costly with regard to school discipline is that the legal challenges produced not only changes in organizational practices, but also undermined the legitimacy of a school's moral authority more generally. That is, schools were likely to reduce their disciplinary responses to student misbehavior while at the same time students became less willing to accept school authority or discipline as legitimate. Legal challenges thus undermined school discipline in multiple ways.

Evidence that organizations adopt new practices in response to legal challenges has been well established in social scientific research.[48] After the Supreme Court's 1975 *Goss v. Lopez* decision extended the right of "rudimentary" due process for public school students faced with short-term suspension and "more formal procedures" for students facing more serious disciplinary sanctions, schools became more reluctant to expel students or discipline them with sanctions other than short-term suspension.[49]

While business firms in the private sector often utilized strategies of "symbolic compliance" when faced with legal challenge,[50] public schools were likely to respond by simply eliminating or reducing practices that were subject to litigation. School administrators had few incentives to maintain school discipline when controlling student misbehavior was difficult to measure and yielded few rewards. School administrators also recognized that utilizing school disciplinary practices aggressively had the risk of attracting not only unwanted negative attention and criticism, but also hostile litigation that could be quite expensive for school districts—in terms of public relations as well as costs for legal counsel—and thus damaging to an administrator's reputation and promotion opportunities. When faced with hostile legal threats, administrators opted simply to reduce the use of school discipline in general, rather than avoid specific practices that courts had questioned.

The effectiveness of school discipline and the related capacity of schools to socialize youth for a constructive role in society was even more threatened by the extent to which "adversarial legalism" undermined the *legitimacy* and *moral authority* of schools as institutions. "Since the mid-1960s," as noted scholar and founding director of the Center for Law and Education, David Kirp, has acknowledged, "little remains about the unreviewability of school disciplinary action."[51] Sociologists have considered legitimacy and moral authority to be the core components of effective discipline ever since Emile Durkheim's critique of the philosophical position of Thomas Hobbes. While Hobbes argued that because individuals were governed by passions and desires, the threat of sanctions from a greater authority was necessary to constrain individual actions and promote social order, Durkheim countered that the strength of external sanctions was ultimately dependent on individuals internalizing restrictions as legitimate normative rules.

Durkheim, like Hobbes, believed that discipline was needed "to teach the child to rein in his desires, to set limits on his appetites of all kinds, to limit and, through limitation, to define the goals of his activity." But the Durkheimian mechanism for imposing discipline was quite different from Hobbesian authoritarian sanctions. Punishment was necessary, according to Durkheim, because it unequivocally communicated that a normative rule had been broken: "it is not punishment that gives discipline its authority; but it is punishment that prevents discipline from losing this authority, which infractions, if they went unpunished, would progressively erode."[52]

Challenges to school disciplinary practices associated with adversarial legalism would be particularly unsettling to the normative order of the school. For Durkheim,

> What lends authority to the rule in school is the feeling that the children have for it, the way in which they view it as a sacred and inviolable thing quite beyond their control; and everything that might attenuate this feeling, everything that might induce children to believe that it is not really

inviolable can scarcely fail to strike discipline at its very source. To the extent that the rule is violated it ceases to appear as inviolable; a sacred thing profaned no longer seems sacred if nothing new develops to restore its original nature.[53]

Successful legal challenges to school authority taught students that school rules were indeed violatable. If youths experienced their first nonfamilial social institution (other than perhaps organized religion) as having rules that were not "sacred," consistently enforced, or necessarily judged as legitimate by outside evaluators, the ability to socialize them to accept the rules of a larger society would correspondingly be undermined.

Changing Court Climates

Schools are organizations and as such exist in specific institutional environments. These environments are critical in shaping individuals' taken-for-granted assumptions about how school practices should be structured. When school officials confront misbehavior that warrants some form of disciplinary response, they attempt to adopt behavior and practices that will be considered appropriate and reasonable in their own eyes and in the judgment of other relevant individuals. In the case of school disciplinary practices, school personnel in recent decades faced quite ambiguous and shifting regulations and assumptions about how disciplinary practices should be applied. In the face of such uncertainty, organizational actors typically look to the external environment for suggestions as to what attitudes and behaviors to adopt. While in the past school personnel might often have looked to local neighborhoods to determine culturally appropriate disciplinary practices, today a school's relevant community is often defined in institutional terms.

Specifically, as contemporary society has experienced changes in technology, significant individual mobility, increased male and female labor market participation away from the home, and a dispersed pattern of spatial organization of metropolitan areas, traditional forms of neighborhood organization have been undermined. Robert Putnam, for example, has noted that over the past few decades not only have voter participation in elections and membership in unions declined, but so too has citizen participation in many local voluntary organizations (such as church-related groups, civic institutions, fraternal organizations, and parent-teacher associations).[54] While many traditional forms of civic community involvement have been in decline, new forms of community organization, activity, and influence have replaced them.[55] In particular, new communities have been organized around shared identities and have often pressed their demands in legal and other (political and professional) *institutional* settings.[56] In many areas of educational practice, courts—not parent-teacher associations or local school boards—have become the primary social context affecting school organization. In other areas of educational practice, educational communities are organized around professional schools, occupational associations of teachers and administrators, and state departments of education. In short, today more than ever a school's relevant community is not just a neighborhood comprised of individuals, but equally an institutional environment made up of courts, professional associations, and other organizations.[57]

Just as school practices are structured by organizational factors that are relatively autonomous from local neighborhood influences, so too are court decisions structured. When making legal decisions affecting school practices, judges do not simply embrace cultural biases of local communities over which they preside, nor do they simply make decisions based on narrow interpretations of legal precedent. Rather, legal decisions emerge through the enactment of the legal process itself as well as through a variety of personal, political, and institutional influences on judicial action. Courts at times act more conservatively than the local communities over which they have jurisdiction; at other times, courts act more liberally. Only in the most general terms, and from the most removed and historically distant point of observation, would one want to assert that law simply reflects the biases of the political culture or ideology of the times. For our purposes, we examine how courts have varied in their opinions related to defining appropriate school discipline, how this variation was not a simple reflection of local political milieus, and how legal decisions were one of the institutional mechanisms whereby larger political and social pressures were translated and communicated to schools—effectively challenging and restructuring school disciplinary practices in complex ways.

In our research we originally examined 6,277 cases and then identified a subset of 1,204 cases that directly involved individuals or organizations contesting a school's right to discipline and control students. Detailed readings of the subset of cases provided a rich qualitative sense of how the issues involving school discipline were understood at the time by individuals having an active role in the judicial proceedings. The set was large enough so that we were also able to analyze patterns systematically through content coding specific details of these discipline cases.

Content coding is a way to measure the presence or absence of particular characteristics found in qualitative records. Specifically, we read cases to identify the direction of the court decision (whether court opinions favored either schools or students), the form of school discipline challenged (suspension, expulsion, corporal punishment, or student transfer), and the type of student behavior that produced the initial sanction (freedom of expression, political protest, general misbehavior, possession or use of drugs or alcohol, possession or use of weapons and violence). In addition, cases were content coded to indicate the race, gender, and disability status of students, if identified, and whether discrimination was alleged. Lastly, we measured several characteristics of schools (including whether it was public or private sector and what grades it covered) and courts (geographic location and jurisdictional level). Our analysis of legal cases thus enabled the identification of systematic variation in characteristics of court cases, while simultaneously allowing in-depth descriptions of important details regarding the substance of the matters contested.

Our research identified several distinct historic periods of court climates related to school discipline. Prior to 1965 and the establishment of the OEO's Legal Services Programs, very few individuals or groups used the legal system at the appellate level to challenge school disciplinary practices. When student discipline was contested in courts, schools were supported in approximately two thirds of the cases. From 1965 to 1968, as Legal Services and other public interest law firms began to devote resources to litigation promoting educational reform, only a few challenges to school disciplinary practices went up to the appellate level. These early legal challenges to school discipline were cases typically involving schools using suspension and expulsion to sanction students for free expression or political protest. In this historic transition period, court decisions were more likely than in later years to favor students. In approximately half of these cases, judges sided with forces challenging school discipline.

A good example of these early challenges to school discipline can be found in a case involving students in Des Moines, Iowa, which by 1969 had worked its way up to the Supreme Court and was decided as *Tinker v. Des Moines Independent Community School District*. The case involved three students in the middle and high schools, children of parents active in the pacifist American Friends Service Committee. The students, with the consent of their parents, wore black armbands to school to "publicize their objections to the hostilities in Vietnam." They were suspended from school until they would agree to appear without the armbands. While lower courts had varying opinions on this case, the Supreme Court found in favor of the students and warned school administrators: "it can hardly be argued that either students or teachers shed their constitutional rights to freedom of speech or expression at the schoolhouse gate."[58]

Subsequent to these early legal challenges, courts between 1969 and 1975 witnessed a dramatic increase in appellate case loads related to school disciplinary practices. Much of this litigation did not emerge spontaneously from grassroots student and parental efforts, but required a supportive legal infrastructure willing and able to devote significant resources to advance challenges at the appellate level. Without institutions like OEO's Legal Services and other public interest law firms, much of this litigation would never have occurred, and even if it had, would likely have been settled by the concerned parties well before the cost and efforts required to advance the cases aggressively through the appellate level. As an early Legal Service manual explicitly noted in 1966: "How can the legal service unit develop test cases to bring about social change and changes in agency practices if the agencies settle the cases before they get to hearing boards or courts?" The report noted how public agencies were often willing to "'back down' on their stands on certain cases in order to avoid litigation."[59] Successful appellate challenges required strategy, tenacity, and institutional persistence. We therefore chose 1969 as the beginning of the student rights contestation period, because it was the year when litigation on this issue dramatically increased, and because it was the date when OEO opened the Center for Law and Education at Harvard to spearhead and coordinate efforts to advance educational law reform.

Prior to 1960 it was difficult to find any appellate cases related to school disciplinary practices and only 72 cases in state and federal appellate courts were found between 1960 and 1968; by contrast, in the student rights contestation period from 1969 to 1975, 76 cases per year occurred on average. There were likely more challenges to school discipline in the case law records of 1969 and 1970 alone, than in all prior years of American history combined. During this period of dramatic increase in legal challenges to school discipline, many of the general patterns found in embryonic form in the 1965–1968 transition years became consistently present at all court levels, including the Supreme Court.

The cases overwhelmingly involved expulsion or suspension of students for misbehavior, often on the grounds of free expression or political protest. Approximately half of appellate court cases involved students disciplined for protest or free expression. The political character of these cases was often clear. Cases such as *Goss v. Lopez*—brought forward all the way to the Supreme Court through the efforts of OEO-sponsored Legal Service offices in Columbus, Ohio, and the Center for Law and Education in Cambridge—attracted *amici curiae* ("friends of the court") briefs from organizations such as the American Civil Liberties Union, the National Association for the Advancement of Colored People, and the Children's Defense Fund, which argued that they had a compelling interest in the outcome of the case. In Chapter 2 we will provide an extensive discussion of the *Goss v. Lopez* case; suffice it to state here that the Supreme Court extended due process guarantees to students subjected to even minor disciplinary sanctions in a case that involved students being suspended for disruptive protest against a school that failed to provide adequate recognition of Black History Week.

Courts in this period remained relatively sympathetic to student challenges and often found in their favor (pro-student decisions occurred approximately 44 percent of the time). It is worth noting that many courts in the South (with the exception of a few conservative state appellate courts) found in favor of students in spite of deeply held conservative regional cultural traditions. Federal district and appellate courts in the South during this time period often had judicial appointments that did not simply mimic local demographic, cultural, or political environments.

During the period of student rights contestation, legal opinions on occasion would be based explicitly on the severe and irreparable psychological harm students had suffered when disciplined by schools. While some might associate such language with cases involving the use of corporal punishment, only four percent of appellate cases involved such forms of discipline, and in these instances courts were not particularly sympathetic to students.

A case in New York appellate courts captured how judges during this period often focused primarily on the well-being of individual students who had been disciplined. The case involved Anna Ladson, an eighteen-year-old public school student who faced long-term suspension and was denied participation in a graduation ceremony after the school charged that she had struck and threatened the principal. The alleged altercation with the principal occurred in the midst of severe racial disturbances, including evacuation because of a bomb threat and "stonings between white and black students."[60] Ladson and her mother challenged the school's right to bar her from the graduation ceremony (the school had scheduled a time when the student could receive her diploma privately). Consistent with the pattern of courts being more likely to favor students during this time period and especially when racial bias was invoked, the court supported the student. As interesting as the decision was the language used in the legal opinion:

> The court is persuaded that *punishment and discipline should be responsive to the educational goals to which the school system is dedicated. Courts are dedicated not only to the administration of laws, but to the pursuit of justice, and the two ideals must come together. The justice of the situation favors graduation attendance.* We have here a student of demonstrated dedication, who has persevered through all of her term in high school and has completed her final year under adversity, even though some of that adversity may be of her own doing. She has been accepted at college. *Her graduation ceremony is important and meaningful to her personally and in her family which has never before had a high school graduate.* She has no other record of school disorder than the one incident here involved. It would indeed be a distortion of our educational process in this period of youthful discontentment to snatch from a young woman at the point of educational fruition the savoring of her educational success. *The court believes that not to be a reasonable punishment meant to encourage the best educational results.*[61]

The court explicitly asserted several interesting propositions. First, it suggested that "justice" was more important than the "administration of law." This part of the decision was quite unusual: typically, judges relied partially on deference to the "administration of law" when supporting students against school authority. Second, the court asserted greater expertise than school officials in determining how educational goals were to be reached. Last, the court emphasized how the school sanction could have damaging effects on the individual punished. During this period judges made fewer claims than in later periods that punishment was either in the long-term best interest of the student or that determinations of these matters must focus on the well-being of the student body as a whole (rather than the individual student bringing the case). The court dramatically concluded its opinion in the case with a clear admission of a pro-student bias: "If an error is being made, the court must err on the side of the youngster seeking to make her way and to fortify her to continue with her education."[62]

A second case two years later, in Ohio, demonstrated similar judicial attitudes toward students and schools. Junior high school student, William Jacobs, had been disciplined for violating the Northwest School District dress code and more specifically for having "long hair." He refused to comply with new regulations prohibiting student mustaches and defining the allowed hair length. The school punished Jacobs by removing him from office as president of the student council, taking him off the honor roll, reducing his grades, and suspending him from school. The student and his mother challenged and overturned the school's discipline in a state trial court. A higher Ohio State appellate court concurred with the lower court judgment; the earlier judges' "carefully drafted" opinion was cited approvingly in the opinion:

> A rule restricting hair length and style and prohibiting mustaches *affects the student in the most intimate and personal way.* History, literature and simple observation make this abundantly clear. Furthermore, 'hair' rules control the student not only during the 35 hours per week he spends in school but control his appearance the other 133 hours of the week as well. It seems belaboring the obvious to point out that *there are thousands of ways for schools to teach discipline and limits and an awareness of relationships with others and with the community without requiring that students cut off their hair and shave their mustaches.* It seems equally obvious that to teach students that they must accept arbitrary authority, particularly in a matter as personal as this, is wholly alien to our concepts of a free society and the dignity of the individual.[63]

In a fashion similar to the earlier New York case, the court justified the decision by invoking the detrimental effects discipline could have on individual students, as well as challenging the degree to which school officials could design school practices with respect to appropriate educational goals.

These twin themes—that courts must protect the well-being of vulnerable children and that school officials do not align school practices with appropriate pedagogical ends—appeared repeatedly in judicial opinions during this time period. The language was applied not simply to students disciplined for freedom of expression or student protest (as in the examples above), but also in cases involving "search and seizure" issues related to the suppression of drug dealing on campus. For example, a seventeen-year-old student in New York had been under observation for six months for alleged drug dealing, was "observed by a teacher, twice during the same morning within one hour, entering a toilet room in the school with a fellow student and both exiting within 5 to 10 seconds," and was subsequently searched in the principal's office. The student was disciplined and turned over to the police after the search uncovered "a vial containing 9 pills" and a wallet with "13 glassine envelopes containing a white powder." The court overturned the punishment and warned school officials: "the psychological damage that would be risked on sensitive children by random search insufficiently justified by the necessities is not tolerable."[64] In later years, judges did not seem to worry so much about the "psychological damage" experienced by students found in possession of significant quantities of illicit substances.

Following 1975 a new period began that coincided not only with a shift in judicial orientation at the Supreme Court, but as importantly with institutional changes in the level of support for aggressive educational law reform. Specifically, in the course of that year federal legislation imposed a Legal Service Corporation to oversee the OEO Legal Service program, with an explicit mandate to curb appellate litigation focused on promoting social reform. In the mid-1970s, corporate and private foundations also became less enthusiastic about funding these pursuits. Likewise, the number of legal challenges declined slightly from its earlier peak level, though it remained significantly higher than it had been before 1969. Specifically, between 1976 and 1992, there were on average 57 cases in state and federal appellate courts per year. As Law and Society scholars have suggested in other areas, prior legal challenges provided individuals with a sense of legal entitlement as well as scripts and strategies to mobilize law when desired.[65] Moreover, the cases involved substantively different matters than the earlier cases. After 1975, protest and free expression issues took up only 8 percent of cases. School discipline was challenged over student use or possession of drugs (16 percent), alcohol (6 percent), weapons (6 percent), violence (14 percent), and general misbehavior (50 percent). Courts also became somewhat less sympathetic to students, deciding in favor of schools at levels similar to those of the early 1960s (that is, in approximately two thirds of cases). This was true even after the content of the cases had significantly shifted from freedom of expression and protest to drugs, alcohol, weapons, violence, and general misbehavior.

While in earlier days judges referred to psychological harm inflicted on individuals and arrogantly held forth on what was appropriate educational practice, later opinions more often took diametrically opposing positions. Judges were likely to acknowledge the need to defer to the authority of school officials in determining appropriate educational practices and to emphasize how the absence of school discipline did damage to the school climate and community as a whole. In short, they tended to see the student body as vulnerable and in need of protection, rather than to define individual miscreants in such terms.

The shift in judicial attitudes was captured well in a 1986 Alabama appellate case involving the expulsion of a student for alcohol possession. Christopher Adams, a ninth grader at Dothan High School, in Alabama, admitted to school administrator Richard Grisby that he had brought alcohol to the campus and allowed a fellow student to drink some, contrary to school rules. Christopher was expelled from October to the end of the spring semester and readmitted the following year. His attempts to challenge the expulsion in court were ineffective. In finding against the student, the judges—unlike in the earlier cited cases—explicitly emphasized deference to local school authorities. "School disciplinary matters are best resolved by the local community school boards and officials," the court found, and should be overturned only in the rare cases when the school actions were "clearly unconstitutional" and when there was a "shocking disparity between offense and penalty."[66] The court also justified its decision in terms of protecting a vulnerable student body as a whole, weighed against the vulnerability of an individual student suffering the school's sanction. As the judges noted,

In the case before us, *the school officials testified that the use of alcohol and drugs had become a very serious problem* in the Dothan City School system. Woodham testified that school officials felt that *making students aware of the possibility of expulsion for possession of alcohol and drugs on school campus would have a significant deterrent effect* on the students. Christopher brought alcohol onto the campus and permitted a fellow student to drink some. The Board's subsequent expulsion of Christopher was a response to what it perceived to be a major crisis of drug and alcohol abuse in the schools. Although Christopher's *punishment may have been severe, we cannot say that, under the above circumstances, it was so severe as to be arbitrary and unjust.* Nor do we find that it was grossly unfair for the school officials to refer Christopher to law enforcement officers. Such action was provided for in the (School's) Code.[67]

Students and parents had entered a new era which continues to this day: underage drinking was no longer dismissed as a relatively harmless right of passage for youth and instead could be subject to serious sanction.

This new emphasis on the vulnerability of the school community and a greater explicit deference to school discretion appeared more frequently and repeatedly in other cases. An Ohio appellate court in 1989 supported school authorities for suspending a high school senior after the student attended wrestling practice with beer on his breath (consumed while the student attended a college visitation day at a local campus). The court made explicit reference to a "growing epidemic of alcohol and drug abuse plaguing young people today."[68] In the context of such an epidemic,

> A school board certainly has the right to prohibit students' use of drugs and alcohol in the school setting. We are all aware of the current drug and alcohol crisis and the need to educate young people as to the hazards of substance abuse. If a school board cannot establish a rule to stop the use of drugs and alcohol among its students absent the students' becoming disruptive, then the school administrators will be helpless to enforce and maintain discipline in our schools.[69]

While student survey data reported that drug and alcohol consumption was actually significantly lower in 1989 than a decade earlier, the perception of an "epidemic" was widespread and was socially significant in its own right.[70]

In a similar move, a Virginia court supported a school's right to expel a high school student for possessing five "Pink Heart" look-alike amphetamines which contained nothing more than 200 milligrams of caffeine. The court argued that

> The school board adopted the regulation and its interpretation of its own regulation should be given considerable deference. That the use of illegal drugs is a matter tearing at the vitals of our society must have been well known to the school board. This school board, having thousands of pupils for whose care and tutelage it is responsible, could not help but be acutely aware of the difficulties posed and the dangers to their charges presented by the presence of illegal drugs, whether in the form of statuto-

rily defined controlled substances or anything else directly related to them, including look-alikes or imitations.[71]

Courts also emphasized the vulnerability of the school community when deciding cases involving weapons. When an Illinois high school's expulsion of a student for carrying a gun on campus was challenged, state appellate courts had little sympathy or concern with the well-being of the student (who, incidentally, had otherwise demonstrated model behavior). Rather, in a curt and forceful decision, the judges noted:

> A high school student ought not carry a .357 Magnum pistol, jammed between his waistband and his belly, with a live round of ammunition in his pants pocket while he is in a lunch line in a high school cafeteria. Expulsion of that student is no abuse of discretion . . . A gun in school is dangerous. A gun in school sweeps all into harm's way. Carrying a gun in school cannot be endorsed. Carrying a gun in school must be condemned. Expulsion is condemnation, appropriate condemnation. This expulsion is not arbitrary, is not unreasonable, is not capricious or oppressive.[72]

Note the strident, defensive language in this case. Indeed, students and parents were now challenging school discipline on procedural grounds that had been legally established in earlier cases of freedom of expression and the right to protest. Students, parents, and schools were now all operating under a shared perception that courts could be effectively utilized to overturn school discipline. In fact, the perception that courts could be used in this fashion was realistic, as a lower court had on procedural grounds found in favor of the student who carried the .357 Magnum.

Yet on the whole courts had become less explicitly worried about the well-being of students who had been disciplined. In North Carolina, for example, Shelly Gaspersohn, a female senior high school student, received corporal punishment from a male assistant principal that left "bruises on her buttocks for approximately three weeks." A psychologist, Dr. Irwin A. Hyman (a noted opponent of corporal punishment) "diagnosed her as having post-traumatic stress syndrome, a psychological condition which leaves a permanent mental scar."[73] Hyman testified that "she had recurring nightmares about the event, she could not talk about it without crying and she had a fear of men who reminded her of (the assistant principal) Mr. Varney." The court was not swayed by arguments about psychological harm, however; the judges asserted that "a teacher has the right to administer corporal punishment to students so long as it is done without malice and to further an educational goal."[74]

At this point judges were not only more likely to endorse school discipline, but also explicitly to recognize the need to support school authority. A Louisiana appellate judge noted in an opinion: "Discipline is a necessary ingredient to public education. If the frail remnants of authority in our society are not to be totally eroded, the disciplinarians in our public school system should be encouraged, not deterred, from enforcing stern but reasonable discipline."[75]

Schools slowly gained strongly sympathetic judicial allies. Certain regions, such as the South and the Western Mountain states, had particularly staunch conservative pro-school court supporters in this period; in other areas of the country, such as California and New York, courts were more favorable to students. We examine these differences in greater detail in Chapter 3.

Although courts became less receptive to arguments in favor of student challenges after 1975, it is worth emphasizing that significant case law affecting school discipline had already been established in the student rights contestation period and continued to be expanded and promoted by liberal advocacy lawyers. For example, not long after the *Goss v. Lopez* decision, the Center for Law and Education published a legal primer of over five hundred pages entitled *School Discipline and Student Rights: An Advocate's Manual*. In the introduction, the author Paul Weckstein—without any reflection on how increased litigation might negatively affect the quality of schooling—summarized the purpose of the document as follows:

> This manual is designed to help students' advocates in their work on school discipline issues—when representing students in school disciplinary hearings, preparing court challenges, or working with groups of students and parents to change school disciplinary policy and practices. It was developed because of the frequency with which we get requests for legal assistance from legal services staff and their clients on school discipline matters.[76]

In 1990, the Center for Law and Education found it necessary to publish a separate publication of nearly two hundred pages devoted solely to updating the earlier document's section on procedural due process rights. By then, the revised legal primer had ten separate sections on application of due process procedures to distinct "specific forms of discipline." The primer described how due process applied in eight areas other than short- and longer-term suspensions, including disciplinary transfer; in-school suspension; removal from particular classes; exclusion from extracurricular activities; exclusion from graduation ceremonies; corporal punishment; exclusion from school buses; as well as in matters related to grading, diploma denial, and other "academic" decisions.[77]

School Adaptations

The implication of these court challenges for school disciplinary practices might seem fairly obvious and straightforward for many readers: courts altered the rules whereby schools had the authority to control student misbehavior, and school discipline correspondingly became less effective. While such a direct connection between law and social organizations might appear intuitively correct, many social scientists would be critical of such an assumption. Specifically, they would argue that variation in court climates over time and across regions was interesting but largely irrelevant, given that public schools tend to ignore external environmental influences altogether. According to educational researchers, public schools have developed institutional cultures that are "encapsulated" and organizational structures that are only "loosely coupled"; schools thus potentially were largely protected from external efforts to alter their behaviors.[78]

Legal scholars such as Gerald Rosenberg have also argued that courts were not always effective in their efforts to change school practices. In *The Hollow Hope: Can Courts Bring about Social Change,* Rosenberg suggested that, contrary to conventional wisdom, the *Brown v. Board of Education* decision had little direct and immediate influence on promoting school desegregation. Ten years after the Federal Supreme Court decision, more than 95 percent of African-Americans in the South still attended completely segregated schools. It was only subsequent federal legislation such as the 1964 Civil Rights Act, plus administrative intervention, local political pressure, and further court challenges that reduced school segregation significantly. Rosenberg noted that courts were often limited in their ability to alter school practices because not only are constitutional rights supporting intervention limited, but the judiciary also lacked independence and competence in formulating and implementing policies.[79]

Other social scientists would also doubt that public school disciplinary practices varied significantly in the United States in the first place. Neo-institutionalists (such as John Meyer, Walter Powell, Paul DiMaggio, John Chubb, and Terry Moe) would likely argue that public schools were subject to common organizational environments and thus share common practices. Although their theories support the notion that courts could heavily influence school practices and schools could change over time, these scholars would not expect significant variation in either court climates or school disciplinary practices across American states in a given year.[80]

We have already described significant variation in court climates. We must therefore now ask: To what extent does discipline in public schools vary? Were differences in court climates systematically associated with how schools disciplined children? While there is no existing data that could answer these questions unequivocally, we were able to provide suggestive answers by relying on multiple indicators from a variety of sources. Thus we examined administrative reports of the use of corporal punishment in public schools from 1976 to 1992 that were collected by the U.S. Department of Education's Office of Civil Rights. We also examined administrative reports on whether public schools in 1980 and 1990 had adopted a set of particular school rules applying to closed campus, dress codes, hall passes, and smoking. We also explored 1980 and 1990 student survey results to assess the degree to which public school students believed that discipline in their schools was strict and fair. Lastly, we examined surveys of public school teachers in the early 1990s that probed whether school rules were being enforced by teachers and whether the principal enforced student conduct and supported teachers in their efforts to discipline youth. Given the data limitations, our results are not definitive, but we were able to identify suggestive findings that provide the best possible estimates of the effects that court decisions had on school disciplinary practices.

First, our data suggested that school disciplinary practices and student-teacher perceptions of them varied systematically in the United States. For example, in 1976 virtually every state in the country reported the use of corporal punishment in public schools. In the decade and a half following 1976, public schools in most areas of the country began to eliminate the use of this form of discipline. In the deep South, however, public schools did not end the use of corporal punishment; in fact in the early 1990s corporal punishment in these states was practiced more often than in the 1976 reports. These differences in state use of corporal punishment were closely associated with our measures of court climate. Public schools in states with more hostile court climates (that is, with higher rates of pro-student decisions in courts with direct jurisdiction over school practices) had lower rates of corporal punishment generally and more of them quickly discontinued the use of the practice.

Once corporal punishment was eliminated in state schools—partially, we believe, in response to hostile courts climates—it was quite unlikely to return, regardless of subsequent conservative changes in the direction of court decisions. This institutional finality occurred because elimination of the practice in a state's public school system created taken-for-granted assumptions amongst local educators that the use of the practice was ill-advised and "unthinkable" as an appropriate method. How these assumptions created obstacles that would resist challenges from subsequent shifts in political and judicial opinions was captured well in the debate around 1996 legislative efforts to reintroduce corporal punishment in California schools. Liberal newspaper editorials commented that "it seems incredible in this day and age that anyone would have to argue the case"[81]; Democrats in the state assembly were reported "aghast at the testimony"[82]; and the state superintendent of public schools worried about "teachers having that sort of responsibility, let alone liability."[83] The sponsor of the legislation commented in frustration over the lack of Republican Party unity on the issue: "Some young Republicans have never lived under anything but the psychobabble of touchy-feely, feel-good . . . and all that . . . They totally misunderstood what I was trying to say."[84] Conversely, in locations where corporal punishment had not been eliminated, court decisions began to lean more heavily in favor of school authority, and schools not only continued the use of corporal punishment but often actually increased the application of this sanction.

In other areas of school discipline, we were able to identify clear associations between court climates and school disciplinary practices. When court decisions were more hostile to school authority, schools tended to have fewer rules and teachers and administrators were more reluctant to enforce rules and utilize discipline aggressively. School personnel in these settings probably had increased apprehension that their exercise of authority could be effectively challenged in courts. Students in these settings might also have been quicker to confront school personnel attempting to control disorder with the now all too common classroom refrain: "I'll sue you!" While we have no direct measure of the legal perceptions of students and staff in existing data sets, we do have results that examine these issues indirectly. We find that when court climates were more hostile to school discipline, teachers reported fewer positive responses to prompts such as "rules for student behavior are enforced by teachers" and "the principal enforces student conduct rules and supports me."

In our review of existing ethnographic, survey, and historical research on the changing experience of teachers during this period, we were also able to uncover a great deal of additional evidence in support of our contention that legal challenges undermined teachers' willingness to exercise authority. Ellen Jane Hollingsworth, Henry Lufler, and William Clune in the late 1970s surveyed 207 Wisconsin teachers and found the widely held attitude that "the courts were robbing teachers and administrators of the opportunity to discipline students the way they once did." While 25 percent of teachers reported that they "weren't sure" about the effect of court decisions, 59 percent reported that "teachers and administrators have been hampered by court decisions in their application of discipline," and 45 percent reported that "too much interference from courts" was a "very important" cause of school discipline problems.[85] Gerald Grant, in his historical account of the transformation of a New York state public high school, suggested a similar role court decisions played in shaping the perceptions and actions of school personnel:

> In the past decade many teachers came to recognize that neither the law nor the parents were behind them. What happened in the 1970s at Hamilton High was not unique. Teachers often thought the law reflected distrust of their judgment or intentions, and was a weapon for disciplining them rather than their students. Where the law once upheld the teacher's right to exercise reasonable corporal punishment, they could now be threatened with a suit for child abuse or dismissal.[86]

Educators could no longer assume that courts would support them. Whereas teachers trained in the 1930s were taught to do whatever was necessary to "get order" in the classroom and to remember when wavering that "you have the law back of you, you have intelligent public sentiment back of you,"[87] by the late 1970s teacher training often included instructions on recognizing the legal limitations of teachers' classroom disciplinary discretion. Books instructing educators on effective discipline began to have chapters with ominous titles such as "How to Work Within the Legal Limits of Proper Disciplinary Action" and included recommendations that educators should ensure that their districts "establish adequate liability insurance," "supplement this coverage through additional insurance available from many professional organizations," and "negotiate a 'hold harmless' clause in their master contract" to protect them "from litigation that may occur after they have left the system."[88]

We also found clear associations between court climates and student perceptions of school discipline. In particular, we were interested in whether court climates were associated with student perceptions of strict discipline, and equally, whether they were related to student perceptions of fair discipline. Student reports of the strictness and fairness of discipline suggest the degree to which court decisions hostile to school authority have affected the level of discipline (measured partially by student perceptions of strictness) and have undermined the legitimacy of school discipline. We found that when courts were supportive of student rights, students reported that school discipline was both less strict and less fair: that is, schools were less likely to apply discipline and the limited discipline they did apply was considered even less legitimate than elsewhere. When courts supported school authority, students were more likely to report that discipline was both stricter and fairer.

Strictness and fairness of discipline were themselves interrelated, and this relationship produced interesting regional variations in the findings. Students were most likely to report that school discipline was unfair in the same instances when discipline was also reported as least strict. In school settings with little discipline, authority often could appear arbitrarily exercised and unjust. As students reported increasing levels of the strictness of school discipline, higher levels of fairness were also reported up to a certain point. When students reported the highest levels of school strictness, however, they said that discipline was applied less fairly than when school discipline was reported at a more moderate level of strictness. This curvilinear association suggests that students believed that increased strictness was legitimate at moderate levels; if discipline became too strict, however, it was often viewed as authoritarian and lost some of its legitimacy. The interesting regional variation identified in our research involved perceptions of school discipline in the South. In 1980 students in Southern states reported high levels of both strictness and fairness in school discipline. By 1990, however, Southern states again had high reports of strictness (consistent with our findings of increased use of corporal punishment there), but students had begun to perceive the discipline as less fair than in many other settings, an evaluation that suggests they viewed their schools as too strict and authoritarian.

Moral Authority, School Discipline, and Student Socialization

Academics and educators have long debated how disciplinary practices might affect student outcomes. We believe that by ignoring the degree to which the effectiveness of school discipline is related to legitimacy and moral authority, much of the recent debate and prior research on the subject has limited utility.

At a practical level, school discipline can generate student compliance and peer pressure toward academic performance. In recent work, James Coleman and his associates argued that private schools outperform public schools in part because they were able to maintain stricter disciplinary climates with less absenteeism, vandalism, drug use, and disobedience.[89] Sociologists Tom DiPrete, Chandra Muller, and Nona Shaeffer also found that rates of misbehavior during the senior year were lower in schools that had a higher frequency of disciplining sophomore students.[90] Conservatives have long argued that without proper order and discipline, schools were unable to function properly and thus provide little education.[91]

Progressive liberal educators have countered these arguments on both theoretical and empirical grounds. Theoretically, the challenge largely relied on the work of John Dewey, who argued that traditional authoritarian disciplinary practices alienated students from educational institutions. Authoritarian discipline served "to cow the spirit, to subdue inclination" and to increase "indifference and aversion" to schools.[92] Dewey maintained that students would develop productive internal self-discipline only when schools changed their curriculum to engage individuals' interests as active learners.

Dewey argued that the most strict school authority could accomplish would be to create an external appearance of student orderliness. If the teacher is "a good disciplinarian, the child will indeed learn to keep his senses intent in certain ways, but he will also learn to direct his fruitful imagery, which constitutes the value of what is before his senses, in totally other directions."[93] This external appearance of orderliness carries significant pedagogical costs: "To repress interest is to substitute the adult for the child, and so to weaken intellectual curiosity and alertness, to suppress initiative, and to deaden interests."[94] Progressive educators thus argued that if traditional authoritarian disciplinary practices were eliminated from public schools, students would be less alienated from their educational environments and more likely to remain in school and apply themselves to their studies.

Empirical research has suggested that use of strict disciplinary practices, such as corporal punishment, could lead to lower educational achievement and higher rates of delinquency.[95] Researchers also argued that these school practices could foster the formation of oppositional peer groups that resisted formal education.[96] In schools where teachers and students were from different racial backgrounds, "principled opposition" to the use of school discipline was particularly likely.[97] In racially mixed school settings nonwhite students might both perceive use of school discipline as particularly unfair and resist school authority in ways that would lower their educational achievement.[98]

While conservative critics of public education have attributed the failure of public schools to lax discipline, liberals have argued, conversely, that regimentation and overly strict discipline alienated students and reduced the effectiveness of schools. Both of these claims have some merit: school discipline was ineffective when it was either too strict or too lenient. What both liberals and conservatives usually missed, however, was the central principle underlying effective school discipline and accounting for the paradox that school discipline would have limited utility when perceived as either too harsh or too permissive. For discipline to be effective, students must actually internalize school rules. This internalization occurs much more readily when school discipline is equated with the legitimately exercised moral authority of school personnel. If school discipline is perceived as either too lenient or too strict, it would lose legitimacy. Moreover, when courts challenge the authority of school personnel to exercise control over their campuses, the moral authority of school discipline is also undermined.

Our belief in the significance of moral authority led us to focus on the effects on student outcomes of their perceptions of fairness and strictness of school discipline. Rather than focus solely on the effects of school discipline on student performance on standardized tests, we identified a broader set of outcomes (such as willingness to disobey rules, student disruption of class, fighting in school, and adolescent arrest) that have often been associated more with youth socialization than educational achievement. We were constrained in this analysis by limitations in existing observational data, but still identified a set of suggestive findings.

Our research indicates that when discipline was perceived as both fair and relatively strict, schools were successful in promoting educational achievement and youth socialization. Students in such schools were more likely to demonstrate commitment to the educational process, and had better grades and higher test scores. Conversely, they were less likely to assert that it was acceptable to disobey rules or to report being arrested as adolescents. Overly strict schools, however, risked being considered authoritarian, unfair, and illegitimate. Schools perceived as both strict and unfair yielded negative consequences in certain areas. Students in these schools had lower grades, were more apt to report a willingness to disobey rules, and had a higher incidence of arrests.

Our research identifying associations between student perceptions of school discipline and subsequent student outcomes suggests that the problem is not simply that school discipline is either too strict or too lenient. Rather, discipline is often ineffective—and at times actually counterproductive or detrimental to students—because the school's legitimacy and moral authority have been eroded. Courts were partially responsible for this situation, as they have challenged schools' legal, moral, and discretionary authority in this area. Hampering public schools' capacity to socialize youth effectively has become a particularly acute problem in recent years, as changes in the way we live have simultaneously reduced parental supervision and parental involvement in children's lives. Specifically, changes in the organization of economic production and the transportation system began to remove adult male workers from proximity to their children early in the twentieth century. More recent changes dramatically increased the number of mothers working outside the home.[99] Today schools must accept greater responsibility for the socialization of youth; yet, simultaneously, their authority to assume such a role has been seriously undermined by court decisions.

School disciplinary climates, while important for all students, were likely to be of greatest significance to youth at risk for delinquency and incarceration. Educational reforms aimed solely at improving test scores often implicitly assumed that students finished high school, received some additional training, and then commenced work. Such assumptions were erroneous for many students. High schools now rarely provide vocational training, so graduates who do not successfully complete any subsequent training are ill-prepared for the labor market. Instead of preparing students for school-to-work transition, disorder in urban public schools and the absence of vocational programs often mean a transition only from school to prison.

School socialization was likely a significant factor in determining whether students were subsequently oriented toward work and capable of being employed in a stable manner—that is, failure in the labor market was often partially the result of inadequate socialization of young adults, who failed to embrace conventional attitudes, dispositions, and activities. School failures in this area have been growing in recent years, as U.S. youth incarceration rates have increased dramatically. From 1980 to the mid 1990s, the number of individuals in jails and prisons has tripled from around 500,000 to more than one and a half million. The majority of these individuals were young males with little education. The percentage of incarcerated who were African-American has increased from one-third in the 1960s to over one-half today. We demonstrate specifically in Chapter 5 that African-American students have been particularly adversely affected by failures in public school discipline.

Outline of Our Presentation

From an analysis of court decisions, we move to the effects of court decisions on school discipline, and to how school discipline affected student outcomes. Chapter 2 identifies the general pattern of state and federal appellate court decisions from 1960 to 1992 and describes the methodology we used to identify and analyze court data. We describe the extent to which legal challenges to school discipline have varied over time with respect to: 1) the amount of litigation; 2) the type of school discipline being challenged; and 3) the type of student infraction that led to school sanction. In addition, we also discuss Supreme Court decisions during this time period that dealt with school discipline.

We continue our examination of court decisions in Chapter 3, applying traditional techniques of statistical analysis to school discipline appellate court cases. Specifically, we analyze factors that were related to the likelihood that court decisions favored students. After controlling for factors related to specific cases coming before judges, we identified variation across regions and jurisdictions, as well as over time, in the probability of pro-student court opinions. The analysis also allowed identification of how particular aspects of the cases (such as student and school characteristics) affected legal outcomes.

In Chapter 4, we examined with the limited observational data currently available the extent to which variation in court climates was one of the factors related to school disciplinary practices and the related student and faculty perceptions of school discipline. We identified associations between measures of court climate produced in our earlier analysis of court climates and student, teacher, and administrator outcomes in four nationally representative data sets (Office of Civil Rights Elementary and Secondary School Survey, High School and Beyond, the National Educational Longitudinal Study, and the School and Staffing Survey).

Chapter 5 explores how perceptions of school discipline at the student level affected educational achievement and youth socialization. Although our measures of school discipline and youth socialization were limited to imperfect observational data found in existing nationally representative sources, we examined the extent to which perceptions of school discipline were associated with a broad range of outcomes related to educational achievement and successful youth socialization. We identified the degree to which the moral authority of school discipline was associated with improvement in test scores, student grades, and the likelihood of high school graduation. We further examined student commitment toward school and attitudes toward disobeying rules; and also modeled teacher reports of student disruptions in class, as well as student reports of fighting and adolescent arrest. In addition, we explored educational characteristics other than discipline that have been suggested by extensions of Emile Durkheim's work to areas of schooling, youth socialization, and criminology more generally.

In Chapter 6, we discuss the implications of our research findings for educational policy inherent in the two central propositions of our research: 1) that the moral authority of public schools has been undermined by the institutional environment in which they are situated; and 2) that moral authority is central to a school's ability to promote academic achievement and socialize youth effectively. In this concluding chapter we move away from narrow social scientific discussion of our empirical findings to offer more speculative policy-focused discussion related to the results. At the school level we consider a recommendation that in order for schools to reduce student disorder, school personnel should become more responsive and proactive in disciplinary approach, intimate in structuring educational involvement through reducing school or class size, and relevant in curricular offerings. At the societal level, we explore recommendations that due process rights for students be limited to cases in which students face long-term exclusion (such as suspension for several weeks or expulsions) as well as those in which their First Amendment rights have been implicated. In addition, we discuss briefly how our research might inform debates over zero-tolerance policies, voucher initiatives, and educational law reform efforts more generally.

We then conclude the book with a detailed set of tables in a methodological appendix. The appendix provides technical description of our analysis and data sets, as well as complete statistical results of our modeling. While the text of the book was written for a larger public audience, the appendix will be of interest primarily to social scientists.

2

Student Rights versus School Rules

With Irenee R. Beattie

CENTRAL HIGH SUSPENSIONS FOLLOW ROW
Central was closed about 11 A.M. Friday. School officials said the
closing came after an estimated 75 to 150 Negro students ram-
paged through halls, setting off fire extinguishers and breaking
windows in interior doors and glass over pictures hanging in the
corridors. Students involved in the disorder have been suspended
. . . [and will] not be allowed to return to school until they and
their parents have conferences with Central officials . . . [The
school principal] said he does not know how long it will be before
the conferences are held and students under suspension are readmitted.

—*THE COLUMBUS DISPATCH*, FEBRUARY 27, 1971

In the winter and spring of 1971, student suspensions from public high
schools made headlines in Columbus, Ohio. Suspended students then claimed
unfair disciplinary treatment and brought court cases against the Columbus Public School District. Such court challenges by students against
school rules and practices had become common in the early 1970s, and
would continue as an important feature of schools' institutional landscape
in subsequent decades. An overarching aim of this book is to understand
how the characteristics of schools' organizational environments influenced
the practice of discipline. Because students and their advocates used the
courts in adjudicating disputes over school discipline, these institutions
played an important role in guiding the use of discipline in schools. Before
we demonstrate the effects of court cases on school practices in later chapters, we need to understand the pattern of court decisions and how the elements of specific court cases shaped judicial outcomes. This chapter ana-

lyzes appellate court cases from 1960 to 1992 that involved a conflict between students and school officials over school discipline.

To introduce some of the issues raised in court conflicts between students and schools over discipline, we again turn our attention to the student unrest reported in Columbus, Ohio, in 1971. At Central High School during a patriotic assembly, according to principal Calvin Park, a "group of black students apparently were disgruntled because there was no special assembly for an observance of Black History Week and scores of students refused to return to classes from the assembly in protest."[1] The students continued to demonstrate the following week. McGuffey Junior High and Marion-Franklin High also experienced numerous bouts of "racial tension" involving hundreds of students in February and March 1971. School principals responded swiftly to these disturbances and disciplined many students in an effort to regain control over the schools. As a result, around 75 students were suspended from Central High. Though only excluded from school for a period of ten days or less, suspended students received no hearing, no formal notification of the specific charges against them, and no opportunity to present evidence on their own behalf. Many suspended students claimed that they had only watched and had not taken active part in the disturbances. But the full suspensions were carried out and became part of the students' permanent records.

Together with their parents, a few of the aggrieved students linked up with the local chapter of the NAACP and expressed their outrage over the suspensions. The local branch of the organization held a meeting for students affected by the discipline and their parents with two public interest lawyers contacted by I. W. Barkan, a lawyer who had frequently worked with the NAACP. Barkan contacted Denis Murphy, a local civil rights lawyer, who agreed to work on the case *pro-bono*. Through Murphy, the aggrieved students linked up with Ken Curtin, an OEO legal service lawyer based in Columbus, who previously had successfully challenged public schools over student rights issues in federal district court.[2] On the basis of the considerable strength of the individual student cases, the lawyers selected nine named plaintiffs to litigate on their collective behalf; Lopez was chosen as the first named plaintiff, because he was articulate and his name sounded "ethnic." All of the families were eligible for free legal services from Columbus Legal Services; Murphy remained active in the case on a *pro bono* basis. Curtin contacted Peter Roos and Eric Van Loon, lawyers at OEO's Center for Law and Education in Cambridge, Massachusetts, who provided essential and sophisticated appellate legal expertise. According to Curtin, all legal actors aiding the students were clear about the explicit aim of the case: to set up a federal appellate-level challenge that was potentially capable of establishing student rights to due process as broadly as possible in school disciplinary procedures.[3] Hence lawyers committed themselves not merely to challenging "the ten day suspension law on the grounds that it was too long to permit without due process," but instead, according to Roos, "to go all the way and say that any suspension for more than a trivial period of time required due process."[4]

As a result of these contacts with the NAACP, OEO Legal Services, and Murphy, nine suspended students brought their grievances to the courts. Court disputes over school discipline had become frequent by the early 1970s. Some school discipline challenges would first be tried in various state courts, then upon appeal enter federal district and appellate courts, before ultimately being considered by the Supreme Court of the United States. Because these students challenged the constitutionality of a state law empowering principals to suspend students with few procedural guidelines, their case skipped the state courts and headed straight to the federal judiciary. By contesting not just the school's record of disciplinary sanction in student records, but also the constitutionality of state law, lawyers strategically denied school officials the latitude of settling the case easily and thereby avoiding lengthy and costly litigation. In the *Lopez v. Williams* case before the United States District Court in Ohio, the student complainants detailed their suspensions, while principals and administrators offered their account of events.[5]

Dwight Lopez, a 19-year-old student at Central High School testified

> that in late February, 1971, there was tension at Central High School over Black History Week. On the morning of February 26, 1971, he had a free study period in the lunch room. While he was in the lunch room, black students came in and started overturning tables. Dwight Lopez testified that he and several of his friends walked out of the lunch room. He testified that he took no part in the unlawful activity and that he did not violate any school rule or any other rule.[6]

After the events in the lunch room, all students were sent home. Later that day, the school principal called Lopez at home to notify him that he was suspended, but did not indicate the reasons for his punishment. A letter from the principal to Lopez's parents subsequently leveled the accusation: "today a group of students disrupted our complete school program.

Dwight was in the group."[7] The letter also advised that Lopez and his parents would need to appear before the Board of Education before he would be allowed to return to school. When Lopez and his parents tried to attend the scheduled meeting, however, several hundred people had blocked the entrance of the building in protest of the board's policies. Because the family missed the meeting, the school district transferred Dwight to an adult school, without his consent. Though he eventually received his diploma, the suspension remained a part of his permanent school record.

The other aggrieved students gave similar accounts; they did not have hearings and were not told the specific charges and evidence against them before being suspended. Finding for the students and against the school, the District Court stated:

> The primacy of the educator in the school has been unquestioned by the Courts. The Courts have consistently reaffirmed the right of school administrators to manage their school systems without interference from the Courts, so long as the basic commands of the Constitution are honored . . .
>
> The Courts have vigorously asserted the right, and indeed the duty of school administrators to prohibit student behavior which materially disrupts classwork, endangers property or interferes with the rights of other students . . . Remembering that school officials are better suited to make decisions affecting their institutions, the Court nonetheless is Constitutionally bound to insure that the student be afforded the minimum procedural process mandated by the Constitution . . .
>
> Due process is not a straitjacket imposed by the Courts upon educators. The minimum requirements of notice and a hearing prior to suspension, except in emergency situations, does not require inflexible procedures . . .
>
> In the present case plaintiffs were not accorded a hearing . . . There is no evidence in the record that any of the plaintiffs voluntarily relinquished their right to a hearing.
>
> The Court holds that plaintiffs were not accorded due process of law, in that they were suspended without hearing prior to suspension or within a reasonable time thereafter.
>
> The Court orders that references to the suspensions . . . be removed from all records of Columbus Public Schools.[8]

Although the judge was careful to state the primacy of school officials in matters of school discipline, the decision still eroded the authority of school personnel by applying the principle of constitutional limitations to their actions.[9]

The school appealed the decision to the U.S. Supreme Court, in a case then called *Goss v. Lopez,* which subsequently defined legal precedent on these matters for decades. The school argued that education was not a constitutionally protected right, so the students had no reasonable claim to an uninterrupted education. The Court rejected this argument and found that state laws directing local officials to provide free education to all and making school attendance compulsory for children of a certain age created circumstances where the students had reasonable claims to public education. The court chided that "[h]aving chosen to extend the right to an education . . . Ohio may not withdraw that right on the grounds of misconduct, absent fundamentally fair procedures to determine whether the misconduct has occurred."[10]

In a six to three majority decision, the Supreme Court affirmed the district court opinion and ruled that the suspensions were invalid and that students' records should be expunged of any reference to them. The Justices reflected on the importance of following the Due Process Clause when schools imposed even short-term suspensions, stating that

> our schools are vast and complex. Some modicum of discipline and order is essential if the educational function is to be performed. Events calling for discipline are frequent occurrences and sometimes require immediate, effective action. Suspension is considered not only to be a necessary tool to maintain order but a valuable educational device. The prospect of imposing elaborate hearing requirements in every suspension case is viewed with great concern, and many school authorities may well prefer the untrammeled power to act unilaterally, unhampered by rules about notice and hearing. But it would be a strange disciplinary system in an educational institution if no communication was sought by the disciplinarian with the student in an effort to inform him of his dereliction and to let him tell his side of the story in order to make sure that an injustice is not done.[11]

This decision was a victory for the students. Indeed, what the Court decreed was that the school principal, the Board of Education, and even the State of Ohio had not provided enough procedural safeguards to ensure that the students' constitutional rights were not violated.

But this decision was not unanimous. Other Justices believed that the

Court had gone too far with this ruling—giving students rights that encroached upon the ability of schools to discipline their charges effectively. In the dissenting opinion, Justice Powell, who was a former school board member, sounded an alarm, warning that the majority decision

> unnecessarily opens avenues for judicial intervention in the operation of our public schools that may affect adversely the quality of education. The Court holds for the first time that the federal courts, rather than educational officials and state legislatures, have the authority to determine the rules applicable to routine classroom discipline of children and teenagers in the public schools.[12]

Further, the dissenters recognized that schools played a critical role in socializing students in ways beyond classroom learning:

> The State's generalized interest in maintaining an orderly school system is not incompatible with the individual interest of the student. Education in any meaningful sense includes the inculcation of an understanding in each pupil of the necessity of rules and obedience thereto. This understanding is no less important than learning to read and write. One who does not comprehend the meaning and necessity of discipline is handicapped not merely in his education but throughout his subsequent life. In an age when the home and church play a diminishing role in shaping the character and value judgments of the young, a heavier responsibility falls upon the schools. When an immature student merits censure for his conduct, he is rendered a disservice if appropriate sanctions are not applied or if procedures for their application are so formalized as to invite a challenge to the teacher's authority—an invitation which rebellious or even merely spirited teenagers are likely to accept.[13]

This statement suggested that the dissenting Justices feared that any court intervention in the operation of school discipline would severely undermine school authority and encourage students to rebel.

On the surface, the dissents seem to support Durkheim's conception of moral authority. Yet the Justices' "rules-for-the-sake-of-rules" approach differed from Durkheim's advocacy of moral authority in two important ways. First, rather than highlight the importance of schools working to help students develop an internalized appreciation for appropriate rules, the dissenting opinions advocated a school discipline that emphasized "the necessity of rules and obedience thereto." Durkheim argued, in contrast, that "an act is not moral, even when it is in substantial agreement with moral rules, if the consideration of adverse consequences has determined it."[14] Merely following the rules to avoid being punished, according to Durkheim, would not lead to the development of a moral character. Instead, schools should foster the *internalization* of the moral ideas behind the rules, not the rules themselves. Second, the dissenting Justices appeared attuned to the *individual* consequences of unenforced rules, whereas Durkheim concerned himself with the *collective* social processes underlying moral authority in schools that affected students as a group. We note these distinctions to emphasize the degree to which pro-school judicial decisions tended to embrace a conservative Hobbesian, rather than a Durkheimian orientation. Legal justifications emphasizing the intrinsic value of external sanctions to regulate individual behavior were particularly unfortunate in this context, as this approach had been widely rejected in dominant professional pedagogical approaches in currency at the time. Because conservative judges failed to articulate arguments that appreciated the extent to which school discipline required internalization, moral authority, and legitimacy, their pro-school opinions found fewer political allies among educational professionals threatened by the litigation than one would ordinarily expect.

Other than the opinions of the Supreme Court Justices, what was the relationship between the moral authority of school officials, courts, and student behavior during this time? *Goss v. Lopez* gives some clues about where to look in greater depth for the answers. In this well-known case, the students proceeded through the courts with favorable verdicts. Were such outcomes typical? How have decisions in school discipline cases varied over time and in different jurisdictions? If the students had been subjected to corporal punishment rather than suspension, would the outcome have been as likely to favor the students? If the students had been suspended from school for smoking marijuana in the bathroom rather than protesting race issues, would the courts have decided this case differently? Observing a variety of court cases over time and across legal jurisdictions allows us to trace the pattern of court decisions and later explore how court cases can potentially shape student outcomes.

Following the *Goss v. Lopez* decision, the headlines in local Columbus papers read "High Court Rules in Student Favor."[15] What were the social implications of the Supreme Court of the United States ruling for a group of minority youth and against the school district and the state? Whatever the consequences, it was clear that the ramifications extended beyond the specific students and school directly involved. Around the country, headlines such as this—announcing court decisions for and against students in disputes over school discipline—were bound to gain the attention of students, parents, teachers, and principals alike. It was the direction of the decision, emphasized in these headlines, rather than the precise legal reasoning behind it, which took on social meaning in the court of public opinion. The relation between courts and school discipline therefore extended beyond legal details identifying limitations of due process guarantees. More important than specific changes in case law was the overall change in the general climate created by the pattern of outcomes found in school discipline court cases.

Case Law versus Court Climate

A narrow look at the relationship between school discipline court cases and school practices might suggest that case law changes emerging from a given case determine such a relationship. Case law, a corollary of common law, is simply "the law created by judges when deciding individual disputes or cases,"[16] and it should be distinguished from law created by legislation or written in statute books. Case law is the compendium of legal precedents set by judges' decisions that lawyers and judges must pay attention to as they craft arguments or decisions based on precise questions of law.

A court climate, on the other hand, has little to do with what is written in each specific court decision. Written case law is ambiguous, with judges and lawyers constantly offering new interpretations of the finer points of a given court decision. It is also particular, hinging upon the specific facts of a given case. Social scientists who study judicial decision-making argue that "to the extent that facts and laws are ambiguous, federal trial judges' perceptions and interpretations are the product of judicial discretion, even when judges are 'simply' evaluating facts, law and the fit between the two. This exercise of discretionary judgment is, after all, why we call them 'judges.'"[17] Liberal exercise of judicial discretion was not limited to lower courts. Legal historian Laura Kalman, for example, has described the judicial deliberative process Supreme Court Justice Abe Fortas occasionally adopted: "Fortas sometime wrote draft opinions without legal citations in them, then ordered his law clerks to 'decorate' them with the appropriate legalese. That did not mean that Fortas knew the supporting law was there.

It meant that he considered law indeterminate and did not care about it much at all."[18]

While the Fortas example might be particularly pronounced and egregious in its apparent disregard of judicial etiquette, most serious observers of the Court have recognized the degree to which judicial discretion has often been exercised without full regard to legal precedent. Given judicial discretion and the inherent ambiguity of law, we believe that organizations—and more particularly, school administrators and teachers in charge of school discipline—are more likely to attune themselves to a diffuse court climate rather than narrow case law.[19] Such a climate is by definition not particularistic: it is the aggregation of all decisions emanating from judges with direct jurisdiction over a given area. So, although case law and the court climate are shaped from the same building blocks—judicial decisions—they differ greatly in their conceptual bases.

Court climate and case law also serve different purposes. Judges and lawyers are necessarily interested in case law in order to craft arguments and ground decisions in legal precedents as applied to a particular case at hand—such, after all, are the professional requirements and institutional basis for their occupations. However, case law interpretations depend upon the facts in a specific situation. School officials charged with maintaining school discipline must undertake a course of action that generally follows the case law trends, yet at the same time does not cause undue strain on the administration of discipline in schools. The interests of school officials were different from those of lawyers and judges; they sought to respond to the court climate in order to remain in compliance with the general sentiment and trends in court decisions, thus avoiding costly and time-consuming legal battles.

It is indeed reasonable for school officials to observe general trends in their respective state and federal courts, rather than specific case law changes. Substantial empirical evidence has suggested that, should a student challenge disciplinary actions in court, the school official's fate will not be decided by a judge on the basis of case law alone. Trial judges, like other political actors, have the discretion to choose between conflicting interests.[20] Over the past 35 years, political scientists and other socio-legal scholars have studied the influence of legal and political subcultures on trial judges and determined that local environmental factors have influenced judicial decisions. For example, researchers have found that the harshness of sentences imposed upon Vietnam War draft resisters was associated with the temporal and spatial variation in public support for the war.[21] More recently, research has suggested that the level of judicial support for environmental regulation was related to the political context of environmental disputes in the states in a given court circuit.[22] Study of federal judicial decision-making also has suggested that the politics of judicial appointments, especially since 1968, has influenced judges' decisions. Research has found that judges who were Carter appointees were twice as likely as Reagan appointees to find in favor of criminal defendants or those claiming civil rights violations.[23] Because social, political, and institutional factors—not just legal ones—influenced judicial decisions, it was logical for a school official to consider general trends in court decisions rather than attempt to interpret and resolve specific ambiguities in case law.

Teachers and school administrators do not have the luxury of paralegals to brief them on the facts of each relevant case that comes before the courts and how such law might apply to daily questions of school practice. Instead, school personnel learn about the court climate from other sources: professional organizations and school or district legal counsel. As a requirement of their jobs, school principals and administrators are expected to be well versed in the school court climate. To this end, professional organizations to which school officials belong have provided them with numerous opportunities to brush up on current trends in school legal decisions. They have published books and journals with information on federal and state court case decisions. For example, the Association of California School Administrators published a *Legal Handbook for California Administrators.* The Massachusetts Secondary School Administrators' Association published *The Alert,* a monthly bulletin containing "legislative information, professional openings and legal summaries."[24] Numerous associations published journals with articles about general trends in cases involving school discipline. The September 1998 issue of the *National Association of Secondary School Principals Bulletin* included articles with titles such as: "The Principal and Student Expression: From Armbands to Tattoos"; "Search and Seizure in the Schools"; and "The Principal and Discipline with Special Education Students."[25] Also, some association websites have provided members-only "Legal Corners." Associations also sponsor conferences and seminars that discussed the school discipline court climate: for example, the School Administrators Association of New York State offers to conduct legal seminars on "Student Rights" and "Student Discipline" at members' local schools.

Further, many school districts employed legal counsel full or part-time to notify administrators about the generalities of relevant case decisions, as well as to represent the district in legal disputes. Legal counsel was often consulted when drawing up school discipline codes in order to ensure the legality of school rules. The national Council of School Attorneys today boasts over 3,000 members.[26] Clearly, many opportunities and organizational structures are available to help school personnel remain informed about changes in local court climates related to school discipline. Yet given the complexity and ambiguity inherent to law in this area, these avenues of legal information were useful in attuning school personnel to general court leanings, but unable to give the last word on judicially acceptable school disciplinary practices in all areas.

School Discipline Court Case Data: 1960–1992

To measure the court climate regarding school discipline, we constructed a data set of appellate court cases at the state and federal levels that involved students (or individuals acting on behalf of students) who were contesting a school's right to discipline and control them. In Lexis-Nexis, we used an overly broad search string to identify 6,277 potentially relevant cases from 1945–1992.[27] A team of researchers read each detailed case decision and determined first if the case was relevant to our topic. We excluded as not relevant all cases involving conflicts between schools and teachers (for example, cases of teacher dismissal); schools and nonstudent outsiders (for example, drug and weapons free zone cases that did not involve students); and student rights cases focused exclusively on free speech issues (not related to the school's use of suspension, expulsion, corporal punishment, or transfer). We included cases involving the use of state agents (such as police) who were acting on behalf of school authority in dealing with students in the vicinity of school grounds. After determining that uniform data were not available for all state courts prior to 1960, we restricted our sample to cases that were decided between 1960 and 1992. A second coder read all cases initially deemed relevant in order to verify whether the cases met our criteria, disqualifying an additional 18 cases as irrelevant. Using these procedures, we created a data set of 1,204 relevant cases.

Analyzing the text of relevant court case decisions, we content-coded the cases to identify 26 variables: state location, court level, case citation, gender of student, race of student, disability status, alleged gender discrimination, alleged racial discrimination, form of school discipline (suspension, expulsion, corporal punishment, or school transfer), type of student misbehavior (alcohol, drugs, violence, weapons, political protest, or general misbehavior), education level, school sector, and direction of court decision. Inter-coder reliability tests suggested coder agreement on approximately 94 percent of coding decisions.[28]

Selection Bias

Social scientists must consider whether a particular data set is subject to problems with selection bias. Selection bias occurs in a sample when the method or criterion used to select the cases results in a sample that differs from the population under investigation in some systematic way. A sample that suffers from selection bias might produce unreliable results. A sociologist who wants to study welfare recipients' experiences with education, for example, would draw a biased sample if she used a list of random telephone numbers to call potential respondents. Clearly, her results would be biased because her method of recruiting a sample would limit cases to only those welfare recipients who could afford a telephone. This would not pose a problem for the research if recipients with and without phones did not differ in their educational experiences and in other respects, but it is logical to assume that they would so differ.

In the present study, might the court case data suffer from selection bias? If we sought to understand all conflicts over school discipline using our court case data, our method would clearly be inappropriate. Missing from this analysis would be all the conflicts between students and schools that never even surfaced in the court system, which we could assume differed in some important ways from those that were eventually adjudicated in the courts. Our research interests are much narrower, however: we seek to understand the school discipline *court climate,* not school discipline conflicts or educational law more generally construed. Thus our underlying population is defined as significant school discipline cases adjudicated in the courts at the appellate level.[29] Our method of creating this data set allowed us to include *all* state and federal appellate court cases dealing with school discipline during the time period of interest. Our sample includes *the entire population* of school discipline cases we seek to understand, so these data cannot be subjected to traditional selection bias critiques. The court climate, by definition, consisted only of disputes that have actually been adjudicated in the appellate courts.

The court climate that we examined was dependent on the action of people bringing and appealing cases in the courts. While individual families with adequate resources could theoretically have advanced litigation independently, appellate court challenges typically involved individuals working with sympathetic institutions, such as OEO Legal Services and other public interest law and advocacy organizations. In the case of *Goss v. Lopez*, for example, the presence of a local OEO Legal Service office that could rely on the expertise of OEO's Center for Law and Education in Cambridge as well as other related organizational resources (such as support from the ACLU), was essential in the case's advancement. Even with this support, however, it would be irresponsible to ignore that certain groups of people had a greater likelihood than others of adjudicating school-student discipline conflicts in court. We know from data from the Office of Civil Rights that minority students were much more likely to be subjected to disciplinary action in schools than were white students. For example, around 40 percent of all suspensions involved nonwhite students, and around 35 percent of all corporal punishments involved minorities during the time period examined.[30] Where race was specified, however, only approximately 10 percent of the school discipline court cases involved a nonwhite student.[31] On the one hand, discipline was practiced disproportionately on racial minorities, yet on the other hand, there was not a similarly disproportionate rate of minority court challenges against school discipline.

Minorities might have confronted financial and social barriers that precluded them from advancing grievances in the courts. While public interest law prior to 1965 was often advanced by the NAACP Fund and usually aimed explicitly at ameliorating racial discrimination and segregation, with the beginning of the War on Poverty and the establishment of OEO Legal Services the focus of law reform shifted from race to poverty. As legal scholars Handler, Hollingsworth, and Erlanger have noted: "by 1967 it was clear that whereas civil rights law had previously been 'in,' poverty law seemed to some extent to have replaced it."[32] While OEO Legal Services and other organizations did still pursue desegregation-related educational law reform, few other efforts were made to address racial disparities in school discipline explicitly through the courts. The prominent role of *Goss v. Lopez* in the corpus of school discipline case law—and the role of racial unrest as a cause for the discipline that was contested in this case—might have given the general public an erroneous impression that race was a prominent feature in court challenges to school discipline. Challenging a school system at the appellate level required either significant political commitment, institutional backing, or substantial financial resources.[33] Filing a court case against a school also required familiarity with, and a certain level of trust in, the court system. Perceptions of racist practices—whether accurate or not—might have led some minorities to the conclusion that the nation's institutions (be they courts, schools, or governments) would not protect their interests. Ironically, some of the findings we present below suggest that nonwhite racial status was associated with a greater likelihood of court decisions in a student's favor. However, this finding does not negate the significant barriers that would have made it less likely for minorities to bring school discipline court challenges than would be the case for their white peers. There is, therefore, a "selection bias" in which cases involving blacks and other minorities were brought forward: probably only the most egregious cases affecting African-American students made their way into appellate courts. We must thus be cautious in interpreting findings suggesting that case decisions might vary by race, because observed differences might be partially due to other factors related to the court trajectories of white and nonwhite grievances.[34]

Appellate Court Cases Over Time

The late sixties and early seventies brought in a new era in which youth gained unprecedented social and legal rights. In 1971, the 26th Amendment lowered the legal voting age to eighteen. In many areas of law, such as free speech and basic civil rights, youth gained legal stature nearly tantamount to that of adults. Not only did such changes contribute to symbolic and real lessening of parental control, but shifts in ideas about adolescent rights also altered conceptions about appropriate school disciplinary practices. Prior to these changes, school authorities were widely viewed as beyond recrimination—students and parents seldom publicly questioned or explicitly challenged their actions. Yet around the same time as citizens began questioning their government's actions in the Vietnam War, students and their parents began confronting school principals and superintendents in the courts over disciplinary disputes. Concurrently, in pedagogical circles educators such as Lawrence Kohlberg, Ivan Illich, and Paolo Freire advanced radical proposals for dramatically altering traditional authority relationships in schools.[35]

How prevalent were appellate cases challenging school discipline before, during, and after this contentious period in U.S. history? How did some central issues raised in court cases change after the Vietnam War era? We will explore the longitudinal aspect of our data set to demonstrate how critical features of these cases varied over time. First, we illustrate how the number of school discipline court cases fluctuated since 1960. Next, we identify changes in the type of student misbehavior at issue in discipline cases over time. Finally, we explore how the form of discipline (such as corporal punishment or expulsion) that produced the legal case varied in different time periods.

Number of Cases

As is readily apparent from Figure 2.1, the sheer number of school discipline court cases expanded greatly since the late 1960s. Prior to 1969, very few school discipline court cases had been adjudicated in the United States. In fact, although we originally collected court cases beginning in 1945, we excluded the years before 1960 from our final data set because there were too few cases in that period to analyze.[36] From 1969 to 1975, school discipline court cases surged. After that time, the level of such cases in the courts remained lower than the peak, but still relatively common and consistent. Clearly, school discipline court climates are a relatively modern phenomenon.

Our analysis of the number of school discipline court cases suggests three distinct time periods. Prior to 1969, we have identified a pre-contestation period in which courts heard very few school discipline court cases. From 1960 to 1968 there was an average of only nine relevant cases per year. This initial time period reveals an emerging and gradually increasing trend of challenging public school administration on student discipline. This increase in litigation was supported institutionally by the growth of public interest legal advocacy organizations and the efforts of OEO Legal Services after 1965. Next was the period from 1969 to 1975 that we have labeled the student rights contestation period, in which unprecedented numbers of school discipline cases were brought before the courts: an average of 76 cases per year. Finally, after students made inroads in the

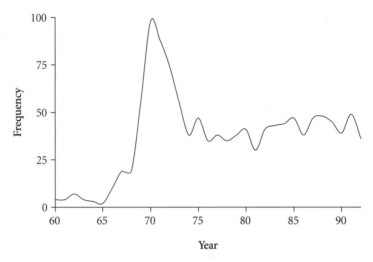

Figure 2.1 Annual number of school discipline court cases, 1960–1992

courts in the early 1970s and institutional support for appellate challenges declined, the number of cases went down slightly, averaging 57 cases per year. We have termed the 1976–1992 years the post-contestation period. Although this period certainly had a lower level of cases than did the contestation period, it was clearly different from the pre-contestation period: students and their supporters were emboldened by their access to the courts from 1969–1975. They had gained legal strategies, case law precedents, a widespread diffusion of a sense of student entitlements to rights, and an institutional infrastructure to maintain support and expansion of these gains. Given these changes, continued challenges to school authority in the courts occurred at levels unimaginable in the early 1960s. In addition, legal gains made in the contestation period were institutionalized in public school practices.

This pattern of expansion in school discipline court cases mirrored broader societal trends both in the courts and in educational institutions at all levels. In 1966, federal rules loosened significantly, allowing for plaintiffs' lawyers to receive a portion of damages assessed for a whole class of people, which contributed to a growth in the prevalence of class action lawsuits. American citizens became increasingly litigious in the decades following the expansion of individual rights promoted by federal legislation and the Warren Court in the 1960s, and institutional changes involving the growth of public interest law. In addition to more court disputes between students and schools, there were more medical malpractice suits, more court challenges over environmental damage, and more litigation challenging numerous public and private institutions.[37] Institutional analysts have argued that it was a period when not just schools, but also private firms faced "legal uncertainty raised by governmental anti-discrimination initiatives" and adopted internal procedures expanding formal and symbolic protections to employees.[38] Hence increased school discipline litigation and school adoption of due process procedures reflected some of the broader changes in the propensity to turn toward courts and invoke individual rights in situations where social conflict with institutions occurred.

As we all know, the late sixties and early seventies was a time of immense social upheaval. Educational institutions at all levels faced challenges to their authority. Most vividly, these disputes occasionally ended in violence, as at Kent State University, where four protesters against the Vietnam War were shot and killed when the University summoned the National Guard to impose order in the spring of 1970—a historic event that occurred less than a year after *Goss v. Lopez* and fewer than 140 miles away. Surviving Kent State students, incidentally, also turned to courts to challenge the harsh and violent suppression of their protest efforts. Elementary and high school students, though engaged in less deadly disputes, were also very active during this period, when individuals in various walks of life were questioning the "establishment."

Form of School Discipline

Each case we examined involved some attempt by a school to discipline a student: discipline ranged from exclusion from a graduation ceremony or sports team to expulsion for the remainder of a school year or indefinitely. Figures 2.2a through 2.2c show the proportion of cases involving various forms of school discipline in each of the three time periods. One thing that remained stable was that suspensions and expulsions were the first and second most common forms of discipline, respectively, that have been adjudicated in the courts. The frequency, however, diminished: while over 60 percent of cases prior to 1976 involved suspension, only 40 percent of subsequent cases involved this form of discipline. This does not mean that the actual proportion of school discipline involving suspensions declined. This

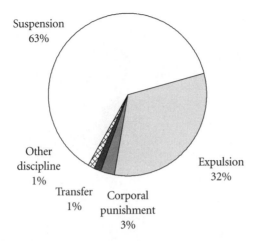

Figure 2.2a Form of school discipline in court cases: 1960–1968 (N=72)

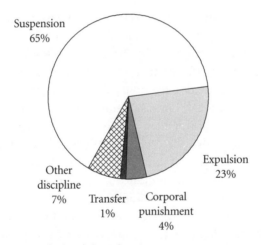

Figure 2.2b Form of school discipline in court cases: 1969–1975 (N=453)

change suggests only that the proportion of school discipline cases adjudicated in appellate courts that involved suspension went down. One explanation for this change might be that after the period of rights contestation, there was sufficient information available to most school administrators about the necessary procedural safeguards to avoid further court challenges in this area.

By contrast, adjudication over student expulsion and the administration

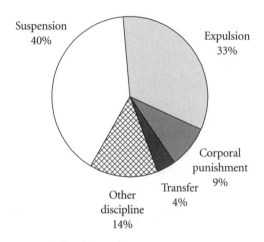

Suspension
40%

Expulsion
33%

Corporal
punishment
9%

Transfer
4%

Other
discipline
14%

Figure 2.2c Form of school discipline in court cases: 1976–1992 (N=679)

of corporal punishment increased. This was surprising, given that the actual use of these forms of discipline had been in decline, according to school administrator reports to the Office of Civil Rights (see Chapter 4). This disparity between the number of court challenges and school use of these practices may have resulted from gains students made in courts. After being accorded additional rights, students and their parents may have become less willing to accept these relatively harsh disciplinary practices without a challenge. Also, the decline in the use of these practices probably corresponded to the development of a court climate that discouraged harsh discipline. Courts have indicated particular concern over the use of expulsion and cautioned school administrators that before abandoning a commitment to the provision of free public education for all children of a certain age by expelling an unruly child, they must have provided the utmost in procedural due process to ensure that the student's rights are protected. We believe these practices declined, in part, because court rulings rendered expulsion too costly as an administrative procedure when a suspension or school transfer could be used as a legally safer substitute.

Type of Student Misbehavior

Dwight Lopez was suspended from school for alleged involvement in a race-related protest; Peggy Strickland was expelled for spiking the school punch with "Right Time" malt liquor; T.L.O. was labeled a delinquent child because her principal found evidence of marijuana dealing in her purse. In these Supreme Court cases and others, the type of student misbehavior—alleged or actual—that led to some form of discipline and a subsequent challenge has changed over time. Figures 2.3a through 2.3c depict the proportion of cases involving various student infractions in both state and federal appellate courts during each of our three time periods. In the pre-contestation period (Figure 2.3a), the majority of cases involved students who were disciplined for some form of political activity (such as civil rights involvement, Vietnam War protest, or free expression). Free expression cases often had explicitly political content, such as putting out an underground student newspaper critical of school policy or of the United States government; growing hair longer than was acceptable under school policies (male); and wearing pants in violation of school dress codes (female). The catchall category, general misbehavior, involved 38 percent of the cases during this period. General misbehavior included causes we could not classify in our other categories. For example, truancy, insubordination, vandalism, and, in one case, stealing muffins from the school cafeteria were all considered general misbehavior. Drug- and alcohol-related infractions combined to make up five percent of the cases in this period, while violence accounted for three percent of the discipline conflicts.

During the student rights contestation period (Figure 2.3b), protest and

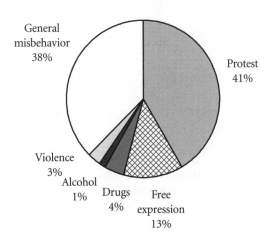

Figure 2.3a Type of student misbehavior in school discipline court cases: 1960—1968 (N=72)

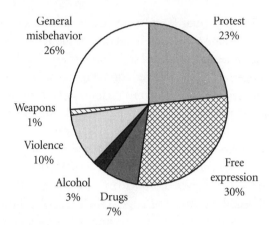

Figure 2.3b Type of student misbehavior in school discipline court cases: 1969—1975 (N=453)

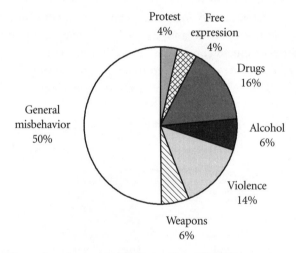

Figure 2.3c Type of student misbehavior in school discipline court cases: 1976—1992 (N=679)

free expression cases continued to dominate school-student court conflicts over discipline. In this period, however, free expression outranked others, comprising 30 percent of all cases. Combined with the 23 percent of cases involving protest, general political agitation again accounted for over 50 percent of all cases, and 26 percent of cases involved general misbehavior.

During the period that student rights were heavily contested, cases involving discipline for weapons violations were introduced in court; there had been no conflicts over such infractions in the earlier period. Relatedly, violence increased from only three percent of all cases during the earlier 1960s to 10 percent of all cases between 1969 and 1975. Drugs and alcohol accounted for 10 percent of all student infractions in these court cases, twice the rate identified in the earlier period.

Finally, in the post-contestation period (Figure 2.3c), the proportion of various student infractions changed substantially. After 1975, free expression and protest each accounted for only four percent of all cases—or six times less than in the prior period. Further, general misbehavior now comprised 50 percent of student discipline court cases. Drug- and alcohol-related infractions were involved in 22 percent of the cases, more than double their representation during the period of student rights contestation. Similarly, violence and weapons combined to account for 20 percent of all cases, nearly twice their proportion during the contestation period. Clearly, the student infractions that came before the court between 1976 and 1992 were far more varied than they were in earlier periods. Our analyses of the features of court cases over time suggest that the court climate was dynamic.

Discipline Cases in the Supreme Court

While we are interested in looking at the school discipline court cases as a whole, we focus here on those that reached the Supreme Court rather than chart minute case law changes in every jurisdiction because such cases have greater sway over the court climate, as all schools in the nation must comply with their rulings. Areas of jurisdiction diminish from the Supreme Court downwards, thereby limiting the direct influence of any given decision. Accordingly, whereas the Supreme Court represented all of the United States, the 12 regional circuits for federal appellate courts and the 94 judicial districts for federal district courts each represented smaller and smaller areas. State court case decisions were even more limited in their impact; these decisions only directly affected the climate within a particular state, unless the decision subsequently was appealed in the federal arena. Here then is a brief overview of the major school discipline disputes in each of the three periods that reached the Supreme Court.[39]

Pre-Contestation: 1960–1968

In this period, school discipline cases did not reach the Supreme Court. Instead, a handful of cases in other legal domains laid the groundwork for subsequent challenges to school discipline. First, in the decision of *In re Gault* in 1967, the Warren Court granted procedural rights to youth in juvenile courts.[40] This ruling was an important prelude to the expansion of student rights, as it extended due process safeguards to youth. In 1968, *Epperson v. Arkansas* involved a teacher's challenge to Arkansas "anti-evolution" law that mandated the firing of any teacher who taught or used a text teaching "that mankind ascended or descended from a lower order of animals."[41] The Court ruled in favor of the teacher, stating that the regulation violated the First Amendment because the reasoning behind the statute was based on religious principles. Although the substance of the case was not directly relevant to school discipline, it became often cited, as it "emphasized the need for affirming the comprehensive authority of the States and of school officials, *consistent with fundamental constitutional safeguards,* to prescribe and control conduct in the schools."[42] Thus, although these cases did not appear in our sample of school discipline court cases, both *Epperson v. Arkansas* and *In re Gault* were important legal precedents for subsequent school discipline cases.

Student Rights Contestation: 1969–1975

Ushering in the period of extensive student challenging of school authority, *Tinker v. Des Moines Independent Community School District* (1969) was the first major school discipline court case to reach the Supreme Court. In December 1965, three Iowa students wore black armbands to school "to publicize their objections to the hostilities in Vietnam."[43] Their fathers filed a complaint in the federal district court to block the school district from disciplining the students. The district court upheld the constitutionality of the school authorities' actions and found these actions reasonable to prevent disturbance of school discipline. On appeal, the judges of the court of appeals were equally divided on the case, thus affirming it without writing an opinion. When the case reached the Supreme Court on appeal, the Court struggled with issues involved in a case that would become a precedent for later judgment of local school disciplinary practices. First, in an oft-cited passage, the majority opinion laid out the issue before the Court:

> It can hardly be argued that either students or teachers shed their constitutional rights to freedom of speech or expression at the schoolhouse gate . . . On the other hand, the Court has repeatedly emphasized the need for affirming the comprehensive authority of the States and of school officials, consistent with fundamental constitutional safeguards, to prescribe and control conduct in the schools . . . Our problem lies in the area where students in the exercise of First Amendment rights collide with the rules of the school authorities.[44]

In the end, the Court decided that

> [a student] may express his opinion, even on controversial subjects like the conflict in Vietnam, if he does so without 'materially and substantially interfer[ing] with the requirements of appropriate discipline in the operation of the school'[45] and without colliding with the rights of others . . . But the conduct by the student, in class or out of it, which for any reason . . . materially disrupts class work or involves substantial disorder or invasion of the rights of other is, of course, not immunized by the constitutional guarantee of freedom of speech.[46]

This case had widespread implications for the expansion of student rights, extending rights to students in public schools that were previously thought to belong only to adult citizens.

This decision encountered strong opposition from a minority of the Court. The opinion of two dissenting Justices, written by Justice Black, warned, "if the time has come when pupils of state-supported schools . . . can defy and flout orders of school officials to keep their minds on their schoolwork, it is the beginning of a new revolutionary era of permissiveness in this country fostered by the judiciary."[47] This was to become the standard argument of subsequent judges' rulings against students or in dissenting opinions in cases where a majority of judges decided against the schools. Allowing students "ostentatiously" to express their opinions in schools, this line of reasoning suggested, would inevitably distract other students and thus undermine school authority:

students, like other people, cannot concentrate on lesser issues when black armbands are being ostentatiously displayed in their presence to call attention to the wounded and dead of the war, some of the wounded and the dead being their friends and neighbors. It was, of course, to distract the attention of other students that some students insisted up to the very point of their own suspension from school that they were determined to sit in school with their symbolic armbands.[48]

Continuing this argument further, the dissenting Justices in *Tinker* argued that the High Court's decision, handed down in February of what would turn out to be a very contentious 1969, was tantamount to handing school control over to students:

School discipline, like parental discipline, is an integral and important part of training our children to be good citizens—to be better citizens. Here a very small number of students have crisply and summarily refused to obey a school order designed to give pupils who want to learn the opportunity to do so. One does not need to be a prophet or the son of a prophet to know that after the Court's holding today some students in Iowa schools and indeed in all schools will be ready, able, and willing to defy their teachers on practically all orders.

This is the more unfortunate for the schools since groups of students all over the land are already running loose, conducting break-ins, sit-ins, lie-ins, and smash-ins. Many of these student groups, as is all too familiar to all who read the newspapers and watch the television news programs, have already engaged in rioting, property seizures, and destruction. They have picketed schools to force students not to cross their picket lines and have too often violently attacked earnest but frightened students who wanted an education that the pickets did not want them to get.

Students engaged in such activities are apparently confident that they know far more about how to operate public school systems than do their parents, teachers, and elected school officials. It is no answer to say that the particular students here have not yet reached such high points in their demands to attend classes in order to exercise their political pressures. Turned loose with lawsuits for damages and injunctions against their teachers as they are here, it is nothing but wishful thinking to imagine that young, immature students will not soon believe it is their right to control the schools rather than the right of the States that collect the taxes to hire the teachers for the benefit of the pupils.

This case, therefore, wholly without constitutional reasons in my judgment, subjects all the public schools in the country to the whims and caprices of their loudest-mouthed, but maybe not their brightest, students. I, for one, am not fully persuaded that school pupils are wise enough, even with this Court's expert help from Washington, to run the 23,390 public school systems in our 50 States.[49] I wish, therefore, wholly to disclaim any purpose on my part to hold that the Federal Constitution compels the teachers, parents, and elected school officials to surrender control of the American public school system to public school students. I dissent.[50]

While *Tinker* did indeed open the door to a broader conceptualization of student rights, would it necessarily lead to the erosion of school authority to the extent suggested?

The next major school discipline case considered by the Court was *Goss v. Lopez* in 1975, the case discussed at length at the beginning of this chapter. This landmark Supreme Court case, decided in favor of the students, granted "rudimentary" due process rights to students suspended from school for fewer than 10 days, and "more formal protections" for students facing longer school exclusion. This case involved significant *amici curiae* briefs. Usually, individuals or organizations that file such briefs have a compelling interest in the outcome of the case, even if they were not directly party to the action. For example, in the Supreme Court abortion case, *Webster v. Reproductive Services,* hundreds of pro-choice and anti-abortion groups filed *amici curiae* briefs urging the Court to decide the case one way or the other.[51] When *Tinker* was decided in 1969, the United States National Student Association urged the Court to decide in favor of the students in an *amicus* brief. When *Goss* came before the Court in 1975, many interested parties joined in filing friend-of-the-court briefs. The Buckeye Association of School Administrators urged the Court to reverse the lower courts and find in favor of the school. Advocating a decision in favor of the students, the outcome which ultimately prevailed, were the following: the National Committee for Citizens in Education, the ACLU, the NAACP, and the Children's Defense Fund. We mention these briefs to show how school discipline court cases had taken on added social meaning and attracted a wide range of institutional involvement during the time period when student rights became highly contested. As was illustrated in Figure 2.1, through the active efforts of institutions such as OEO

Legal Services, the ACLU, and other public interest law advocates, courts at all levels began to experience unprecedented numbers of school discipline cases during this period. Organizations with vested interests in related issues, such as youth advocacy groups and school administrator organizations, pressed for outcomes they deemed favorable to their constituencies.

At the close of the student rights contestation period in 1975, the Supreme Court decided *Wood v. Strickland*. In this case, two Arkansas tenth graders (Virginia Crain and Peggy Strickland), and an unidentified third girl were caught spiking the punch at a home economics extra-curricular activity with two 12-ounce bottles of malt liquor. Initially, no one seemed to take notice of the prank. However, ten days after it occurred, the teacher in charge of the meeting, having heard rumors about the "spiking," questioned the girls about it. She urged them to go to the principal and admit their wrongdoing. They did so, and Principal Waller suspended them from school for the maximum two-week period, subject to approval by the school board. Neither the girls nor their parents opted to attend the board meeting they had been verbally notified about. At the meeting, the teacher and principal initially urged leniency toward the girls for their infraction.

However, as the board was deliberating, the school superintendent called to notify the principal that one of the girls involved in the punch-spiking incident had also participated in a fight that evening at a basketball game. The principal did not reveal the name of the girl involved in the fracas but informed the group that one of the "spikers" had just been involved in a fight. He and the teacher withdrew their recommendations of leniency, and the board voted to expel the girls for the remaining three months of the semester.

Claiming that members of the school board and administration had violated their civil rights, Strickland and Crain subsequently filed a suit for damages and injunctive relief in the federal district court. This court ruled in favor of the school on the grounds that, absent proof of intentional malice on the part of the school officials, they were immune from damage suits. The federal court of appeals, finding that the facts of the case demonstrated a violation of the students' right to "substantive due process," reversed the lower court's ruling and sent the case back to the district court for appropriate injunctive relief and determination of damages. They based this decision on the fact that, according to Arkansas statues, the definition of "intoxicating liquor" included only beverages with an alcohol content exceeding five percent by weight. "Right Time" contained less alcohol than this standard.

Upon appeal, the Supreme Court chastised the court of appeals for being "ill advised to supplant the interpretation of the regulation of those officers who adopted it and are entrusted with its enforcement."[52] All members of the Burger Court joined in overturning the lower court's substitution of their own interpretation of the alcohol regulation for that of the school board. The Court was divided seven to two, however, in deciding the proper standard by which school officials should be judged liable for protecting the procedural guarantees of due process. The school officials claimed that legal precedent gave them absolute immunity from liability for actions conducted while performing their jobs. The district court agreed with them on this point, while the court of appeals found that school officials could be held responsible for compensatory damages to students if they indeed violated their rights. The majority of the Supreme Court Justices rejected the latter argument as too broad, and instead presented somewhat narrower circumstances under which school officials could be held liable for violating students' rights. The decision stated:

> Liability for damages for every action which is found subsequently to have been violative of a student's constitutional rights and to have caused compensable injury would unfairly impose upon the school decision-maker the burden of mistakes made in good faith in the course of exercising his discretion within the scope of his official duties. School board members, among other duties, must judge whether there have been violations of school regulations and, if so, the appropriate sanctions for the violations. Denying any measure of immunity in these circumstances "would contribute not to principled and fearless decision-making but to intimidation."[53]

The imposition of monetary costs for mistakes which were not unreasonable in the light of all the circumstances would undoubtedly deter even the most conscientious school decision-maker from exercising his judgment independently, forcefully, and in a manner best serving the long-term interest of the school and the students. The most capable candidates for school board positions might be deterred from seeking office if heavy burdens upon their private resources from monetary liability were a likely prospect during their tenure.[54]

School officials should be accorded neither absolute liability nor absolute immunity when exercising discretion in disciplinary actions. An appropriate standard for determining a school administrator's liability involved both objective and subjective tests of good faith in undertaking a disciplinary action. Thus,

> in the specific context of school discipline, we hold that a school board member is not immune from liability for damages . . . if he knew or reasonably should have known that the action he took within his sphere of official responsibility would violate the constitutional rights of the student affected, or if he took the action with the malicious intention to cause a deprivation of constitutional rights or other injury to the student.[55]

A school board member must therefore have "knowledge of the basic unquestioned constitutional rights of his charges."[56]

The two dissenting Justices found the expectation of school officials to attune themselves to the court climate extreme. They stated:

> The Court's decision appears to rest on an unwarranted assumption as to what lay school officials know or can know about the law and constitutional rights. These officials will now act at the peril of some judge or jury subsequently finding that a good-faith belief as to the applicable law was mistaken and hence actionable . . .
>
> There are some 20,000 school boards, each with five or more members, and thousands of school superintendents and school principals. Most of the school board members are popularly elected, drawn from the citizenry at large, and possess no unique competency in divining the law. Few cities and counties provide any compensation for service on school boards, and often it is difficult to persuade qualified persons to assume the burdens of this important function in our society. Moreover, even if counsel's advice constitutes a defense, it may safely be assumed that few school boards and school officials have ready access to counsel or indeed have deemed it necessary to consult counsel on the countless decisions that necessarily must be made in the operation of our public schools.[57]

Wood v. Strickland had an important consequence for school personnel: it significantly raised the stakes for teachers and administrators' failure to attend to variation in court climates. By legally allowing students to hold principals, school board members, and others financially accountable for violating constitutional rights, the decision made it virtually mandatory for school personnel to keep tabs on local court decisions. Further, the case was decided in an era when school districts' retention of legal counsel was not as commonplace as it has now become. Indeed, it probably did much to stimulate the emergence and growth of opportunities for in-house school district legal counsel. For example, in 1967 the National School Board Association had felt compelled to create the Council of School Attorneys "to improve legal representation of our nation's public schools and thereby reduce the economic impact of adverse legal decisions on education resources."[58] But seven years later (by 1974, a year before *Wood v. Strickland*) only 250 attorneys had joined as members. By 1977, however (two years after the decision), the membership in the organization had tripled to around 700. Subsequent growth has continued, with 1,800 members by 1984 and over 3,000 licensed attorneys affiliated with the organization and working on behalf of public schools in 2002. External adversarial legal challenges to schools inevitably created internal demands for greater reliance on educational law expertise. For example, David Kirp and Mark Yudof, the founding director and an affiliate of OEO's Center for Law and Education, respectively, would in 1974—with "handsome financial support provided by the Ford Foundation and Carnegie Corporation"—publish the 750-page tome on *Educational Policy and the Law.* Given "a revolution in the relationship of law to social policy . . . [t]he law, the courts and the law schools will never be the same," Nathan Glazer noted in the preface. "To contracts and torts have been added education and many other special fields."[59]

While the *Wood v. Strickland* case might have done much to focus the attention of school personnel and to increase demand for educational law expertise, in practice legal efforts to hold public officials personally responsible for their actions have been difficult and relatively rare. Nonetheless, students and legal actors interested in expanding their professional influence could clearly use this case to advance their ends.

Post-Contestation: 1976–1992

In this third period, the institutional infrastructure that promoted litigation in this area was severely weakened, and the Supreme Court took a decidedly pro-school turn. Although the Court continued to hear school discipline cases, it was generally less favorable toward students than it had been in the earlier period. In 1977, for example, the Burger Court ruled in *Ingraham v. Wright* that corporal punishment could not be construed as "cruel and unusual punishment" under the Constitution and thus could continue to be administered in schools. In this case, two boys who attended Charles R. Drew Junior High School in Dade County, Florida, were reprimanded for minor infractions with corporal punishment. James Ingraham and Roosevelt Andrews argued that the disciplinary paddling had violated their constitutional rights and they sought damages and declaratory relief in the courts. The federal district court and the court of appeals both found in favor of the school and dismissed the complaint, holding that there were no constitutional grounds for relief. The Supreme Court affirmed this ruling.

In the Dade County school district where the incidents occurred, corporal punishment was authorized under certain specific guidelines:

> The authorized punishment consisted of paddling the recalcitrant student on the buttocks with a flat wooden paddle measuring less than two feet long, three to four inches wide, and about one-half inch thick. The normal punishment was limited to one to five "licks" or blows with the paddle and resulted in no apparent physical injury to the student. School authorities viewed corporal punishment as a less drastic means of discipline than suspension or expulsion. Contrary to the procedural requirements of the statute and regulation, teachers often paddled students on their own authority without first consulting the principal.[60]

In the case of these two students, the Court record suggested that the punishment deviated somewhat from those guidelines.

> Because he was slow to respond to his teacher's instructions, Ingraham was subjected to more than 20 licks with a paddle while being held over the table in the principal's office. The paddling was so severe that he suffered a hematoma requiring medical attention and keeping him out of school for several days. Andrews was paddled several times for minor infractions. On two occasions he was struck on his arms, once depriving him of the full use of his arm for a week.[61]

Though the punishment in this case was more severe than district guidelines would generally allow, the issue before the Court did not concern the severity of the beatings, but rather the constitutionality of corporal punishment. The challenge to this practice was based on the Eighth Amendment protection against cruel and unusual punishment, and whether students facing such punishment were entitled to a hearing and notice, before being paddled, in accordance with the Due Process Clause of the Fourteenth Amendment.[62]

The case was decided in a close five to four decision in favor of the school. The majority stated:

> In view of the low incidence of abuse [by teachers and administrators punishing students via corporal punishment], the openness of our schools, and the common-law safeguards that already exist, the risk of error that may result in violation of a schoolchild's substantive rights can only be regarded as minimal. Imposing additional administrative safeguards as a constitutional requirement might reduce that risk marginally, but would also entail a significant intrusion into an area of primary educational responsibility. We conclude that the Due Process Clause does not require notice and a hearing prior to the imposition of corporal punishment in the public schools, as that practice is authorized and limited by the common law.[63]

This majority decision essentially maintained the status quo regarding the use of corporal punishment in schools and ended the general expansion of student rights through Supreme Court case law that had occurred between 1969 and 1975.

The dissenters, though not advocating the abolition of corporal punishment entirely, found the majority extreme in their view that the Eighth Amendment does not apply to schoolchildren.

> Today the Court holds that corporal punishment in public schools, no matter how severe, can never be subject of the protections afforded by the Eighth Amendment. It also holds that students in the public school systems are not constitutionally entitled to a hearing of any sort before beatings can be inflicted upon them.[64]

They argued that the protections against cruel and unusual punishments should be extended to students on the grounds of this comparison:

> if it is constitutionally impermissible to cut off someone's ear for the commission of murder, it must be unconstitutional to cut off a child's ear for being late to class. Although there were no ears cut off in this case, the record reveals beatings so severe that if they were inflicted on a hardened

criminal for the commission of a serious crime, they might not pass constitutional muster . . .

The essence of the majority's argument is that schoolchildren do not
need Eighth Amendment protection because corporal punishment is less
subject to abuse in the public schools than it is in the prison system.
However, it cannot be reasonably suggested that just because cruel and
unusual punishments may occur less frequently under public scrutiny,
they will not occur at all. The mere fact that a public flogging or a public
execution would be available for all to see would not render the punishment constitutional if it were otherwise impermissible . . . In short, if a
punishment is so barbaric and inhumane that it goes beyond the tolerance of a civilized society, its openness to public scrutiny should have
nothing to do with its constitutional validity . . .

I am therefore not suggesting that spanking in the public schools is in
every instance prohibited by the Eighth Amendment. My own view is
that it is not. I only take issue with the extreme view of the majority that
corporal punishment in public schools, no matter how barbaric, inhumane, or severe, it is never limited by the Eighth Amendment.[65]

This close decision illustrates how the slim majority that decided in favor
of students in earlier times had shifted. Thus the Burger Court had decided
in *Goss v. Lopez* that the rights of due process protected by the Constitution
not only applied to criminals being punished by the state, but also to
schoolchildren facing short-term suspension for minor infractions. By the
late 1970s, however, the Supreme Court's composition and inclination had
changed so that protections for criminals against "cruel and unusual punishment" and for due process were narrowly found not to apply to students
facing corporal punishment.

In 1978, *Carey v. Piphus* continued the pro-school trend in the Supreme
Court. This relatively minor case involved a boy in elementary school suspended for wearing an earring, and a high school student suspended for
smoking marijuana in school. The lower courts established that both boys
were denied due process per the rulings of *Goss v. Lopez*, and the Supreme
Court heard the case to determine whether, on the basis of *Wood v. Strickland*, the students could claim substantial damages for these violations
from school officials, as the court of appeals held. In a unanimous decision, the Supreme Court ruled that "in the absence of proof of actual
injury, the students are entitled to recover only nominal damages."[66] In

this case, the judges sent the case back to the district court to determine whether the students' suspensions were justified. If so, the students "nevertheless will be entitled to recover nominal damages not to exceed one dollar"[67] from the school officials. Without proof that they had suffered emotional or material distress from the schools' actions, students could not justify the receipt of large amounts in damage claims.

In another minor case in 1982, *Board of Education of Rogers, Arkansas v. McCluskey,* the Court decided a case that had little, if any, constitutional significance. The case involved the suspension of a student who got drunk off campus, then returned to school. The lower courts found that the school rule on which the school board based the suspension was vague and did not explicitly prohibit alcohol consumed off school grounds, so the decision to suspend the boy should not stand. The Supreme Court, against the vocal opposition of Justice Marshall, heard the case and found for the school (six to three), thus overturning the lower court's ruling. In his dissent, Marshall seethed:

> The case is not of sufficient importance to warrant full briefing and argument. It is not worthy of an opinion signed by a Member of this Court . . . Today we exercise our majestic power to enforce a School Board's suspension of a 10th grade student who consumed too much alcohol . . . If the student had been unjustly suspended, I wonder if the Court would consider the matter of sufficient national importance to require summary reversal. I doubt it.[68]

Marshall clearly believed that the Court was abusing its discretionary power to select which cases to hear. During this time, however, the Burger Court was under increased pressure to limit the scope of legal gains made by students in earlier decisions.

In 1985, the Court heard its first major case regarding drug possession in school: *New Jersey v. T.L.O.* This landmark case involved a New Jersey high school student, "T.L.O.," who was caught smoking in the girls' bathroom. When the principal searched her purse for cigarettes, he turned up evidence of marijuana (rolling papers) and intensified his search. Additional "rummaging" turned up a small amount of marijuana, a pipe, a number of empty plastic bags, a good sum of money in one-dollar bills, an index card containing a list of those students who owed T.L.O. money, and two letters that implicated her in dealing. The juvenile court admitted this evidence, and T.L.O. was proclaimed a delinquent and sentenced to probation. On appeal, lower federal courts were mixed as to whether the evidence should be suppressed because the principal's search of the purse could be held to violate Fourth Amendment protections against unreasonable search and seizure.[69] In a split decision, the majority of the Supreme Court ruled that, unlike the police, school officials should be able to search students without a warrant or probable cause. In contrast to police searches, the legality of their search would depend on the "reasonableness, under all the circumstances, of the search." Although they found that the Fourth Amendment indeed applied to school officials, they suggested that the standards of reasonableness for a search depended on the context. The Justices noted that

> a few courts have concluded that school officials are exempt from the dictates of the Fourth Amendment by virtue of the special nature of their authority over schoolchildren . . . Teachers and school administrators, it is said, act *in loco parentis* in their dealings with students: their authority is that of the parent, not the State, and is therefore not subject to the limits of the Fourth Amendment. Such reasoning is in tension with contemporary reality and in the teachings of this court . . . If school authorities are state actors for the purposes of the constitutional guarantees of freedom of expression [see *Tinker v. Des Moines,* 1969] and due process [see *Goss v. Lopez,* 1975], it is difficult to understand why they should be deemed to be exercising parental rather than public authority when conducting searches of their students . . .
>
> Today's public school officials do not merely exercise authority voluntarily conferred on them by individual parents; rather, they act in furtherance of publicly mandated educational and disciplinary policies . . . In carrying out searches and other disciplinary functions pursuant to such policies, school officials act as representatives of the State, not merely as surrogates for the parents, and they cannot claim the parents' immunity from the strictures of the Fourth Amendment.[70]

Further, "although the underlying command of the Fourth Amendment is always that searches and seizures be reasonable, what is reasonable depends on the context within which a search takes place."[71] Granted, even students in public schools, unlike, say, inmates in prison cells, have reasonable expectations of privacy. Nevertheless,

> Against the child's interest in privacy must be set the substantial interest of teachers and administrators in maintaining discipline in the classroom

and on school grounds. Maintaining order in the classroom has never been easy, but in recent years, school disorder has often taken particularly ugly forms: drug use and violent crime in the schools have become major social problems.[72]

In striking this balance, the Justices opined: "It is evident that the school setting requires some easing of the restrictions to which searches by public authorities are ordinarily subject."[73]

Specifically, the requirement of obtaining a warrant was "unsuited to the school environment" and would "unduly interfere with the maintenance of the swift and informal disciplinary procedures needed in the schools." Further, a "school setting also requires some modification of the level of suspicion of illicit activity needed to justify a search."[74] In most settings, a search must be based on "probable cause." Yet this standard was not the only way to comply with the Fourth Amendment's requirement that a search be reasonable.

> A search of a student by a teacher or other school official will be "justified at its inception" when there are reasonable grounds for suspecting that the search will turn up evidence that the student has violated or is violating either the law or the rules of the school. Such a search will be permissible in its scope when the measures adopted are reasonably related to the objectives of the search and not excessively intrusive in light of the age and sex of the student and the nature of the infraction.[75]

The majority agreed that teachers and administrators have other things to worry about than determining whether they had "probable cause" to conduct a search.

In their partial dissent, Justices Brennan, Stevens, and Marshall agreed with the majority that Fourth Amendment protections did apply to school personnel conducting searches. They did warn, however, that

> Today's decision sanctions school officials to conduct full-scale searches on a "reasonableness" standard whose only definite content is that it is *not* the same test as the "probable cause" standard found in the text of the Fourth Amendment. In adopting this unclear, unprecedented, and unnecessary departure from generally applicable Fourth Amendment Standards, the Court carves out a broad exception to standards that this Court has developed over years of considering Fourth Amendment problems. Its decision is supported neither by precedent nor even by a fair application of the "balancing test" it proclaims in this very opinion.[76]

They argued that the new standard of "reasonableness" would result in uncertainty among teachers and administrators, making efforts to comply
with this standard nearly impossible because of the lack of precedent.

Further, the dissenters believed that in this case the Court should have
upheld lower court decisions ordering the suppression of evidence of marijuana use and sale that was found in the course of a search for cigarettes.
They argued,

> Mr. Choplick [the principal] overreacted to what appeared to be nothing
> more than a minor infraction—a rule prohibiting smoking in the bath-
> room of the freshmen's and sophomores' building. It is, of course, true
> that he actually found evidence of serious wrongdoing by T.L.O., but no
> one claims that the prior search may be justified by his unexpected dis-
> covery. As far as the smoking infraction is concerned, the search for ciga-
> rettes merely tended to corroborate a teacher's eyewitness account of
> T.L.O.'s violation of a minor regulation designed to channel student
> smoking behavior into designated locations. Because this conduct was
> neither unlawful nor significantly disruptive of school order or the edu-
> cational process, the invasion of privacy associated with the forcible
> opening of T.L.O.'s purse was entirely unjustified at its inception.[77]

Unfettered opportunities to search students in schools, the minority suggested, sent a message that was incompatible with American values and
law. The dissenting opinion closed:

> The schoolroom is the first opportunity most citizens have to experience
> the power of government. Through it passes every citizen and public of-
> ficial, from schoolteachers to policemen and prison guards. The values
> they learn there, they take with them in life. One of our most cherished
> ideals is the one contained in the Fourth Amendment: that the govern-
> ment may not intrude on the personal privacy of its citizens without a
> warrant or compelling circumstance. The Court's decision today is a cu-
> rious moral for the Nation's youth. Although the search of T.L.O.'s purse
> does not trouble today's majority, I submit that we are not dealing with
> "matters relatively trivial to the welfare of the Nation. There are village
> tyrants as well as village Hampdens, but none who acts under color of
> law is beyond reach of the Constitution."[78]
>
> I respectfully dissent.[79]

This decision, like *Ingraham v. Wright* before it, signified the Court's
renewed willingness to consider constitutional rights less applicable to

schoolchildren than to other citizens. The minority clearly indicated their concern about the broader implications of the outcome in their closing words.

The next major school discipline case to reach the Supreme Court was *Bethel School District v. Fraser* in 1986. Like *Tinker v. Des Moines,* this case dealt with questions about the freedom of speech accorded to students in public schools. Specifically, the Court agreed to hear the case to decide "whether the First Amendment prevents a school district from disciplining a high school student for giving a lewd speech at a school assembly."[80] Matthew Fraser, a student at Bethel High School in the state of Washington, gave a speech nominating a fellow student for student government office. His speech was full of overt sexual metaphors. Prior to delivering the speech, he discussed it with two of his teachers, both of whom suggested that it was inappropriate and that it might have "severe consequences" if delivered at an assembly of 600 students, but they did not actively prohibit him from giving it. Fraser went ahead with the following:

> I know a man who is firm—he's firm in his pants, he's firm in his shirt, his character is firm—but most . . . of all, his belief in you, the students of Bethel, is firm.

> Jeff Kuhlman is a man who takes his point and pounds it in. If necessary, he'll take an issue and nail it to the wall. He doesn't attack things in spurts—he drives hard, pushing and pushing until finally—he succeeds.

> Jeff is a man who will go to the very end—even the climax, for each and every one of you.

> So vote for Jeff for A.S.B. vice-president—he'll never come between you and the best our high school can be.[81]

As Fraser spoke, a school counselor noticed that "some students hooted and yelled; some by gestures graphically simulated the sexual activities pointedly alluded to" in the speech. Some students "appeared to be bewildered and embarrassed by the speech." In addition, "one teacher reported that on the day following the speech, she found it necessary to forgo a portion of the scheduled class lesson in order to discuss the speech with the class."[82]

The day after the speech, the assistant principal called Fraser into her office and notified him that the school officials thought his speech had violated a school prohibition against obscene language. The rule stated, "Conduct which materially and substantially interferes with the educational process is prohibited, including the use of obscene, profane language or gestures."[83] Fraser admitted to the deliberate use of sexual innuendo in his speech; he was then informed that he would be suspended for three days and removed from the list of candidates for speaker at the school's commencement exercises.

Fraser requested a review of the disciplinary action through the school district's grievance process. The hearing officer concurred with the assistant principal in determining that the speech Fraser delivered was "indecent, lewd, and offensive to the modesty and decency of many of the students and faculty in attendance at the assembly."[84] Fraser served two days of suspension and was allowed to return to school on the third day. Fraser and his father then brought legal action against the school district in the federal district court, alleging violation of his First Amendment right to freedom of speech. The court found for the student and awarded Fraser $278 in damages, $12,750 in litigation costs and attorney's fees, and enjoined the school district from preventing him from speaking at commencement ceremonies. Fraser's classmates had elected him by write-in ballot to give the commencement speech, which he ultimately delivered. The school district appealed this decision to the court of appeals, which affirmed the earlier judgment in favor of Fraser and held that the speech in this case was indistinguishable from the armband protest in *Tinker*. Further, the court rejected the district's argument that it had an interest in protecting an essentially captive audience of minors from lewd and indecent language and that it had the power to control the language used during a school-sponsored activity.

The district then appealed to the Supreme Court, in which a majority sided with the school and reversed the lower court decisions. The Court pointed out the role of schools in socializing youth:

> The process of educating our youth for citizenship in public schools is not confined to books, the curriculum, and the civics class; schools must teach by example the shared values of a civilized social order. Consciously or otherwise, teachers—and indeed the older students—demonstrate the appropriate form of civil discourse and political expression by their conduct and deportment in and out of class. Inescapably, like parents, they are role models. The schools, as instruments of the state, may determine that the essential lessons of civil, mature conduct cannot be conveyed in a

school that tolerates lewd, indecent, or offensive speech and conduct such as that indulged in by this confused boy.[85]

Continuing the Court trend that viewed youth as possessing different rights under the Constitution than adults, the majority stated,

> The First Amendment guarantees wide freedom in matters of adult public discourse . . . It does not follow, however, that simply because the use of an offensive form of expression may not be prohibited to adults making what the speaker considers a political point, the same latitude must be permitted to children in a public school. In *New Jersey v. T.L.O.* . . . , we reaffirmed that the constitutional rights of students in public school are not automatically coextensive with the rights of adults in other settings . . .
>
> Surely it is a highly appropriate function of public school education to prohibit the use of vulgar and offensive terms in public discourse . . . Nothing in the Constitution prohibits the states from insisting that certain modes of expression are inappropriate and subject to sanctions . . . The determination of what manner of speech in the classroom or in school assembly is inappropriate properly rests with the school board.[86]

The majority argued that this case differed from *Tinker* because the sanctions imposed upon Fraser for his "offensively lewd and indecent speech" were unrelated to any political viewpoint, as had been the case when students were punished for wearing armbands to protest the Vietnam War in *Tinker.*

In their dissenting opinions, Justices Marshall and Stevens argued in favor of upholding the lower court decisions for the student. Marshall thought the Court should decide for the student because "the School District failed to demonstrate that the respondent's remarks were indeed disruptive."[87] Justice Stevens argued that the concept of what was "offensive" changed over time, therefore if offensive speech was punished, students must be given fair warning about the scope and content of prohibited speech. He drew upon an example from his youth:

> "Frankly, my dear, I don't give a damn."
>
> When I was a high school student, the use of those words in a public forum shocked the Nation. Today Clark Gable's four-letter expletive is less offensive than it was then. Nevertheless, I assume that high school administrators may prohibit the use of that word in classroom discussion

and even in extracurricular activities that are sponsored by the school and held on school premises. For I believe a school faculty must regulate the content as well as the style of student speech in carrying out its educational mission. It does seem to me, however, that if a student is to be punished for using offensive speech, he is entitled to fair notice of the scope of the prohibition and the consequences of its violation. The interest in free speech protected by the First Amendment and the interest in fair procedure protected by the Due Process Clause of the Fourteenth Amendment combine to require this conclusion.[88]

To Justice Stevens, the school rule against offensive speech was unclear and inapplicable in this case because the school did not prove that disruption occurred and Fraser used no explicitly obscene language in the speech. "What the speech does contain is a sexual metaphor that may unquestionably be offensive to some listeners in some settings."[89] But an impartial judge could not conclude that this metaphor fell under the purview of the school rule. Thus it was unfair to hold the student accountable when it was unclear that "the speech was so obviously offensive that an intelligent high school student must be presumed to have realized that he would be punished for giving it."[90]

Justice Stevens concluded that the setting and community norms should be taken into account:

It seems fairly obvious that respondent's speech would be inappropriate in certain classroom and formal social settings. On the other hand, in a locker room or perhaps in a school corridor the metaphor in the speech might be regarded as rather routine comment. If this be true, and if respondent's audience consisted almost entirely of young people with whom he conversed on a daily basis, can we—at this distance—confidently assert that he must have known that the school administration would punish him for delivering it?

For three reasons, I think not. First, it seems highly unlikely that he would have decided to deliver the speech if he had known it would result in his suspension and disqualification from delivering the school commencement address. Second, I believe a strong presumption in favor of free expression should apply whenever an issue of this kind is arguable. Third, because the Court has adopted the policy of applying contemporary community standards in evaluating expression with sexual connotations, this Court should defer to the views of the district and circuit judges who are in a much better position to evaluate this speech than we are.[91]

In this last school discipline case to reach the Supreme Court during the period under investigation in this book, it was evident that the balance of the Court remained decidedly pro-school.

In the major cases heard between 1976 and 1992, the Court determined that the Eighth Amendment protections against cruel and unusual punishment, Fourth Amendment protections against unreasonable search and seizure, and First Amendment rights to freedom of speech did not apply equally to students in public schools as to adults outside of such settings.

But the story about the clash between student rights and school rules does not end with the Supreme Court. Indeed, the cases discussed above were only the proverbial "tip of the iceberg" of court disputes over school discipline. While the Supreme Court deliberated these cases, numerous others were heard in state and lower federal courts and were influential in creating variation in court climates facing school actors.

Key Actors in the Rights vs. Rules Arena

Our discussion of Supreme Court cases reveals that diverse individuals and organizations may play a role in a given case. An exploration of the key actors involved in school discipline court cases and their interests—both institutional and personal—in the outcomes should yield important insights. Clearly, the actors were numerous and their interests conflicted. Educational policy that emerged from this interaction thus by definition was unplanned, haphazard, and contradictory.

Institutional actors played an essential role in the emergence of this field of law: without these advocacy organizations, disputes between students and schools would unlikely have reached into the appellate courts in the unprecedented manner that occurred from 1969 onward. Educational litigation in this area was explicitly stimulated by the federal government's establishment of the OEO Legal Service Program in 1965 and the Center for Law and Education in 1969. Private and corporate foundations also encouraged litigation by their support for public interest legal advocacy organizations. By 1975, however, these assorted government and nonprofit advocacy organizations lost much of their support for continuing law reform efforts in this area.

These groups—as well as local and state government offices, professional organizations, and associations that represented school administrators and teachers—had clear interests in the outcome of school discipline court cases, and worked for particular court outcomes. Professional groups representing teachers and administrators, predictably, often urged decisions for the school. Conversely, advocacy groups such as the Children's Defense Fund and the ACLU often argued in favor of the students. Both types of groups contended that cases had wider importance than might appear on the face of it. School administrator associations bolstered the claims of school officials involved in the cases by arguing that deciding for the student would erode the legitimacy and authority of school personnel, not just for the district involved, but for all schools. Groups filing briefs for students suggested that student rights generally—not simply the rights of the few students involved in a given case—were in danger of being trampled upon if the courts failed to decide for the student(s).

In addition to students and school officials, lawyers representing these two sides also were important actors in the rights versus rules contest. First, lawyers representing the students were at times associated with powerful national groups such as the ACLU or NAACP. In addition to protecting the rights of particular student litigants, these groups often had specific political agendas and ideologies that these lawyers were committed to advancing. For example, "the mission of the ACLU is to assure that the Bill of Rights—amendments to the Constitution that guard against unwarranted governmental control—are preserved for each new generation."[92] Therefore, in a particular case, an ACLU-affiliated lawyer, whether employed directly with the organization or working in private practice in a *pro-bono* capacity, may have been fighting for Dwight Lopez's right to due process, but the lawyer's larger interest, by virtue of the group represented, was to protect all students from unwarranted government-exercised authority. Likewise, "the principal objective of the NAACP is to ensure the political, educational, social and economic equality of minority group citizens of the United States."[93] National groups were not interested in every school discipline case, of course, but became involved when a case touched upon core organizational principles. In these cases, attorneys clearly had interests that extended beyond the particular case at hand.

Of course, many attorneys representing students were not affiliated with such groups. In these cases, the interests of the lawyers were the same as those in any legal case: they would rather win than lose. In some situations, attorneys agreed to forgo payment unless their clients prevailed and were granted attorney's fees. In other cases, the legal representatives required the same payment as they would in any other litigation. In a handful of cases, judges noted that the student's parent was serving as his or her attorney. The interests of the lawyers in such cases were clearly tantamount to those of any supportive parent: they believed their child's rights were infringed upon and wished for them to prevail. Lawyers, in addition, had a professional interest: winning a successful precedent-setting appellate court case carried with it significant prestige and rewards.

Lawyers representing the schools—increasingly retained as full-time employees of the districts—also had interests in court outcomes. School counsel often advised school districts on legal aspects of disciplinary codes and punishment to avoid litigation in the first place. So, in school discipline court cases, these lawyers often defended their own advice on acceptable disciplinary practices. According to one publication, "The recruitment, selection, and retention of legal counsel is crucial to a school district. Few decisions can impact the efficient functioning of a school district as significantly as the retention of legal counsel. School attorneys are required to "wear many hats" in order to be responsive to the school district's multitude of legal needs."[94] Not only were these attorneys attempting to win cases for their client; they were also vindicating their own advice and providing a justification for their institutional positions.

Judges who heard school discipline cases, and the institution of the judiciary as a whole, also had important interests in these cases. Some judges considered school discipline to be wholly the business of the school officials.

By accepting an education at public expense pupils at the elementary or high school level subject themselves to considerable discretion on the part of school authorities as to the manner in which they deport themselves. Those who run public schools should be the judges in such matters, not the courts. The quicker judges get out of the business of running schools the better. I have no intention of becoming a tonsorial or sartorial consultant of boards, superintendents and principals. Except in extreme cases the judgment of school officials should be final in applying regulation to an individual case.[95]

Others were quicker to side with the student:

we find unpersuasive the argument that to hold such school regulations unconstitutional would open the floodgates to litigation by students challenging all sorts of school regulations and practices. To fail to hold such arbitrary regulations unconstitutional because of fear of opening the floodgates to litigation, some meritorious and some not, would be an abdication of the judiciary's role of final arbiter of the validity of all laws, and protector of the people, young and old, from the governmental exercise of unconstitutional power.[96]

Clearly, different judges came to hear a case with conflicting ideological notions about what the proper role of the judiciary should be in settling school discipline disputes. Thus, one judge may have had an "interest" in maintaining school authority with little court intervention, while another judge may have had an "interest" in vigorously protecting the rights of students. Others may have had few preconceived opinions on the matter.

The level of the judge's courtroom probably dictated to some degree his or her interest in a case. Courts at the state level, and even some district courts, were more likely to employ judges who lived in the area in which the court resided. While this may not determine a judge's decisions in one way or another, it adds a layer of complexity, given personal connections with the community or individuals involved in a case. Obviously, this would be less of a factor when a case originating in Tennessee was heard in Ohio when it reached the United States Court of Appeals in the Sixth Circuit.

The willingness of students and their families to contest school practices was, of course, a necessary ingredient in the formation of a court climate. Unlike in many areas of educational law targeted for reform (for example, fiscal equity litigation), in matters of school discipline aggrieved individuals would be "walking through the door" of local Legal Services offices in search of legal redress and remediation.[97] The fact that prior to 1960 only a handful of disputes between students and school officials made their way to the appellate courts suggests that, in the absence of this institutional Legal Service and advocacy infrastructure, individuals did not have the wherewithal to challenge school practices frequently enough at the appellate level to develop a corpus of law in this area. In addition to changes in the legal environment, other social factors—such as the increasingly litigious nature of American society, the expansion of youth rights under the Warren Court, and an overall questioning of entrenched authority—conspired to open the door for students to challenge school discipline not just in the classroom, but now also in the courtroom. One can view such legal challenges as vainglorious attempts by students to "save face" in the eyes of their classmates, as valiant efforts to challenge unconstitutional school rules and practices, or as some combination of the two. Indeed, court records indicate that both types of motivation entered into play. Regardless of the underlying personal incentives to bring grievances to court, individual students subjected to discipline have a particular interest in avoiding sanctions and continuing their education without obstacles.

Along with students, parents—who often are the named litigants in cases involving minors—also have personal interests in school discipline court challenges. Schools were traditionally considered acting *in loco parentis,* or in place of the parent, when disciplining students. But when parents disagreed with school actions, these disagreements could lead to court challenges. For example, a judge in the Superior Court of New Jersey noted in his opinion in T.L.O.'s case that *in loco parentis,* "which is usually applied for the purpose of protecting a child, is being used here to strip the juvenile of constitutional protection. It would be rare parents indeed who would turn their daughters over to the police the first time they find her to possess or even distribute marijuana."[98] Likewise, Dwight Lopez's mother would probably have been willing to listen to his side of the story about the extent of his involvement in the cafeteria unrest before pulling him out of school and forcing him to attend an alternative school. Not many of the cases we reviewed would get far without the consent and financial or logistical support of parents. Parents' interests in school discipline court cases were often very similar to those of students: they wanted their sons and daughters to have access to quality education of their choosing. Further, they wanted to be sure, when schools were entrusted with the job of disciplining their children, that they were not doing so in ways that were discriminatory or violative of basic rights. It is important to note, however, that students did not always have the backing of their parents, a fact that judges occasionally noted in their decisions. Sometimes parents' interests were in conflict with those of students—such parents often gave no opinion of the conflict over discipline, or offered support for the school. Nonetheless, in the majority of cases parents supported their children's court challenges. Without such support it was too hard for students to take challenges to school discipline into the courts.

On the other side of conflicts was the broad category of "school officials"—which included principals, school board members, superintendents, teachers, and the institutions that represented them. These actors had both individual and institutional interests in the outcomes of cases involving challenges to school discipline. At the institutional level, officials must maintain order in the schools. To do so, it is imperative that students and parents view schools' disciplinary decisions as legitimate. Court challenges to these decisions were in many ways an affront to the legitimacy and moral authority of school actions. If Johnny could get away with smoking in the boys' room without risk of punishment because of some procedural technicality related to due process violation, then other students may come to believe that the school was an ineffective and illegitimate enforcer of rules.

Aside from defending the legitimacy of school authority, school officials—especially school board members and superintendents—were interested in minimizing the financial costs of such cases to the district. Court challenges to school discipline imposed significant financial burdens on school systems, both in terms of the cost of hiring lawyers and the time spent by school officials in answering these challenges. Yet the eagerness of schools to appeal cases that had been decided in favor of students makes it clear that interests in legitimating school authority tended to outweigh considerations of monetary costs.

Court records conveyed the sense that a given teacher or principal also felt that his or her personal legitimacy as an enforcer of school rules was being challenged on an individual level. One can be sure that students in general were aware when teachers and principals' disciplinary actions were being challenged in the courts, and these officials may, rightfully, be concerned that a court case was being viewed as a referendum on their authority. In reality courts rarely ruled on the particular actions of a school official, but rather on more general procedural and constitutional issues. Nevertheless, the fact that an external legal forum existed for students to challenge school discipline suggested that teachers' actions were not beyond reproach, as they may have been considered in times gone by. Individual school officials, especially those on the "front lines" of imposing discipline, often tried to convince courts that deciding in favor of a student would undermine their ability to maintain order in schools. In conjunction with the argument that these cases undermined institutional legitimacy, the contention that individual legitimacy was also at risk bolstered a position that many judges found compelling.

Recognizing the different institutional and personal interests that were at issue in school discipline court cases is important for several reasons.

First, it illustrates that any given school discipline case was not simply a clash between rights and rules, but also a clash of individuals and institutions. Second, the motivation of litigants helped shape the court climate: if neither students and their parents nor schools cared enough to appeal school discipline case outcomes, there would be no court climate to examine. Third, recognizing the role of institutional actors reminds us that individuals within the educational system do not simply respond to narrow case law readings, but actively and formatively interact with court climates by contesting decisions as well as reconstructing the social meaning of the decisions in their daily lives and practices.

3

How Judges Rule

With Irenee R. Beattie

> Living by rules, sometimes seemingly arbitrary ones, is the lot of
> children. School is of necessity made up of "rules." They establish
> the time for beginning class, recess, exercise, study periods, out-
> side assignments, athletic activities, playground conduct, use of
> parking and other school facilities such as lockers—all inexorably
> intertwined with academic, personal, artistic, and cultural pur-
> suits . . . We must be wise enough to perceive that constant judi-
> cial intervention in some institutions does more harm than good.
>
> —*MERCER V. BOARD OF TRUSTEES, NORTH FOREST*
> *INDEPENDENT SCHOOL DISTRICT (1976)*

The judges' written opinion in this case was indicative of a pro-school
tendency in court decisions that was particularly noticeable after 1975.
During the earlier student rights contestation period, judges tended to
adopt pro-student orientations. In 1969, at the start of that period, for example, a pro-student court of appeals decision noted that "to uphold arbitrary school rules which 'sharply implicate basic constitutional values' for
the sake of some nebulous concept of school discipline is contrary to the
principle that we are a government of laws which are passed pursuant to
the United States Constitution."[1] Written opinions in school discipline
court cases thus tended to be either pro-school or pro-student, with a limited number of decisions falling into a gray area. In this chapter we seek to
find out which factors influenced the direction of court decisions.

By analyzing how decisions in school discipline cases varied over time
and across states, we can measure court climates empirically—that is, determine the extent to which courts were pro-school, moderate, or pro-
student. While many studies of educational law have focused exclusively on
Supreme Court decisions, our analyses are significantly broader and in-

clude the entire sample of school discipline appellate court cases at the state and federal levels. Only a handful of these cases were ever eventually considered by the Supreme Court: 99 percent of our court cases were from courts other than the Supreme Court. Supreme Court judges often expressed annoyance and irritation that they even had to consider cases involving school discipline. Clearly, though, the Supreme Court had the largest jurisdiction and the greatest nationwide impact . Yet we believe that it was the amalgamation of school discipline case decisions from all appellate court levels that shaped court climates.

In this chapter we describe the structure of appellate court decisions using data on the population of school discipline court cases. We describe how the outcomes of school discipline court cases varied, and look for factors internal to the cases that influenced court decisions. Identification of systematic variation in decisions in these cases facilitates a deeper appreciation for the actual substantive character and internal logic of this sociolegal field. Throughout, we include excerpts from the case decisions themselves to illustrate our findings.

Our analyses here are not intended to identify all the societal and institutional factors affecting court decisions—such an endeavor is well beyond the scope of this book. Law and society scholars, however, have repeatedly disproved the formal legal model which posits that a judge's decision in a given case was based solely on the particular facts, legal precedents, and legal issues at hand.[2] Instead, such varied factors as local organizational environment, demographic characteristics, the politics of judicial appointments, and judges' political attitudes affect judicial outcomes.[3] Here we focus on more limited factors internal to a case, such as the race of the student, the type of misbehavior for which the student was disciplined, and the school practice implicated. These factors are likely quite similar to those that concerned school personnel. Although we use statistical models to understand the influence of various factors on court decisions, in many ways we simply mimic the process through which a person, such as a school administrator, might come to formulate an impression of a court climate. Monitoring the decisions in certain locations, for certain types of student infractions or certain forms of discipline, a school administrator would probably develop a similar understanding of the court climate as we do below.

Case Factors

Time Period

Along with features of school discipline cases that varied over time, court decisions and thus the court climate, too, have changed. Figure 3.1 charts the predicted probability of a court decision in favor of a student litigant from 1960 to 1992. One should think of these probabilities as the percentage likelihood of a pro-student outcome in a case, after controlling for how the case was unusual with regard to other factors that influenced the outcomes, such as region and type of student disciplinary infraction. Figure 3.1 thus shows that students had a 49 percent likelihood of a case being decided in their favor if it was decided in the mid- to late sixties. Before that time and since the early eighties, the likelihood of pro-student outcomes has hovered between a more modest 35 and 40 percent. We use predicted probabilities of pro-student outcomes throughout the remainder of this chapter to illustrate the relationship between various factors and court case outcomes.[4]

If one compares the results in Figure 2.1 to those depicted here, it is clear that the beginning of the student rights contestation period in 1969 was almost immediately preceded by a period of time (around 1967) when stu-

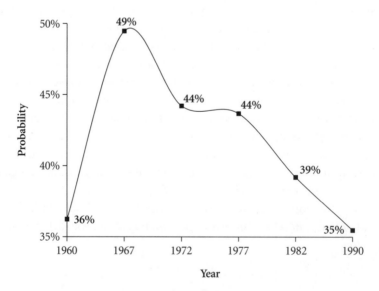

Figure 3.1 Predicted probability of pro-student decision

dents had the greatest likelihood of prevailing in a student discipline case. Further, during the contestation period of 1969 to 1975, when an average of 76 school discipline appellate court cases came up per year, the probability of pro-student outcomes remained steady at around 44 percent. It was not until the contestation period had already ended, and institutional support for appellate court challenges from OEO Legal Services and other public interest law advocacy organizations had diminished, that the likelihood of a student-favored outcome dropped back below 40 percent.

One factor in particular manifested varying outcomes in different time periods, and may account for some of the differences we observed above. When the student misbehavior involved free expression, such as a challenge to school regulations about dress or hair length, the likely outcome in such a case varied depending on when it reached the courts. In the pre-contestation period from 1960 to 1968, free expression cases had only a 19 percent probability of a pro-student outcome, while other types of infractions were far more likely (38 percent) to have a favorable result. In contrast, free expression cases heard after 1969 enjoyed a 44 percent probability of a pro-student outcome, even though cases involving other infractions had only a 33 percent probability of a favorable decision. This may be so because the issues involved in free expression cases differed from one period to the next.[5]

Region

One might anticipate stereotypical regional patterns in judicial decisions, such as a conservative South less favorable toward African-American students or a liberal West more favorable to student protesters. Yet the regional patterns we uncovered were more complex and unexpected. First, most regions have generally been less favorable toward students than the Northeast states under the jurisdiction of the First and Second Federal Circuit Court of Appeals. The Midwest, Mountain, Mid-Atlantic, and South regions were all significantly more pro-school than was the Northeast. Western states, under the jurisdiction of the Ninth Federal Circuit Court of Appeals, were slightly more favorable toward schools. The results show that judges in Northeast states—an area of the country where many of the top law schools as well as educational law reform organizations are located—have found greater merit in student claims against schools than in other areas of the country.

Figure 3.2 maps whether relevant decisions in a given state were pro-

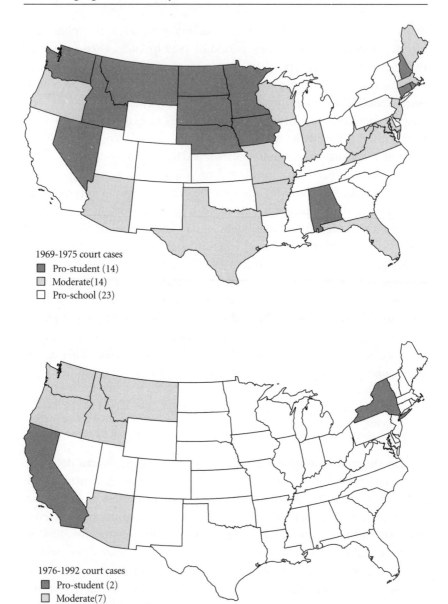

Figure 3.2 Court climates involving school disciplinary practices, 1969–1975 and 1976–1992

student, moderate, or pro-school.[6] Over the entire period, courts were generally pro-school, with only about 35 percent of all cases being decided in favor of students.[7] During the contestation period, however, 15 states, mostly concentrated in the Mountain and Midwest regions, tended to favor students in their decisions. The South at the time had a somewhat less consistent and more liberal pattern of court decisions than subsequent to this period. In part this was because federally appointed judges motivated by civil rights concerns occasionally overturned state decisions when race was involved. During the post-contestation period, appellate courts with jurisdiction over only two states—California and New York—continued to decide cases generally in favor of students. Also while the 1969–1975 period was characterized by 14 moderate states, the 1976–1992 period had only seven moderate states, clustered primarily in the West and Mountain regions. In addition to illustrating state and regional differences in case outcomes, these maps reinforce that the probabilities of pro-student outcomes as presented in Figure 3.1 declined after 1975.

Court Level

We have already seen some differences in school discipline cases depending on court level. In general, cases heard in state high courts were more favorable towards student than those heard in federal courts. However, as Figure 3.3 shows, state courts at all levels were far less favorable toward students in cases of discipline for involvement in political action. On the other hand, federal courts, though generally somewhat less student-inclined on nonpolitical cases than state courts, were more favorable than state courts in cases involving political protest. State courts had a 44 percent probability of a pro-student decision in nonpolitical cases, compared to a mere 15 percent probability of this decision when the student infraction involved political action. Federal courts were likely to be less favorable to students in nonpolitical cases (32 percent), but more favorable in political action cases (29 percent) than the state courts. State courts probably referenced a narrower range of relevant law, and also might have been influenced by intense local pressure to maintain school authority; federal courts—often in distant locations—were perhaps more immune from such pressures.

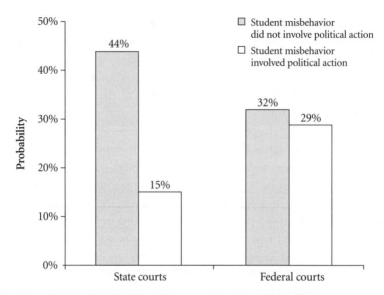

Figure 3.3 Predicted probability of pro-student school discipline court case decision by political action and court level (based on Table 3.B)

School Sector

Although we focus most of our attention on public school discipline, the various voucher initiatives now being introduced or considered make it important to note some differences in court treatment of public versus private school disciplinary court cases. Because private schools are not state institutions, they are not bound by the same constitutional regulations as public schools. Therefore students wishing to challenge private school disciplinary actions have had fewer arguments with which to fashion their case. Accordingly, cases against private schools were only 25 percent likely to be decided in favor of students, lower than the probabilities in public schools.[8]

For example, private school student Mark Geraci was expelled from St. Xavier High School after he "aided and abetted" an extramural friend who came onto school grounds to throw a pie at one of Geraci's teachers. The court records state:

On the final day of the school year Tom McKenna, a student at Moeller High School, entered St. Xavier High School, went to the classroom where Mark Geraci and his classmates were taking a final test and threw a

meringue pie in the face of Mr. Downie, the teacher. Pandemonium en-
sued involving teachers and students. By Mark's own testimony, . . . he
and some fellow students had decided it would be a "funny prank" to get
McKenna to "pie" Mr. Downie. "I called Tom . . . and he said he would go
along with it."[9]

Although Geraci had not collected any money to pay McKenna for the
deed, McKenna told Geraci when the two spoke the night before the last
day of school "he might come over and do it anyway." Geraci provided no
overt verbal encouragement to McKenna, but did provide him with information on which door of the school building to enter, which classroom
Mr. Downie would be teaching in, and even helped him secure transportation from his own school. The school charged that Geraci, counter to
school codes of conduct, had committed "an act patently immoral, detrimental to the reputation of the school" and violative of his duty to exercise "common sense, mature judgment and Christian charity." The court
agreed with the school, stating that "Geraci's acts constituted a breach of
the contract with St. Xavier [that is] fully supported by the evidence."
While such a harsh punishment for being a mere accessory to a youthful
prank might have been overturned for a public school student, Geraci's expulsion was upheld in the Ohio State Court of Appeals. As in other cases
involving private schools, judges here pointed out that public and private
schools were different under the law. With regards to the due process
clause, judges in *Geraci v. St. Xavier* stated that "a private school's disciplinary proceedings are not controlled by the due process clause, and accordingly such schools have broad discretion in making rules and setting up
procedures for their enforcement; nevertheless, under its broad equitable
powers a court will intervene where such discretion is abused or the proceedings do not comport with fundamental fairness."[10]Clearly, this differed
from judicial pronouncements, in *Goss* and elsewhere, about the primacy
of due process required in public schools.

   In another case involving a private school, Barry Flint and Donald
Plaisance were caught violating the smoking rules at St. Augustine High
School. The rule stated: "Students are forbidden to smoke within two
blocks of the school grounds. Violation of this rule incurs a fine of ten dollars for those who smoke as well as for those present in a gathering where
this rule is being violated. Violators may not return to school until the fine
is paid. *Repetition will result in dismissal.*"[11]The school had a new principal,

and he expelled Plaisance and Flint after they had been caught smoking near school many times, although the dismissal portion of this rule had not previously been enforced. A lower state court had overturned the boys' expulsion from school, but the Court of Appeals of Louisiana ruled:

> Fundamental rights of all parties are very much at issue here. We do not consider the basic due process rights of Flint and Plaisance to be any less important or any less deserving than those of St. Augustine High School which also clearly requires protection if it is to survive as a private, properly disciplined, functioning institution of learning.
>
> We have not sought to balance the one against the other. We have only concluded that the procedure followed by St. Augustine High school in the cases involving these two young men is not such as to require the State of Louisiana, through its judicial system, to intercede.
>
> St. Augustine himself observed that when he was in Rome he fasted on the days set aside for that purpose by the Romans, though they were not the same as the days that he fasted while at home. He thus may be considered the original author of the oft-used phrase: "When in Rome do as the Romans do."
>
> These young men were obliged, while at St. Augustine High School, to do as they were required by the rules of the school—which they deliberately chose to ignore. Having determined, as we do, that such due process rights as they were entitled to in the premises have not been so violated as to sully the school's action, we reverse the judgment of the Civil District Court.[12]

This finding is interesting in light of work by sociologist James Coleman and his colleagues.[13] Their research on the superior academic performance of private school students suggested that school climate and student behavior have contributed to differences in pupil achievement. Peer climates have been more conducive to learning in private schools, with fewer fights and threats to teachers than in public schools. Part of the advantage of private schools was found in their greater degree of family and community involvement. This social connection and closure—or "social capital," as Coleman termed it—among family, community, and school made it easier for private schools to enforce rules and norms than was the case for relatively socially disconnected public high schools.

Coleman has asserted that "the private school is an agent of the family rather than an agent of the larger society."[14] In this area it was an advantage for private schools that they were not state institutions—courts afforded them much greater discretion and latitude in the manner whereby they disciplined their students. This judicial restraint has allowed private school officials the capacity to discipline students aggressively without imminent threat of court challenges. A private school may expel troublemakers, rule-flouters, and revolutionaries with little fear of recrimination; public schools may not. Surely this has contributed to shaping peer climates and learning environments in private schools to a much greater extent than the general and diffuse "social capital" that Coleman found there. The court climate thus has likely contributed in important ways to public-private differences in educational outcomes. Ironically—in the name of formalizing and guaranteeing equality of treatment—courts may have exacerbated educational inequalities.

Though in general private schools have been given more leeway in the governance of their schools, disputes over rules that parents or students were not notified about or that appeared to be based on some school official's "personal beliefs" have not resulted as favorably for schools as other types of cases. For example, in *Fiedler v. Marumsco Christian Church,* a white girl, Lisa Fiedler, was expelled from a private Baptist school for having a purported romantic relationship with a black boy and fellow student, Rufus Bostic. Although the school admitted students of all races, Aleck Lee Bledsoe, principal of the school and pastor of the associated church, "personally had a position against [interracial dating] as pastor and principal"[15] and argued that his stand was based on church doctrine and the Bible. After several unheeded warnings not to talk to Rufus, Lisa was expelled from school. Pastor Bledsoe spoke with Lisa's father and was persuaded to readmit her after a few days, but once he learned that the Fiedlers had contacted the NAACP regarding the original expulsion, he rescinded his offer of readmittance. The federal district court accepted the argument of the church that "as a matter of firm religious conviction based on their interpretation of the Bible, interracial marriage, interracial dating, and interracial romantic relationships violate the tenets, doctrines, and beliefs of the fundamentalist Christian faith as held and practiced by the defendants."[16]

Upon appeal, the district court's decision was reversed. Appellate justices opined that the personal beliefs of the pastor, not the deeply held religious beliefs of the entire faith, motivated the school's actions.

Bledsoe himself testified that his position was the position of the church and was based on the Bible; that he had preached about it from the pulpit though he could not remember how many times; that he had had no negative feedback from the sermons that he had preached. He said that he believed "socially [interracial romantic relationships] would be a real problem." . . . Nothing other than Bledsoe's own conclusions indicates that his conviction regarding interracial romantic relationships is shared by the institution or that it is, in any event, more than a "personal preference." The institutional belief indeed is apparently one of racial equality and Bledsoe's belief is in no way reflective of that stance. The district court's contrary finding, offered without benefit of factual analysis, is not supportable by any interpretation of the evidence offered at trial.[17]

This result notwithstanding, courts generally accorded more autonomy to private schools in disciplining their students.

Race

The important *Brown v. Board of Education* desegregation decision was handed down in 1954, six years before our analysis began. Our court case data contain several examples of discipline for infractions in schools in which race was a factor—*Goss v. Lopez,* for one, which we discussed at length in the previous chapter. Additional cases were fought on the grounds of alleged racial discrimination in the implementation of school disciplinary sanctions.

Subsequent to the court decision in *Brown,* race remained an important factor shaping educational experiences. In appellate court cases involving school discipline, students who were explicitly identified in court records as being nonwhite were actually more likely to prevail over school authority. In some types of cases in high federal courts, nonwhite students were especially well situated to win legal challenges. Specifically, nonwhite students who were expelled from school could expect a 91 percent probability of a pro-student outcome in federal appeals or the Supreme Court (compared to a 38 percent likelihood of a pro-student outcome for a white student). In these cases specific federal laws that guarantee equality of treatment with respect to race were most readily applied.[18] This relationship is illustrated in Figure 3.4. In state and lower federal courts, an expulsion case had a much lower probability of a pro-student outcome: 52 percent for a

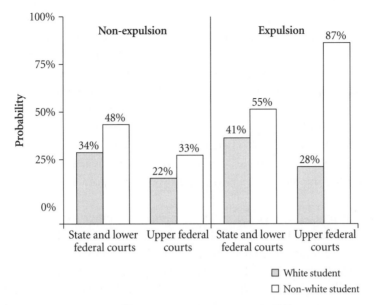

Figure 3.4 Predicted probability of pro-student school discipline court case decision by student race, expulsion, and court level (based on Table 3.B)

nonwhite student and 40 percent for a white student. Though all courts were more likely to favor a nonwhite student than a white student, regardless of the punishment imposed, this finding must be qualified by considering potential selection bias. Possibly only the most egregious cases of minority student rights violations ever made it to the courts, due to scarcity of financial resources and trust in the court system. These unusual cases would attract the interest and legal expertise of advocacy groups such as the ACLU and NAACP, in addition to OEO Legal Services.

In May 1963, Linda Woods, a "Negro girl living in Birmingham, Alabama" was arrested and charged with parading without a license at a "peaceful demonstration against racial segregation"[19] that took place on Saturday, when school was not in session. Several weeks later, the principal gave Woods—along with several other students who had been at the demonstration—a letter suspending her from school for the remainder of the term for her involvement. Woods filed a class action suit in the United States District Court on behalf of all the aggrieved students: the district court ruled in favor of the school and described the demonstration for which students had been sanctioned:

> This Court was shocked to see hundreds of school children ranging in age from six to sixteen running loose and wild without direction over the streets of Birmingham and in the business establishments. It is due to the patience and good judgment of the people of Birmingham and the police officials particularly that no one was seriously injured on May 7, 1963, when the demonstrators were allowed by the police department and city officials of Birmingham to parade within a certain designated area, and the hundreds of school children in the parade refused to stay within the boundaries of the parade area, broke through the police and for some forty-five minutes ran wild over the city of Birmingham.[20]

The district court judge continued, "This Court cannot conceive of a Federal Court saying to the Board of Education . . . made up of dedicated, courageous, honorable men that they should take no action under the circumstances." He also indicated that he had the assurances of the school officials that "the suspension or expulsion of no child will be upheld by the School Board . . . due to prejudice, anger or in retaliation." The expulsions were carried out. Upon appeal, the U.S. Court of Appeals reversed in favor of the students: "We are fully aware of the reluctance with which Federal Courts should contemplate the use of the injunctive power to interfere with the conduct of state officers. But when there is a deprivation of a constitutionally guaranteed right the duty to exercise the power cannot be avoided."[21] In this case, the appeals court ruled, the district court should have issued a restraining order enjoining the school district from expelling the students for the remainder of the school year.

Racial dynamics were especially evident in similar class action suits against school districts. In such cases, a large group of students claiming to represent an entire class of students (such as African-American high school students in a particular district) alleged that a school or district practiced racially biased enforcement of rules or imposition of sanctions. In the mid-1970s in Erie, Pennsylvania, a group of high school students joined with the Erie Human Relations Commission, a local civil rights group, to file a case against school officials alleging violations against students' rights in meting out punishment. The school district routinely moved misbehaving students out of their regular schools and into the New Directions Center, a facility for disruptive students, where classes offered at the regular school were often not available. Further, the complaint alleged that the punishment was disproportionately used to sanction African-

American students for their misbehavior. Attempting to mediate between the school district and the students, the district court helped both parties draw up a consent decree stating a mutually agreed upon solution to the problem.

On numerous occasions after the decree was established, students returned to court to argue that the district was not satisfying its end of the bargain. While the district court repeatedly buckled under the pressure from school officials to abandon the consent decree, the U.S. Court of Appeals stepped in on three occasions to require the district court to enforce the decree and protect students from inequitable imposition of disciplinary consequences. This was another important example of high federal courts taking a pro-student direction when cases involved strong exclusionary sanctions against minority youth.[22]

This is not to say that courts always favored minority youth. When students were involved in activities that courts tended to view with particular disfavor, such as student protest, the outcome was less likely to be pro-student. Likewise, when the imposed discipline was less harsh than an expulsion or other long-term removal from regular classes, high federal courts were not as prone to favor minority students. For example, in Arkansas in the late 1960s, a group of 29 black students stood up and walked out of a pep rally during the playing of "Dixie," widely considered as a symbol of Southern white racism because of its association with the Confederacy during the Civil War. The students who walked out of the assembly were suspended from school for five days. This action followed attempts by African-American students in the recently integrated school to convince school officials to abandon the playing of the divisive tune at school events.

Jonesboro High School voluntarily commenced operating a unitary school system in 1966. The school had thus operated as a completely integrated school without any abnormal problems for the first two years of total integration. For many years the playing of the song "Dixie" at pep assemblies had been permitted. For these first two years, black and white students participated in curricular and extracurricular activities together.

At a faculty meeting on September 26, 1968, one of the members stated that a few individual requests had been made to omit the playing of "Dixie" at pep assemblies as the song allegedly was offensive to Negro students. The school authorities concluded to experiment with the discontinuance of the playing of "Dixie" at pep assemblies but without any notice or publicity. This was done for approximately a month during which time there were complaints from white students and parents about discontinuing playing "Dixie" as it had been on the program for many years. On October 25, 1968, the committee decided to submit the matter to a vote to determine how many students were in favor of the continued use and how many were opposed. The vote being favorable to the playing of the tune, it was announced that thereafter attendance at the pep assemblies would be optional.[23]

Some African-American students opted not to attend the pep rally at all, while others saw it as an opportunity to protest a practice they considered offensive.

Two suspended students filed a class action suit against the school, alleging that leaving the pep rally was an action protected by the Free Speech Clause of the First Amendment, akin to wearing armbands in protest of the Vietnam War. The district court agreed with the school in finding that the students' silent procession out of the assembly created a disturbance. The court of appeals upheld this decision and engaged in a historical interpretive analysis of "Dixie" to determine whether the song was "racially abusive." Their review indicated that "Dixie" was a "typical American song with a gay and catchy tune" that was written by a Northerner as a "walk-around" for minstrel shows. On the basis of their research, the judges concluded, "[W]e cannot say that the tune 'Dixie' constitutes a badge of slavery or that the playing of the tune under the facts presented constituted officially sanctioned racial abuse. Such a ruling would lead to the prohibition of the playing of many of our most famous tunes."[24] Clearly, the court was unwilling to entertain the notion that the racist history of minstrels as a tool to ridicule African-Americans, the use of the song by the Confederacy during the Civil War, or the racially divided opinion toward the song among students might somehow justify the protesters' actions. This case again illustrates that courts have been less favorable to African-American students when lesser sanctions than expulsion were contested.

Type of Student Misbehavior

We have already shown that the type of student misbehavior at issue in court challenges has changed over time. How dependent was the court climate on the type of infractions committed by students?

FREE SPEECH AND FREE EXPRESSION.   In general, courts were more favorable toward free expression cases than they were toward other types of
student misbehavior during the second and third time periods. In the pre-
contestation period (1960–1968), however, free speech and free expression
cases had only a 19 percent probability of a pro-student decision, while
other types of student misbehavior enjoyed a 38 percent probability of
success. During and after the student rights contestation period (1969–
1992), free speech and expression cases had a higher probability of pro-
student outcomes than cases dealing with other student infractions (44
percent compared to 33 percent probability of a pro-student outcome).[25]
These results suggest that after an initial hesitation to equate the individual
freedoms of youth in schools with those of adults, courts subsequently became more amenable to affording students basic rights to freedom of
speech and expression, especially when exercising these rights did not appear substantially to disrupt school operations.

The disputes over free expression can be broken down into two basic
types of student rights that confronted the courts: appearance (especially the length of boys' hair and whether girls were allowed to wear
pants) and speech (especially as published in student newspapers). Although cases dealing with freedom of expression were clearly political in
some ways, we separate them from other politics cases (like student protest against the Vietnam War) because these disputes were generally not
"collective action" as were cases we explicitly labeled "political." These cases
involved the rights of schools to restrict individual expression in fashion
or words.

HAIR AND APPEARANCE.   Beginning in the mid- to late sixties, styles in
the United States shifted: young men began growing their hair longer than
had been fashionable in previous years. This style was frequently referred
to in court records as the "Beatle haircut," after the British foursome. These
hairstyles often flatly violated school regulations for appearance and dress,
and schools often suspended "long-hair boys" until they complied with
regulations. Many students contested these disciplinary actions, arguing
that the rules unnecessarily infringed upon their rights of free expression.
Courts were bitterly divided on the issue.

Earlier decisions tended to favor schools. Judges were reluctant to en-
croach upon school officials' judgment on the issue and were persuaded
that young men with long hair were disruptive to an appropriate school

environment. For example, in 1965, the Supreme Judicial Court of Massachusetts ruled:

> An unusual length and style of the hair of a senior male pupil in a public high school could reasonably be regarded by school authorities as inimical to the maintenance of proper decorum and discipline in the school and to the proper operation thereof, and action by the authorities suspending the pupil from the school until he had had an "acceptable haircut" was within the authorities' discretionary powers and could not be disturbed by the courts, even though the pupil was a professional musician to whose "image" as a performer and professional success the length and style of his hair was essential . . .
>
> [If schools could not control student appearance,] those in charge of our schools would be virtually unable to cope, on a day to day basis, with the problems of management and discipline to which the unpredictable activities of large groups of children may give rise . . .
>
> We are of the opinion that the unusual hairstyle of the plaintiff could disrupt and impede the maintenance of a proper classroom atmosphere or decorum. This is an aspect of personal appearance and hence akin to matters of dress. Thus as with any unusual, immodest or exaggerated mode of dress, conspicuous departures from accepted customs in the matter of haircuts could result in the distraction of other pupils.[26]

But "accepted customs" was a vague concept to define. Subsequent cases often involved "hair-splitting" descriptions regarding student styles. In a 1966 case before the United States District Court in Texas, several boys who were members of "a musical group or 'combo' known as Sounds Unlimited"[27] were suspended from school for their hair length. Their feelings about it were quite well known in the local school community, and the court record quoted their song, entitled "Keep Your Hands Off It":

> Went to school, got kicked out,
> Said it was too long, now we're going to shout.
> Keep your hands off it,
> Keep your hands off it,
> It don't belong to you.
> Bopped upon the steps, Principal I met.
> You're not getting in, now what do you want to bet . . .
> Went this morning, tried to get in.

The kids were for us, but we still couldn't win.
Keep your hands off it . . .
HAIR, THAT IS.[28]

Before the court, the parents of the boys in the group testified as to the length of their sons' hair. Stephen Webb's mom stated that his hair "is over his ears, but one can see the lobe of his ear. It is not over his collar, but is over his forehead and down to his eyebrows." Paul Jarvis' mother described "his hair is about 1 inch over his ears and about 1 ½ inches above his eyebrows." The judge summed up this testimony to describe the hairstyle as "in conformity with the so-called 'Beatle' type hair style."[29]

Principal Lanham argued that the boy's hair caused "trouble and commotion," elicited the "exchange of obscene remarks to the long-haired boys," attracted attention, and was disruptive in the classroom. He indicated that he was not unilaterally opposed to long hair, but that he "did not accept the extreme Beatle type hair style."[30] He also suggested that there was a correlation between discipline and dress or attire. The district court found these arguments convincing and ruled in favor of the school. The students appealed to the United States Court of Appeals. In their opinion upholding the ruling of the lower court, the majority of justices described how "a group of boys at his school had decided that a classmate's hair was too long and that they were going to take the matter in their own hands and trim it themselves." Further,

> [o]bscene language had been used by some students in reference to others with long hair and girls had come to his office complaining about the language being used. Also, long-hair boys had been told by others that the girl's restroom was right down the hall. Mr. Lanham mentioned one long-hair boy who refused to go to the boy's restroom until the other boys had left. He referred to other incidents where the boys would eat in the lunchroom only with the girls and never eat with the boys.[31]

The court indicated that the state has an interest in maintaining an effective and efficient school system, and "that which so interferes or hinders the state in providing the best education possible for its people, must be eliminated or circumscribed as needed. This is true even when that which is condemned is the exercise of a constitutionally protected right."[32]

In the dissent to this case, one justice argued that the "long-hair boys" should not be punished for the obscene language and unsavory actions of those who did not like their hair. His words signaled things to come, when courts shifted toward students in these cases. He found flaws with the majority opinion and argued,

> These boys were not barred from school because of any actions carried out by them which were of themselves a disturbance of the peace. They were barred because it was anticipated, by reason of previous experiences, that their fellow students in some instances would do things that would disrupt the serenity or calm of the school. It is these acts that should be prohibited, not the expressions of individuality by the suspended students.[33]

This type of exchange between judges in the minority and those in the majority was not uncommon throughout the late sixties.

In arguments that seem somewhat ridiculous by current standards of appearance, school officials continued to argue that long hair was disruptive. In a 1967 United States District Court case in Louisiana, the Superintendent of Schools was quoted as saying,

> Throughout the realm of professional education there is a distinct and direct relationship between student dress and conduct. From my experience, I know that gross deviation from the norm does cause a disruption of the learning atmosphere and can create an undesirable separateness among students. Furthermore, gross deviation can be and has been dysfunctional in the social adjustment of children. Dress and appearance do have an effect upon conduct and decorum.[34]

Courts were particularly sympathetic to such arguments, and not until 1969 did some courts begin to rule in favor of students in hair length cases.

In a United States District Court case in Wisconsin, the judges were skeptical that long hair symbolized anything deeper or more sinister than fashion. Here, the judges grounded their pro-student decision in empirical social science research. We cite the decision at length to illustrate a growing reliance on integrating the fields of social science and law to challenge traditional school-based forms of authority:

> The record here includes a deposition (taken at the instance of the defendants) by a principal of a public high school in a city about five miles from Williams Bay. In apparent seriousness he testifies: that "extreme hair styling" on boys especially "symbolizes something that I feel is not in the best interests of good citizenship"; that "whenever I see a long-hair

youngster he is usually leading a riot, he has gotten through committing a crime, he is a dope addict or some such thing"; that "anyone who wears abnormally long hair, to the decent citizenry, immediately reflects a symbol that we feel is trying to disrupt everything we are trying to build up and by we I mean God-fearing Americans"; that the students at his high school share his opinion "that long hair symbolizes revolution, crime, and dope addiction"; that in his opinion "wearing long hair is un-American" in this day and age; and that its symbolism renders long hair a distraction . . .

[According to defendants,] in Williams Bay a male high school student whose hair is longer than the Board Standard so departs from the norm that his appearance distracts his fellow students from their school work; and . . . students whose appearance conforms to community standards perform better in school, both in strictly academic work and in extracurricular activities, than those whose appearance does not conform.

With respect to the 'distraction' factor, the showing in this record consists of expressions of opinion by several educational administrators that an abnormal appearance of one student distracts others. There is no direct testimony that such a distraction has occurred. There has been no offer of the results of any empirical studies on the subject by educators, psychologists, psychiatrists, or other experts. Even in the opinions which have been received in evidence, there has been no amplification with respect to what portion of the students are susceptible to such distraction, how frequently susceptible students are likely to be distracted for this reason, how quickly or slowly high school students accommodate to individual differences in appearance, or how the distraction actually manifests itself in terms of the behavior of the distracted students in various learning situations. From the testimony of the educational administrators, it appears that the absence of such amplification is not accidental; it arises from the absence of factual data which might provide the amplification.

With respect to the "comparative performance" factor, this record is equally barren. The expert opinions are fewer than those on the distraction factor. No empirical findings are offered. No hard facts are adduced even from a limited sample to demonstrate that the academic performance of male students with long hair is inferior to that of male students with short hair, or that the former are less active or less effective in extracurricular activities.

Defendants here have fallen far short of showing that the distraction caused by male high school students whose hair length exceeds the Board standard is so aggravated, so frequent, so general, and so persistent that this invasion of their individual freedom by the state is warranted. The same is true of defendants showing with respect to the differential in school performance between male students with long hair and those with short hair.[35]

In the absence of empirical evidence, these judges were unconvinced by what had previously been the standard school argument supporting hair regulations.

Upon appeal, the appellate court upheld the district court's ruling in favor of the student. The majority argued in their 1969 opinion that

the doctrine invoked by the School Board of "in loco parentis" does not bolster its discipline argument. Although schools need to stand in place of a parent, in regard to certain matters during the school hours, the power must be shared with the parents, especially over intimately personal matters such as dress and grooming. Since the student's parents agree with their children that their hair can be worn long and because it would be impossible to comply with the long hair regulation during school hours and follow the wishes of the students and their parents as to hair length outside of school, in the absence of any showing of disruption, the doctrine of "in loco parentis" has no applicability . . .

Discipline for the sake of discipline and uniformity, is indeed not compatible with the melting pot formula which brought this country to greatness.[36]

Although the tide had turned in favor of the students, some judges still argued strenuously in favor of the schools. In the dissenting opinion, one judge expressed concern that the ruling would unnecessarily burden courts with decisions that were rightfully made by school officials:

I think the majority opinion is clearly wrong in its pronouncement "The right to wear one's hair at any length or in any desired manner is an ingredient of personal freedom protected by the United States Constitution." I assume this broad statement includes boys or girls attending High School. If so, the statement is unwarranted. Thus boys, imitating the style of the 'Wild Man from Borneo' with hair unkempt and reaching down to the waist would, according to the majority opinion, have a federal constitutional right to defy school rules and regulations to the contrary.

I assume there are more than one hundred School Boards operating in the Western District of Wisconsin. If the District Judge is to be the arbiter of the length and style of hair and of various other items and practices included in school regulations, he will have little or no time to take care of ordinary federal district court business.[37]

Moving beyond early arguments about long hair being antithetical to proper school "decorum," school officials began arguing that long hair should be banned from school for health and safety reasons. In one case, school personnel argued that the regulation stating that boys' "hair must not be in the eyes, over the ears, or over the collar. Sideburns cut at bottom of ear" was needed to ensure students' physical well-being. Boys with long hair caused a "safety problem in some physical education activities" because hair "constantly falling in the eyes was hazardous in sports such as football, basketball, or softball."[38] Presumably, long hair on girls did not cause similar dangers, since there were no analogous coiffure restrictions on young women. In another case, a judge summed up this now common school officials' argument:

[that] long male hair would constitute a safety hazard in the science laboratory and in shop classes and that it would be extremely difficult to enforce a regulation requiring boys to wear hair nets or caps; that if dress codes and hair style regulations could not be enforced, it could be anticipated that students would go overboard and wear all sorts of extreme costumes and arrive at school in bizarre states of appearance; one experience was testified to in a school where no hair regulation was in effect, in which students began using extreme hair coloring, such as brilliant orange, purple and greens of various shades; that long hair presents a health factor; if there was no hair regulation it would result in friction, fighting and incidents between long and short haired students.[39]

Related to the cases involving hair length were those involving facial hair. In 1969 in the United States District Court for the Southern District of Georgia, the judge who had recently delivered an opinion regarding school desegregation that caused "the elimination of the dual system" of education heard a case involving a student's challenge to a school's prohibition against facial hair. The judge cautioned that orderly school desegregation

is suddenly jeopardized by a lilliput of a lawsuit—a legal controversy that has upset everybody in the school system—a cause celebre that attracted

a courtroom full of spectators when the matter was heard before me . . .
How has this new school crisis come about? What does it involve? It concerns the monumental question of the constitutional right of a student to
wear a mustache in violation of a regulation of the school authorities . . . I
have previously expressed my disrelish of the job thrust upon me of saying how public schools should be run. I not only do not have the time,
but the task is far beyond my competence . . . Once again, I am cast in the
role of a school administrator. With all my overload of work, I must decide the precise point at which the fuzz or down above the lips of a teen-
ager becomes a mustache.[40]

Citing the types of "distraction" asserted by school officials in long hair
cases, the court ruled in favor of the school. The judges rejected the student's argument that a rule forbidding mustache or beard hindered the
"constitutionally protected right to express one's individuality." The opinion stated, "Students wearing mustaches or beards in a high school may be
a distracting influence on a student body which does not wear them.
Teachers have a right to teach in an atmosphere conducive to teaching and
learning and unkempt faces do not contribute much to it."[41] The Court of
Appeals affirmed the ruling, stating that "the entire problem seems minus-
cule in light of other matters involving the school system."[42]

In addition to hair, student clothing options were also often under the
purview of school regulations. In the late sixties and early seventies, rules
prohibiting girls from wearing pants came under fire in the courts. In
1969, Lori Scott, a tenth grader at Hicksville High School, and her female school mates were permitted to wear pants between December 1 and
March 31, when the principal declared the weather too cold for skirts.
However, Lori wore pants to school twice in October and was placed in detention, thus missing her classes, for violating the regulation. She argued
with the school board that her family did not have the financial means to
purchase clothing that would comply with the dress code. The board did
not act to her satisfaction, so she brought a case against the district that
made its way to the Supreme Court of New York. In the decision, the judge
questioned the reasonableness of the no-pants regulation for girls:

Does the proscription of slacks for female students fall within the perim-
eters of the board's authority? The simple facts that it applies only to female students and makes no differentiation as to the kind of slacks man-
dates a negative answer, for those facts make evident that what is being

enforced is style or taste and not safety, order or discipline. A regulation against the wearing of bell-bottomed slacks by students, male or female, who ride bicycles to school can probably be justified in the interest of safety; as can, in the interest of discipline, a regulation against slacks that are so skin-tight and, therefore, revealing as to provoke or distract students of the opposite sex; and, in the interest of order, a regulation against slacks to the bottoms of which small bells have been attached. Such regulations are valid because they relate the prohibition to an area within the board's authorized concerns; the flat prohibition of all slacks is invalid precisely because it does not.[43]

Obviously, the court ruled in favor of the student in this case. Indeed, school rules against girls wearing pants were no longer adjudicated after the early seventies; the pendulum of fashion had swung such that girls and women wearing pants became the norm. Also, forceful court decisions such as that discussed above made challenges on this issue increasingly difficult for schools to defend. Regulations forbidding pants quickly became historical relics once young women in the early seventies fought for and gained new legal standing in many societal arenas.

Fashion, almost by definition, changes with the times. Schools attempting to prescribe proper appearance and dress for their students have faced an uphill battle in the courts since the late 1960s. Courts mostly recognized the rights of students to wear clothes and hairstyles that suited their own personal tastes, rather than the tastes of some school official or a nebulous "community," except where school officials demonstrated reasonable concerns for student safety and school discipline. It is likely that the more permissive school dress codes of today resulted at least partially from the flurry of cases about this issue that were decided in favor of students.[44]

FREE SPEECH.   The right to speak or write what is on one's mind without fear of punishment is a central element of a free and democratic society. But did this right apply to students in public schools? Like the free expression cases involving appearance, those involving speech were more frequently found in favor of students than cases regarding student discipline for political protest or weapons. Nonetheless, the courts have been divided on whether the free speech rights granted to adults applied equally to students.

For example, in 1979 four high school students produced a satirical publication addressed to the school community. They decided to emulate *National Lampoon,* "a well-known publication specializing in sexual satire."[45] The students began preparation of the publication in school but after school hours, with the permission of their teacher (Mr. Mager); most of the preparation took place at home. When Mr. Mager saw a draft of an article that he objected to, he told the assistant principal. The assistant principal called in one of the students and "discussed with him the 'dangers' of publishing material that might offend or hurt others." Specifically, he warned that he had suspended students for a similar publication in previous years. The administrator cautioned the student not to mention particular students and not to distribute the publication on school grounds. In response, the students "deleted several proposed articles and excised students' names from others. Moreover, they assiduously endeavored to sever all connections between their publication and the school. A legend disclaiming responsibility for any copies found on school property was affixed to the newspaper's cover. Indeed, all 100 copies of the paper were produced by the facilities of a community business."[46]

The publication, entitled *Hard Times,* first surfaced within the school when a teacher confiscated a copy from a student and presented it to the principal. Initially, the school took no action, and schoolwide examinations were conducted without incident. But when the Board of Education President learned of the paper through her son, she was "shocked and offended" by the contents. The paper had a banner across its cover disclosing its contents as "uncensored, vulgar, immoral." The judge agreed: "Its thirteen pages are saturated with distasteful sexual satire, including an editorial on masturbation and articles alluding to prostitution, sodomy, and castration."[47]

The students were suspended for five days; this was to be reduced to three days if they submitted an essay on the "potential harm to people caused by the publication of irresponsible and/or obscene writing." They were segregated from other students during study hall periods, lost all student privileges during the period of suspension, and had suspension letters added to their school files. The students challenged these actions in the district court. Both school and students submitted affidavits "to assist the court in gauging the paper's likely impact on Granville's students." The school's experts, three school administrators from neighboring towns, predicted in their affidavits a "devastating" effect on public education. The students' expert, a professor of education, asserted in his affidavit that "no competent school administrator" would claim that *Hard Times* would disrupt the education of high school students.[48]

The district court upheld the school's actions, but the students took the case up to the court of appeals, which overturned the previous ruling. The judges stated:

> It is not difficult to imagine the lengths to which school authorities could take the power they have exercised in the case before us. If they possessed this power it would be within their discretion to suspend a student who purchases an issue of *National Lampoon,* the inspiration for *Hard Times,* at a neighborhood newsstand and lends it to a school friend. And, it is conceivable that school officials could consign a student to a segregated study hall because he and a classmate watched an X-rated film on his living room cable television. While these activities are certainly proper subjects of parental discipline, the First Amendment forbids public school administrators and teachers from regulating the material to which a child is exposed after he leaves school each afternoon. Parents still have their role to play in bringing up their children . . . The risk is simply too great that school officials will punish protected speech and thereby inhibit future expression. In addition to their vested interest and susceptibility to community pressure, they are generally unversed in the difficult constitutional concepts such as libel and obscenity. . . .
>
> When school officials are authorized only to punish speech on school property, the student is free to speak his mind when the school day ends. . . . Indeed, our willingness to grant school officials substantial autonomy within their academic domain rests in part on the confinement of that power within the metes and bounds of the school itself.[49]

The courts jealously guarded free speech rights, even when students were involved.

POLITICS.   Political protest in schools became a force to be reckoned with in the sixties and early seventies. Students waged sit-ins, marches, and boycotts of classes to protest issues ranging from racial discrimination to the Vietnam War to school rules about smoking. To be sure, school officials did not take kindly to the sudden wave of activism on their campuses. Principals and teachers heartily punished students who engaged in political protest at school and sometimes even those whose protest occurred off school grounds. Not surprisingly, students challenged these sanctions in the courts. In fact, between 1960 and 1968, 41 percent of all school discipline court cases involved political protest. During the student rights contestation period, from 1969 to 1975, protest accounted for only 23 percent of cases. More recently, from 1976 to 1992, a mere four percent of cases involved political action. Like school officials, judges—particularly those from state courts—were not sympathetic toward students involved in political action, perhaps because state courts were especially supportive of school officials' actions in such cases.[50]

In 1981, Brazil High School in Indiana experienced disruptions. First, 54 students engaged in a walkout "in protest of the enforcement of certain school regulations dealing essentially with student smoking and student attendance."[51] Further, many of the protesters distributed leaflets to fellow students urging them to participate. The day after the walkout, numerous students attempted to incite another protest by distributing more leaflets. The principal found out who was responsible before another walkout occurred, and called the agitators into his office. Eventually, the students were expelled in October for the remainder of the semester.

The students brought their grievance over the discipline to the federal district court. Because the school had reasonable suspicion that disruption would occur upon distribution of the leaflets, and because of their recent experiences with similar disruptions, the court ruled that the punishment was not excessive. The decision stated that "once a reasonable forecast of material interference with the school's work is made, school officials should be accorded a wide degree of discretion in determining the appropriate punishment to be imposed." Further, the judge ruled

> that a quiet discussion between mature students and a benevolent school administrator is unquestionably preferable to a formal adversary proceeding such as that currently before the Court. Many times a patient response rather than discipline and expulsion is the better remedy. It is a judgment call and . . . the Court will not substitute its judgment for that of the school officials.
>
> It is hopeful that this decision will not be interpreted so as to result in a "chilling effect" on students advocating constitutionally protected conduct. On the other hand, the Court does not intend that this ruling shall give to the school officials a license or invitation to prohibit conduct that is constitutionally protected . . . A variation in the facts as to time, place and manner could very well change the result.[52]

This decision illustrates the degree to which courts were not particularly sympathetic to students challenging school discipline arising from political protest.

DRUGS AND ALCOHOL.   School discipline cases involving alcohol and drug use increased since the 1960s, especially since the mid-seventies. The courts have been especially supportive of school discipline where student drug use or possession was concerned. On average, students caught under the influence, in the act, or with the goods, who subsequently challenged their punishment in the appellate courts, had only a 23 percent probability of prevailing compared to the 40 percent probability of a decision in their favor when they challenge the discipline for *anything other* than drugs. School discipline cases involving alcohol have not resulted in as many pro-school case outcomes as those involving drugs.

In one fairly recent drug case, athletes Darcy Schaill and Shelley Johnson challenged their school district's random urinalysis program testing all student athletes for drug use, claiming it was unconstitutional. The federal court of appeals indicated that participation in athletics is voluntary, and thus if the girls wished to avoid being tested, they could opt out of sports. The justices stated that they were mindful of student rights,

> [h]owever, we recognize that, if students are to be educated at all, an environment conducive to learning must be maintained. The plague of illicit drug use which currently threatens our nation's schools adds a major dimension to the difficulties the schools face in fulfilling their purpose— the education of our children. If the schools are to survive and prosper, school administrators must have reasonable means at their disposal to deter conduct which substantially disrupts the school environment. In this case, we believe that the Tippecanoe County School Corporation has chosen a reasonable and limited response to a serious evil.[53]

When drugs were involved, courts were also willing to uphold schools' rights to involve the criminal justice system in punishing the student. Courts upheld the sentencing of a sixteen-year-old boy for dealing marijuana at school to involuntary confinement in a "youth camp." In a 1988 case in the Supreme Court of Nevada, the opinion indicated that even when the sole reason for incarcerating a student was for the "deterrent effect," justices still supported involving the criminal justice system:

We deem the deterrence of others from engaging in drug sales in our schools to be "sufficient reason" to incarcerate a youth adjudged to be guilty of such criminal conduct, and we see the juvenile court as having acted in an eminently wise and prudent manner in deciding upon this disposition. . . . Scott is described in the record as a "middleman in drug sales" among high school students. If such a person can be adjudged guilty of drug sales in the schools and escape any punitive sanction, the law and its moral force are indeed in jeopardy. To maintain the integrity of our drug laws some punishment must follow, as it did here, from the violation of these laws.[54]

Cases of drug and alcohol violations illustrated the increase in litigation that involved not only school rules, but also state and federal laws. Clearly, courts were more favorable towards harsh sanctions against students when they had transgressed regulations in these areas.

VIOLENCE AND WEAPONS.　Students who were caught fighting on school grounds or who brought weapons to school faced severe disciplinary consequences. Those students who challenged penalties in the courts faced an uphill battle. Our analysis shows that when violence and weapons were involved, courts were somewhat more likely (about 9 percentage points) to support a school's right to discipline, even if this also meant bringing in the police and applying a criminal delinquency charge. We also found that violence and weapons cases represented increasing numbers of school discipline court cases over time. In the post-contestation period, these infractions combined to account for fully 20 percent of court cases. This was certainly up from the 1960s, when weapons cases were less than one percent, and violence cases were only three percent of the total.

Judges have repeatedly supported stringent school policies against weapons. In Missouri on September 27, 1988, eighth-grade student Art King was suspended from school for the remainder of the semester for bringing a butterfly knife to school. He argued in court that although the district had meted out an equivalent punishment to two other boys earlier that semester for similar infractions, his own suspension was unduly harsh because he had a superior academic and disciplinary record relative to the other offenders. The court found in Art's favor, but the Missouri Court of Appeals reversed in favor of the school. The court stated that the superintendent was within reason to ignore academic records in making punishment decisions. The judges summarized the superintendent's testimony:

> [He stated] that anyone who brings a knife to school creates a potentially dangerous situation. Because the District needed to emphasize the inherent danger in these situations, he reasoned, it should not impose disparate punishments on students who bring knives to school. He concluded that uniformity in punishment helped prevent such dangerous occurrences. Although we may question the wisdom of his methods, we cannot categorize as unreasonable the District's uniform policy of suspension for possession of knives at school . . .
>
> Art's violation of school policy triggered the District's use of its discretionary power. In imposing the suspension, it acted within the scope of its discretion, and we cannot say that it abused its discretion.
>
> We might have reached a different decision, but we may not substitute our judgment for the District's as to matters within its discretion.[55]

Especially when dealing with the growing problems of violence and weapons in the schools, judges have tended to defer to school officials.

School officials have significant leeway to search students they have suspected of possessing a weapon. In an early Supreme Court of New York gun possession case, judges in 1978 found in favor of the school and argued:

> In the case now before us, we are dealing with a 14-year-old boy, in a school, with a loaded weapon in his pocket. There is no doubt in our minds that a school official has the right to "frisk" a child based on a reasonable suspicion that he has a gun. Police officers are given that same standard when searching adults for guns. It would be absurd to have a higher standard for those with a quasi-parental obligation than for police officers who approach an adult on the street. The mere fact that a child may have a loaded gun in a school creates exigencies affecting the security of all of the children in the school.[56]

More recent cases have continued to echo this sentiment: school officials suspecting weapon possession must be allowed to search students in order to maintain safety in the schools.

Violence or weapons decisions in favor of students generally hinged on procedural problems in implementing punishments. Fifteen-year-old Ted

Warner left class without permission; his teacher, Mr. Dinn, subsequently "backed him up against a wall"[57] with his hands on Warner's shoulders. Warner then allegedly struck Mr. Dinn in the stomach, causing him to double up in pain, and was then ordered to the principal's office. In a preliminary hearing, rather than rule immediately on the delinquency charges against Warner, the court ordered a full hearing because there was evidence that the same teacher had been involved in altercations with other boys. At the formal hearing, when Warner's attorney attempted to cross-examine Mr. Dinn about his previous conduct, the judge sustained the objection of the prosecutor:

> *The Court:* What would [Mr. Dinn's past] have to do with Ted, here, hitting the teacher?
> *Attorney:* Well, that shows the teacher's previous provocations.
> *The Court:* You maintain there's provocations for a student to hit a teacher?
> *Attorney:* Yes, when he shoves him against the wall, that's provocation.
> *The Court:* I'll sustain the objection. I can't get it through my head, what [that] would have to do with it. I can't imagine any act, that would be sufficient to provoke a student to strike a Teacher, or a Private to strike a Sergeant, or a Sergeant to hit the Captain, or a Captain to slug the Admiral. There's no provocation. . . . We have quite a few people waiting here, and I think I've heard enough of this. Did you want to put on any witnesses, Mister Day [Warner's Attorney]?
> *Attorney:* No, I think not.
> *The Court:* . . . the Court finds Ted Warner to be a delinquent child, and orders him committed to the Trustees of the Indiana Boys' School until he's Twenty One years of age. You'll remain in the custody of the Sheriff for transportation to Boys' School, thank you for coming in.[58]

Upon appeal, the Indiana Supreme Court overturned the delinquency charge, finding the judge's unwillingness to hear evidence about the teacher's past record to be unfair. The court also found that the judge's demeanor created "an atmosphere of impatience in the courtroom, especially in the eyes of a 15-year-old young man."[59] The justices stated:

We are not unmindful of the deplorable rise in the frequency of acts of violence committed by students against teachers in our schools in Indiana and throughout the nation . . . Where school authorities deem the situation in a school or with a particular pupil so intolerable that they feel it necessary to invoke the aid of our courts for remedial action, we should stand ready to do whatever is judicially appropriate to restore peace and order to the academic institution involved.

Notwithstanding our strong sentiments in this regard, we must believe with equal resolve and conviction, that in order for our judicial system to be effective, it must be respected, and in order for it to be respected it must be fair. Convicting a man accused for a dastardly crime by an unfair proceeding or one which appears to be unfair may win favor for the court among the outraged citizenry at the time of the alleged offense. But over the long run . . . the inequitable conduct of the court will invariably prevail in its effect on public opinion . . . the more emotionally charged or heinous the crime, the greater is the need for judicial circumspection in the conduct of the trial.[60]

This unusual pro-student decision in a case involving violence clearly was stimulated by the judge's actions, rather than school practices.

Arbitrary enforcement of rules about weapons has not been viewed kindly by the courts either. Thirteen-year-old Cynthia Jones received a commemorative knife from her father to give to her boyfriend as a Christmas gift. "This was a bone-handled knife with a plate thereon for initials or other inscription. It had no switch mechanism and had to be opened as whittlers have done for generations." Cynthia had a friend who was moving out of town who wanted to see the knife and "Cynthia brought the knife to the school bus stop to show it to her, with the intention of taking the knife home before the school bus arrived. However, the bus approached; and Cynthia, reluctant to face the consequences at home for missing the bus, elected to take the knife with her to school."[61] Once at school, Cynthia was in the bathroom when another student began smoking. A school administrative assistant caught the smoker and searched the purses of all girls in the bathroom at the time. She found Cynthia's knife, and subsequently "Cynthia's school life metamorphosed into a chapter of *Les Miserables*," according to the appellate judge who heard Cynthia's challenge to the prospect of her full school year expulsion. The school took disciplinary action citing a school rule providing mandatory expulsion for "the possession, use or transmittal of a weapon or use in a manner reasonably calculated to threaten any person." Knives were defined in the school board policy as "switchblade, hunting or any knife used to intimidate." In the view of the court, the commemorative knife at issue here did not meet that definition. The judges stated:

> We are as mindful as every member of the School Board of the absolute necessity of preventing violence in school. Every day we must deal with evidence of man's inhumanity to his fellows; and we are as cognizant as all public officials of the necessity for strict disciplinary requirements in the schools. But the School Board cannot have it both ways. If it is going to urge the validity of a mandatory rule of such gravity, then it had better use in its rule making all of the punctiliousness that Seurat did in his painting. Here, it failed to do so by not meeting its definition of knives as weapons.[62]

In this case, the judges found the school's punishment to be too harsh. Such pro-student decisions in cases involving weapons were again exceptional.

OTHER STUDENT MISBEHAVIOR.   Youngsters can be creative in their misbehavior. Since the mid-1970s, the majority of discipline court cases have involved varieties of student misbehavior other than those discussed above. Although the outcomes of these cases did not differ in significant ways from those involving other types of infractions, we discuss one of them here in order to give a flavor of the full range of disciplinary infractions schools, and thus the courts, have faced. Other forms of student infractions that appeared in our data set included insubordination, tardiness, truancy, and theft.

Matthew Manico, whom the judge called "a member of [the] varsity wrestling team, of State championship, and potential Olympic, caliber"[63] was put on athletic suspension in his senior year for theft: he stole muffins from the school cafeteria. He was first given a two-day academic and extracurricular suspension by the principal at South Colonie Senior High School. Next, the athletic director, who is not a specified disciplinary authority, told Manico he was not allowed to participate in the wrestling program for the remainder of the season for his muffin caper. Other school officials were not consulted on this punishment. The Supreme Court of New York noted:

> This Athletic Director may be a paragon of wisdom; he may be endowed by his Creator with superhuman insight and judgment-making ability. But somewhere there surely must be an Athletic Director who is not such a paragon, nor so well endowed.
>
> . . . Assuredly, it was intersession. Many of [the school district's] key employees, including the Superintendent, were out of town. The school was on holiday. *But due process never takes a holiday!"*
>
> Untold numbers of students pass through our school system into the outer world every year. Most of them are fated to live lives of complete anonymity. To only a few is given the brief opportunity to achieve greatness—a momentary point in time when heroes clash, and mortals, by extraordinary efforts, rise above the normal capabilities of humankind to achieve a once and only measure of immortality. Petitioner is one of them, and he is all of them."
>
> This case is not about muffins; it is about due process and jurisdiction.[64]

Form of Discipline

School punishment has taken various forms. Suspensions and expulsions have remained the most prevalent punishments adjudicated throughout the period under investigation. However, the catchall category "other discipline" has become more common in cases since 1976—this would include suspension from a sporting team, barring an individual from graduation ceremonies, or reduction of academic grades. Also, more cases of corporal punishment have come up since this time. Adjudication over suspensions, however, has diminished since 1975. All courts have ruled against schools more frequently if the student challenge involved the especially harsh punishment of expulsion. In the higher courts this was overwhelmingly true when the expelled student was a minority-group member.

EXPULSION.   Of all the disciplinary measures available to school officials, expulsion has provoked the most pro-student outcomes when litigated in the courts. In court cases, the measure ranged from expulsion for the remainder of a semester to permanently.[65] Judges appropriately viewed these cases with great care:

> [A] sentence of banishment from the local educational system is, insofar as the institution has the power to act, the extreme penalty, the ultimate punishment. In our increasingly technological society getting at least a high school education is almost necessary for survival. Stripping a child of access to educational opportunity is a life sentence to second-rate citizenship, unless the child has the financial ability to migrate to another school system or enter private school.[66]

Because expulsion has such serious consequences and states have often implicitly promised to provide public education to students through "compulsory education" laws, courts have repeatedly taken a close look at the facts in these cases and were more likely to decide for students. In Alabama, a 13-year-old was permanently expelled from school for bringing a handgun and bullets to campus. He protested this action in the courts. The appellate judges agreed with the lawyers for the student, who argued that "the child's right to a public education in Alabama has been infringed upon" because state codes mandated compulsory school attendance for every child between ages seven and sixteen. This created "an entitlement to education in this state for children under the age of sixteen."

> This entitlement does not allow the child to escape the consequences of misconduct in a public school, nor does it contradict the inherent authority of a school board to maintain order and discipline in public schools. However, a child's right to education may be improperly infringed upon when a school board takes disciplinary action that is unreasonable and arbitrary.[67]

The judges felt that it was appropriate for them to take into account "the age of the students, their past history of behavior and school performance, and the actual disruptive effects of their conduct [when] determining whether the actions of the school boards were reasonable."[68] In this case, they suggested that permanent expulsion might be unreasonable and sent the case back to the lower court (which had not ruled on this issue when originally hearing the case) to make a final determination.

In other expulsion cases, the infraction was less serious than bringing a gun to school. For example, Leonard Dillon, a high school student, was expelled for kissing a student and showing subsequent disrespect to a teacher. In his case before the federal district court, the record showed that

> On February 3, 1978, Laura Beth Lester, a teacher at North Pulaski High School in Jacksonville, Arkansas, advised Don E. Elkins, the high school principal, that she had found the plaintiff, Leonard Dillon, then a student at the high school, kissing a girl in the hallway and that Dillon had remarked, "What a drag" when told to stop. A few days thereafter, the plaintiff's parents received a "recommendation for expulsion" notice, stating that Elkins was recommending that the plaintiff be expelled for the remainder of the school year.[69]

Ms. Lester did not testify at the school board hearing on Dillon's fate, and thus did not give Dillon a chance to question her interpretation of the events. The judges' decision noted,

> In effect, the Pulaski County Special School District Board upheld the expulsion of the plaintiff simply on the evidence that a complaint had been made concerning his conduct. The identity of the teacher originally responsible for the initiation of disciplinary proceedings against Dillon was known, and she was present at the school board hearing. Certainly in regard to the allegation that the plaintiff had been disrespectful, her testimony was critical. Neither she nor the school board faced any greater loss than a few minutes of their time if she were to be required to explain to the school board the reasons for her report and to submit to cross-examination by the plaintiff's attorney. Under all the circumstances, due process clearly demanded that the plaintiff should have been given an opportunity to question her before the school board at its disciplinary hearing concerning the details of his alleged misconduct.[70]

The court ordered that Dillon be allowed back in school and that the expulsion be removed from his files. This case illustrates that, especially after *Goss v. Lopez*, courts were critical of expulsions in which due process procedures were not strictly followed.

Decisions in expulsion cases after *Goss* mapped out certain expectations for due process in disciplinary proceedings. In overturning the expulsion of a number of students for their involvement in fighting and riots at school, the judge chided:

In an expulsion hearing, the notice given to the student must include a statement not only of the specific charge, but also the basic rights to be afforded the student: to be represented by counsel, to present evidence, and to confront and cross-examine adverse witnesses . . . Defendants next argue that even if the notice was defective, the court must still determine whether the plaintiffs were given a fair and impartial hearing. Defendants misapprehend the meaning of notice. It is not "fair" if the student does not know, and is not told, that he has certain rights which he may exercise at the hearing.[71]

The argument suggests that the courts viewed expulsion as a severe form of discipline with grave consequences for a student's future. Boards of education were thus required to ensure absolute fairness and adopt formal proceedings that mimicked those found in courts of law.

Not all school discipline cases dealing with expulsion result in pro-student decisions. Sometimes judges made distinctions between students involved in the same incident with regards to the severity of their infraction. In Arizona's Court of Appeals, the court distinguished between students who merely possessed drugs and were thus suspended from school, and the student who had distributed the drugs, who was expelled. The opinion stated:

A student may be suspended or expelled for behavior inimicable to the welfare of other students . . . Here, the School Board, in recognizing the dangerous condition created on school premises by the possession thereon of drugs, enacted a rule proscribing such conduct for the protection of the pupils. We are all aware of the fact that the schools of today are beset with problems of drug abuse and therefore are unable to say that the School Board abused its discretion in imposing the severe sanction of expulsion on a student who distributed drugs to fellow students.[72]

Further, judges often justified expulsion because of the supposed "deterrent effect" it had on student misbehavior. For example, a student caught smoking marijuana in school was expelled, and the U.S. District Court in Kentucky ruled in favor of the school:

It is unlikely that the right to a free, public education, however important it may have become as a practical matter, could be said to be a fundamental right rooted in the history and traditions of our people to the extent that the state could not abolish it, if done in a nondiscriminatory manner . . . There is no constitutional right, fundamental or otherwise, to smoke marijuana in school. Nor, is there anything unconstitutional about having discipline in a high school even strict discipline.

There is no constitutional right to be free from an appropriate degree of discipline, if one is affiliated with an organization where discipline is necessary, such as a team, a military unit, a police force, or a high school. . . .

Although the measures taken by the defendant here were drastic, drastic measures are needed. The public and private schools across our country are experiencing dire difficulties to the extent that their effectiveness, and even sometimes their very existence, are seriously threatened. Abuse of alcohol and drugs is a prime factor in this crisis. Thus there is a rational basis for the statute authorizing expulsion for possession of alcohol and drugs in school and for the action of the Board in the individual case. The defendants were justified in taking this situation into account in imposing the stringent sanctions they did upon the plaintiff. They were justified in considering, as courts do in imposing criminal sentences, the deterrent effect on other students, and to use strict discipline to keep drugs out of their school.[73]

In this case (and in others) justices agreed with school arguments that sometimes the damage to one individual's future could be justified for the good of all students.

Unlike expulsion, suspension, corporal punishment, transfer, and other punishments have relatively equivalent results in the courts. Two forms of discipline have become more commonly contested in the courts since 1976: "other" discipline and corporal punishment.

"OTHER" DISCIPLINE.   Just as student disciplinary infractions have become increasingly varied, the legal challenges to school disciplinary strategies have also become more diversified since the period of student rights contestation. In the 1960s, only one percent of school action that was adjudicated involved a form of discipline other than suspension, expulsion, corporal punishment, or transfer. Since 1976, 14 percent of cases were student challenges to other forms of discipline.[74] Creative disciplinary measures have always been used in conjunction with more standard forms of punishment. But the increase indicated either that "other" forms of discipline have become a more prominent disciplinary action, or that legal advocates have attempted to expand due process rights beyond matters of suspension and expulsion. Documents produced by legal advocacy groups, such as the Center for Law and Education, suggest at a minimum that expansion of due process guarantees beyond the areas initially adjudicated in the *Goss v. Lopez* case was an explicit organizational goal.[75]

"Other" punishments include grade reduction and exclusion from extracurricular activities. Courts could be critical of new forms of punishment on grounds that they differed from "tried and true" traditional discipline. For example, courts were skeptical in a case of Elinor Hamer, who "left school during the lunch period on an emergency matter without advising any teacher or staff member."[76] The student returned to school the next Monday, with a note from her mother excusing her absence. The principal told her that because she had left school without informing any teacher or staff of her absence, her report card grades in missed subjects would be reduced 3 percent. Although some teachers refused to give this penalty, others complied. When Hamer and her parents appealed to the school board to hear her grievances, the board refused. The court ruled in favor of Hamer: "In our view plaintiff's complaint is sufficient to require appropriate response by the Board and a hearing to determine whether her right to due process has been violated by procedural infirmities or substantively by the application of arbitrary grade reduction penalties."[77] The form of discipline imposed was deemed to have "no reasonable relationship to the disciplinary objectives sought . . . by the Board."[78]

CORPORAL PUNISHMENT.   Corporal punishment, some might argue, is an extremely harsh form of discipline. Indeed, many states—primarily in the Northeast and Midwest—no longer allow school officials to inflict it on students. Students who challenged corporal punishment in the courts, however, did not meet especially favorable outcomes. If anything, these case outcomes tended to be somewhat more pro-school.

In a 1982 case, Keith Rhodus, a student at Southside Junior High School in Louisiana, was disciplined by a teacher, Mr. Dumiller. Dumiller administered corporal punishment, which consisted of "striking him eight times in the kidney area"[79] with a wooden paddle. School district regulations mandated that students not be paddled more than three times, and that another teacher be present when corporal punishment was administered. Even though Dumiller overlooked these guidelines, the United States District Court ruled against the student. The court found that ignoring the guidelines caused no violation of Rhodus's constitutional rights, thus he was not entitled to damages from the district or the teacher.

Conclusion

Court cases dealing with school disciplinary issues were ultimately related to broader social phenomena than the specifics of the case. Because court decisions were strongly related to student and school demographic and institutional characteristics, the court climate was clearly associated with social factors in any given case, such as the student's race and region of residence. Also, many interested parties beyond the students and school personnel, such as parents, lawyers, and at times national advocacy organizations, were involved in the creation of the court climate through their actions at various stages in these disputes.

The judicial system was the institutional arena where broader disputes about the meaning of education were aired and resolved. School discipline cases, therefore, touched upon conceptions of proper school authority and the importance of discipline, but also involved broader matters such as racial tension and inequality, federal and state versus local school control, perceptions of youth culture and counterculture by school personnel and judges, conflicts over what precisely was meant by "free public education," and regional differences in conceptions of acceptable types of student behavior.

Courtrooms were responsible for many changes in American schools: racial desegregation, school financing overhauls, new interpretations of principles of separation of church and state, and the expansion of student rights. Whether by design or by consequence, court expansion of youth rights in general and student rights in particular have contributed to a changing school environment. Prior to the late 1960s, school actors remained relatively unchallenged both in the public discourse and in court testimony. Afterward, the increased threat of court challenges to school discipline made it paramount for school officials to consider the court climate when writing school dress codes or administering a paddling. By definition, the court climate differed by location and time period, and thus has had varying implications for school practices.

Particular internal characteristics of cases contributed to court decisions in unique ways. Discipline disputes between private schools and their students were more likely resolved in favor of the school. If the form of discipline was expulsion, rather than some other action (such as corporal punishment or suspension), the courts were more likely to rule for the student. If the expulsion involved an African-American student, federal courts were overwhelmingly likely to find in favor of the student. Federal courts were also more likely than state courts to find for students when they had been disciplined for involvement in political action. State courts, however, were more pro-student in cases that did not involve political protest. There were also regional differences in the treatment of various types of student infractions. These were among the myriad factors that influenced the court climate that school personnel faced.

Through the efforts of students and their legal advocates, student rights were clearly expanded by the courts. Indeed, many groups, such as OEO Legal Services, the ACLU, and the Children's Defense Fund, actively campaigned for students to gain legal rights and protections tantamount to those enjoyed by adults. But did the expansion of student rights have unintended consequences? How did the court climate relate to broader trends in school discipline as a whole? Was the court climate we have delineated related to student perceptions of school discipline and in turn student achievement and socialization?

4

From the Bench
to the Paddle

With Richard Pitt and Jennifer Thompson

"What I know about court cases," one teacher reported, "I picked up in the teachers' lounge. I guess they affect male teachers more than females, because men are more likely to be physical with students." "I learned about court cases in *Newsweek*," said another. A third teacher suggested, "It all depends on who you grab. Grab the dumb ones—they don't know what the hell to do. Don't grab a lawyer's kid."

—TEACHER OPINIONS REPORTED IN HOLLINGSWORTH,
LUFLER AND CLUNE (1984)

Having uncovered much about the new legal environment schools have faced, we have yet to demonstrate that changes in it have affected how schools actually interact with students. Public schools could conceivably— if they were truly "encapsulated," "insulated," or "loosely coupled" to their external environments, as some social scientists maintain[1]—simply ignore both hostile and sympathetic court decisions.

We believe, however, that students, teachers, and administrators were far from oblivious to court climates. While most of them were not versed in the intricacies of particular case law and were unable to manipulate the contradictory and ambiguous character of decisions—as the opinions of teachers cited in the epigraph suggest—they were quite sensitive to whether courts in general would "back them up" or "take the other side." Hollingsworth, Lufler, and Clune, for example, studied how disciplinary practices were embedded in teacher and student perceptions of legal rights in three Wisconsin high schools in the late 1970s. They found that neither teachers nor students had an accurate understanding of case law, but both groups were well aware of the direction that the judiciary followed and altered their school practices accordingly. In surveys of 207 teachers at the three schools, 45 percent felt that "too much interference from courts" was a very important cause of school discipline problems, and 59 percent agreed with the statement that "teachers and administrators have been hampered by court decisions in their application of discipline." Teachers' actual understanding of case and statutory law was imperfect:

> The feeling that the courts had gone "too far," then, was based on a substantial misunderstanding of specific decisions and statutes. Teachers thought that the courts had entered a variety of areas where no decision at all had been rendered and saw due process as more complete in exclusion cases than the skeletal due process afforded by *Goss*. An unanticipated consequence, then, of increased litigation in the education area has been the feeling on the part of teachers that their behavior has been more substantially circumscribed than is actually the case.[2]

Hollingsworth, Lufler, and Clune's survey suggested that students at these same schools also had little understanding about the specific protections afforded them by statutes and court decisions.[3]

Court climates were communicated to educators in a number of ways. Professional associations, for example, had an interest in inflating the threat of hostile legal actions, because they could then position themselves as a necessary institutional ally, protector, and buffer for their members. Gerald Grant's history of Hamilton High, for example, noted how judicial proceedings in nearby localities were communicated and amplified in union newsletters. Grant, analyzing archives of the *New York Teacher*, found that

> The Median teachers' union published cases of teachers whose jobs had been jeopardized when child-abuse machinery was invoked against them. A teacher in another school district who had restrained a rowdy and abusive student was charged with child abuse. It took months to close the case and expunge it from state records. Another teacher, accused by a student he had physically prevented from disrupting a test in school, said: "Next morning the police came to my home and arrested me. They led me out of my home in handcuffs."[4]

Hollingsworth, Lufler, and Clune described a similar pattern of how court decisions were communicated to teachers in Wisconsin high schools:

Teachers who had never personally been involved in court cases and who had never known a teacher who had been involved felt threatened by lawsuit. The sense that they might be sued was translated into two related teacher behavior changes. Classroom teachers reported that they were far less physical in their dealings with students than they used to be, and they also reported they wanted to have much less to do with school discipline generally. The feeling that they wanted "out of discipline" was enhanced by local teacher union activities. Union leaders had been trying in Middle City, unsuccessfully, to have language placed in the union contract which would relieve teachers of some obligation to spend times in halls and washrooms where many discipline problems occur. Union bargaining language included vague statements about teacher liability and may have increased teacher concern in this area.[5]

Professional associations often also sold the names and addresses of their members to organizational entrepreneurs who trafficked in inflating legal threats and then providing protection against such challenges. For example, an advertisement for a subscription to *School Law Bulletin* promised to help "quickly resolve common, legally-charged situations" and offered a free special bonus report on "Your Right to Discipline: How far can you go and still avoid litigation?"[6] Another recent mass solicitation for legal insurance offered an "Educational Professional Liability Plan" for only $100 per year. The plan boasted covering 150,000 educators nationwide and offered to pay 90 percent of attorney fees (after a $100 deductible) if one was accused of "a broad range of exposures associated with your educational duties," including "criminal charges arising out of corporal punishment."[7]

A study by Henry Lufler argued that "courts have increased the insecurity of teachers as they deal with the average discipline problems that take place within the school."[8] Surveying teachers at the school, he found

a great deal of misunderstanding about what the courts have said, and an overwhelming pattern of overestimating the extent to which courts have told teachers what they can and can't do within the classroom. A few basic decisions in the area of school discipline, like suspension hearings before students are suspended from school, in teachers' minds have been viewed as permitting students to have lawyers when they are about to be suspended from school. So there's this pattern of exaggeration. What that has done is cause a lot of teachers to get out of the business of disciplining students. To a certain extent, courts have become alibis, used by teachers who don't wish to discipline students.[9]

Despite much anecdotal and testimonial evidence of a relationship between court climates and school disciplinary practices, there have been few efforts to identify it systematically and empirically.[10] Attempts to establish such a relationship are plagued by several methodological hurdles. These obstacles include inadequate observation of court climates, limited data on school practices, and problems inherent in attempts to establish causation from identifiable patterns of association among variables in observational data. Before moving ahead with our analysis, it is worth discussing each of these methodological limitations so the reader is alerted to the tentative nature of our analysis. The research in this book is ground-breaking in its use of the techniques of social scientific measurement to establish that such associations exist; we hope that social scientists will take our initial research as an invitation to explore these critical issues further.[11]

Methodological Obstacles

Measuring Court Climates

Our measure of court climate is admittedly rather crude. We have identified court climates around schools simply by considering the direction of all prior court decisions related to student discipline in jurisdictions that have direct authority over a public school in a state. To gauge the relevant court climate for a public school in Des Moines, Iowa, we thus considered all prior judicial decisions that emanated from the Iowa Court of Appeals, the Iowa State Supreme Court, the Northern and Southern Iowa Federal District Courts, the Eighth Federal Appellate Court, and the Federal Supreme Court. Our measure is constructed by considering all of these court decisions as having equal weight; assigning the court decisions the value of $+1, 0,$ or -1 depending on whether the ruling respectively was pro-school, neutral, or pro-student; and then calculating a value for the average of court decisions found in these cases.

There are multiple alternative approaches for moving from court decisions to court climates. Rather than assuming that all cases have equal weight, for example, we could have used information provided in legal data sets to identify the frequency with which particular decisions are subsequently cited in later court opinions—that is, we could have weighted particular court decisions (such as *Goss v. Lopez*) more heavily than other local court decisions that are handed down and then possibly forgotten. We could have also considered cases decided in nearby jurisdictions that were surely reported in local papers and thus could have possibly affected the opinion and practices of school actors. We also could have "controlled" for the particular details of the court cases (information which was identified from our content coding) and created an "instrumental variable" measure of court climates that was relatively unaffected by the particulars of the cases brought before judges.

We chose to rely on the simpler method because it yields a clearer, more straightforward and easily understood measure that approximates the tenor of court climates that would likely affect schools. While one could plausibly argue the merits of an alternative methodological approach, we have embraced the simplest operationalization of court climates for this analysis. In this first attempt to establish empirically a relationship between court climates and school disciplinary practices, we simply want to suggest the general importance and existence of this relationship, rather than definitively identifying its size or magnitude.

Measuring School Disciplinary Practices

The second methodological obstacle we face in establishing the relationship between court climates and school disciplinary practices is inadequate data on school disciplinary practices over time. Unfortunately, individuals in schools have not been repeatedly and systematically asked relevant questions about school disciplinary practices, the perceptions of their legal rights, or their impression of local court climates.[12]

We attempt to overcome this limitation by relying on multiple sources of data on school practices that were collected by researchers and government agencies for other purposes. In particular, we make use of data from the Office of Civil Rights' *Elementary and Secondary School Civil Rights Compliance Report* (1968–1992), the *High School and Beyond Study* (1980–1982) of sophomores and seniors, the *National Educational Longitudinal Study* (1988–1992) of eighth to twelfth graders, and the *School and Staffing Survey* (1990–1994) of teachers, as well as additional information on characteristics of locales identified from several supplementary sources.[13] These diverse sources of educational data provide useful multiple indicators of the relevant phenomenon. In addition, we supplement our original analysis with excerpts from prior ethnographic research on schools as well as journalistic accounts that lend support to our interpretation of results identified in the analysis.

First, we examine in detail the use of corporal punishment in schools over time. The Office of Civil Rights has collected detailed school-level information on the use of this practice over a number of years. Because of the controversial nature of this practice, it serves as an excellent *marker* for the use of *authoritarian* discipline in schools. Second, we examine administrator reports of the use of particular school rules from 1980–1990. Third, we examine teacher reports of the extent to which they believe schools have the authority to enforce and employ school discipline. Lastly, we examine student perceptions of school discipline, with attention focused on the extent to which individuals perceive their schools' discipline as being both strict and fair. While student and teacher reports of school discipline are clearly subjective—that is, a "strict" school can have different meanings for different individuals—we employ extensive controls for social background and individual characteristics to adjust for the subjective character of the reports. Our statistical analysis thus "adjusts" or "controls" for factors such as the extent to which African-Americans are more likely than whites to report that their schools are stricter and the degree to which women are more likely than men to report that their schools are fairer.

Establishing Causation

Social scientists are ideally interested in identifying not simply how two variables are related—for example, that stricter school disciplinary practices occur in settings where pro-school court climates exist—but in establishing that a *causal relationship* between the phenomena is present. The demonstration of such causality is particularly difficult with observational data.

One problem is that of reverse causation—that is, one might argue that it is the variation in school disciplinary practices that produces change in the direction of court decisions, rather than the other way around. Plausibly, stricter schools might be more likely to have their practices opposed as inappropriate by hostile court decisions. Although this argument is clearly reasonable and might explain court interventions in many areas of social life, we do not believe that it fits the case of school discipline. Specifically, the analysis in Chapter 3 has demonstrated that authoritarian disciplinary practices such as corporal punishment are not more likely to receive court sanction than any other disciplinary measures.[14] In addition, our findings will indicate an association between pro-school court decisions and stricter school disciplinary practices. In the area of school disciplinary practices and the law, causality largely runs in the direction of courts influencing schools disciplinary practices, not vice versa.

Another difficulty is that attempts to demonstrate causality are also always open to the critique of omitted variable bias—that is, that the relationship identified is possibly spurious. For example, one could argue that if the practice of corporal punishment persists and flourishes in schools in states with particularly pro-school court climates, it is not because of the effects of courts as such. Rather, court decisions and school practices could *both* be shaped by a larger conservative political culture or other demographic factors, and schools thus might be sensitive to general cultural influences and inattentive to actual court decisions. Much of the previous research in the law and society tradition has embraced models assuming such diffuse sets of pressures, and has thus been content simply to relate general historical changes in law and organizational behavior to larger and more indirect (as well as often vaguely identified) social influences. For example, sociologists such as Frank Dobbin, Lauren Edelman, John Meyer, John Sutton, and their colleagues have discussed how processes associated with legalization (such as expansion of due process rights) have transformed firms through the expansion over time of human resource departments and the formalization of related personnel procedures in these settings. These neo-institutionalists have tended to attribute these changes not to any specific laws or court decisions in particular, but rather to "a wider transformation in the relationships among the state, organizations and individual citizens" that occurred over the past few decades.[15] Their approach is consistent with Gerald Rosenberg's suggestion that courts tend to affect societal outcomes only indirectly. According to Rosenberg, "a court's contribution, then, is akin to officially recognizing the evolving state of affairs, more like the cutting of the ribbon on a new project than its construction."[16]

Social scientists who attempt to identify direct effects of factors such as court climate, instead of patterns of broader historical change, attend to this problem by "controlling" in their statistical modeling for plausible sets of alternative factors that could influence the phenomenon that one is attempting to explain.[17] We adopted such an approach here and incorporated extensive controls for a range of individual and social characteristics that were likely to influence school disciplinary practices independent of court climates. At the state-level these include the strength of Republican Party control of state government; the percentage of a state's population that belongs to Christian denominations associated with the religious right;[18] the educational level of the population; the bureaucratic character of the state's school system; as well as racial demographic factors. When analyzing reports of administrators and teachers, we also included measures of school grade level, urban/suburban/rural differences, gender, race, age, and teaching experience. When student data is used, even further controls can be employed such as family background, academic experience, and state-level "fixed effects" for other unmeasured state factors.[19]

Attempts to establish causation are also particularly difficult when data do not explicitly have a longitudinal character. Ideally, one would want a set of schools measured over time, with subsequent efforts then directed at demonstrating that when court climates change, practices in school change. With the data we have available for the analysis in this chapter, we can only occasionally employ such an ideal design. Our data on corporal punishment is closest to this methodologically desirable character and will be examined fully. In other places, we attempt to approximate a longitudinal design by pooling individual student and administrator data from the early 1980s and early 1990s for analysis in models with state-level "fixed effects" that identify the effects of court climate on school practices over time and across legal jurisdictions. Finally, we will also present additional analysis that is simply cross-sectional in character—that is, analysis that examines the relationship between court climates and school practices at one point in time while controlling for a range of confounding factors.

Given these methodological constraints, we were tempted in this project to be satisfied simply by identifying broad historical changes in the legal environment, in a manner similar to prior empirical work on effects of Equal Employment Opportunity legislation on expanded legalization within business firms. While our findings are not inherently inconsistent with approaches that emphasize the role of broader social forces, we have attempted a more ambitious analysis that identifies effects of variation in court climates. Such a perspective highlights the extent to which judicial actors have "relative autonomy" to decide court cases, and social agency in influencing outcomes in organizations under their jurisdiction. Our approach thus argues against structural determinism; at the same time we appreciate the extent to which American political institutions are structured both to empower the judicial branch with unique powers, and to segment that influence across distinct state and federal levels. Meaningful variation occurs not just over time, but also across state and federal courtrooms—our analysis intends to test the degree to which this variation is associated with the practices of organizations such as schools. While we cannot hope definitively to isolate causal effects related to court decisions, our identification of robust direct associations between court cases and school disciplinary practices and perceptions of those practices suggests that court climates are indeed implicated in variation in these organizational practices over time and across legal jurisdictions.

Corporal Punishment in Public Schools, 1976–1992

Any attempt to examine variation in school disciplinary practices cannot avoid this politically and ideologically charged issue. Corporal punishment is, at its most basic level, "the intentional use of physical force upon a student as punishment for any alleged offense or behavior."[20] In the modern context, corporal punishment has been under attack for a number of reasons that have little to do with either the potential benefits or risks involved in its use. In the modern era, Michel Foucault has reminded us, punishment has moved from disciplining the body physically to surveillance, isolation, and other techniques of social control.[21] Relatedly, sociologist Pierre Bourdieu has described the emergence of a set of professional practices and beliefs that have sought to displace the expertise of "unknowledgeable" parents with the "rigorous" and "scientific" knowledge of university-trained experts.[22] While judgments about the benefits or harms of corporal punishment are largely beyond the scope of this project,[23] we are quite interested in tracing the changes in the use of this practice for what it tells us about the potential role of how court climates affected school disciplinary practices generally.

Corporal punishment serves as an excellent marker for how school disciplinary practices have changed over time. The Office of Civil Rights has collected detailed records of the use of corporal punishment in public schools since the mid-1970s. The effects of court climate on the use of this practice will be particularly interesting, since there is little evidence from case law that courts have sought to constrain the use of this practice. In the previous chapter, our analysis of the direction of court decisions suggests that courts were not particularly inclined to rule in favor of students when cases involved corporal punishment. For example, in 1977, when the Supreme Court had a chance to rule on the use of the practice, the Court held that the Eighth Amendment ban on cruel and unusual punishments did not apply to corporal punishment inflicted by teachers or principals in public schools.[24] While courts have been reluctant to strike down corporal punishment through case law, it is worth emphasizing that the general direction of court decisions has influenced public school use of this and other disciplinary practices. In jurisdictions that have been particularly pro-school, were school authorities more likely to either continue or increase the use of corporal punishment?

States and school districts have differed on what disciplinary infractions resulted in corporal punishment, who administered it, and how it was administered. In some school districts corporal punishment has been treated as a low-level penalty and used before others, such as suspension or even detention. In other districts it has been used only as a last resort or "after all other methods of discipline have proven ineffective."[25]

In twenty-six states and most American urban school districts, corporal punishment is currently proscribed altogether.[26] States that have banned the practice include Alaska, California, Connecticut, Hawaii, Illinois, Iowa, Maine, Massachusetts, Michigan, Minnesota, Montana, Nebraska, Nevada, New Hampshire, New Jersey, New York, North Dakota, Oregon, Rhode Island, South Dakota, Utah, Vermont, Virginia, Washington, West Virginia, and Wisconsin. Some states have embraced contradictory laws: for example, Ohio has a 1993 law that "bans" corporal punishment, but it allows school districts to enact policies permitting it.[27] Other states, at the district level, have reduced the number of corporal punishment incidents to such a low level that they have practically ended the practice entirely. Those states are Arizona, Colorado, Delaware, Idaho, Indiana, Kansas, Kentucky, Maryland, Ohio, and Pennsylvania.[28] In addition to these eleven states that still allow it as a penalty for misbehavior, thirteen others let their school districts decide whether or not corporal punishment will be used and how it will be administered. In several Southern states, corporal punishment in schools actually increased in the 1980s and early 1990s. Figure 4.1 uses data from the Office of Civil Rights to produce maps of the rate of corporal punishment within states from 1976 to 1992. In these maps the reader should focus on broad patterns of variation across regions, since measure-

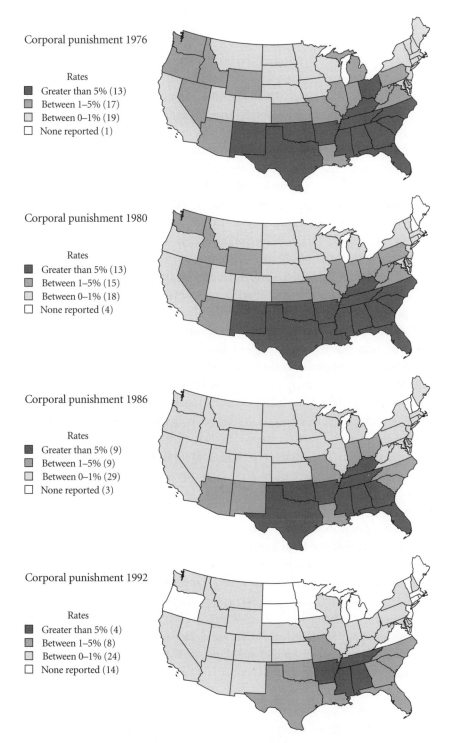

Corporal punishment 1976

Rates
- ■ Greater than 5% (13)
- ▨ Between 1–5% (17)
- ▢ Between 0–1% (19)
- ☐ None reported (1)

Corporal punishment 1980

Rates
- ■ Greater than 5% (13)
- ▨ Between 1–5% (15)
- ▢ Between 0–1% (18)
- ☐ None reported (4)

Corporal punishment 1986

Rates
- ■ Greater than 5% (9)
- ▨ Between 1–5% (9)
- ▢ Between 0–1% (29)
- ☐ None reported (3)

Corporal punishment 1992

Rates
- ■ Greater than 5% (4)
- ▨ Between 1–5% (8)
- ▢ Between 0–1% (24)
- ☐ None reported (14)

Figure 4.1 Changes in state rate of corporal punishment: 1976–1992

ment of specific state-level variation is often based on inadequate numbers of observations within states and thus fails to represent state-level averages accurately. Over the sixteen-year period examined, however, a pattern of corporal punishment increasingly concentrated in the Deep South is clearly manifested.

Depending on the locale, the inappropriate behavior that led to corporal punishment may have been either a major or minor infraction. This determination was rarely made and codified at the state level. School districts themselves usually created a hierarchy of consequences used to determine at which level of behavior a student would incur this particular penalty. Sometimes called a "discipline ladder," this hierarchy was usually organized at the level of offense. Therefore, as in the case of the Arkansas Cave City School District, a student who misbehaved could be spanked as a first-offense penalty, given in-school suspension for a second offense, and given an out-of-school suspension for the third offense.[29] In this hierarchy, spanking was perceived as a less serious disciplinary approach. If a student's behavior was especially egregious, he or she may bypass the corporal punishment phase entirely and be suspended. In some Mississippi school districts, the discipline ladder has six steps. If the students were not referred to the office during a probationary period (usually 10 to 20 days), they were removed from the ladder entirely.[30] Otherwise they proceeded through the various steps. The first three of the six steps include corporal punishment. Therefore, if a student was disciplined three times in a month, it was likely that at each occasion the student would be spanked. This may explain why Mississippi had the highest rate of corporal punishment in the nation in the early 1990s.

How corporal punishment was administered also differed by state, by district, by school, and even by the age of the student receiving the punishment. The usual method of administration was paddling, usually with an open hand, a paddle, or a ruler. Open-hand spankings were usually reserved for small children and were seen as useful for the "immediate correction of misbehavior."[31] They were used less as punishment than as a way to get a wayward child's attention. In fact, some states make it quite clear that this particular kind of spanking should only be used for younger children:

> In addition to paddling, the Board recognizes that there are instances where the open palm of the hand on the buttocks, in the case of K-6 students, is an appropriate method for the immediate correction of misbe-

havior. However, the use of the open palm of the hand on the buttocks may not be substituted for paddling in private if the intensity and duration of the punishment is intended to be more than a means of getting the student's attention. The Board considers the use of the open palm of the hand on the buttocks inappropriate under any circumstances with regard to middle and senior high school students (6–12) where higher maturity levels require the use of a different approach to correct misbehavior.[32]

For a corrective measure, most schools turned to some kind of paddle, usually wooden, as the method of delivery for corporal punishment penalties. Descriptions of these paddles ranged from the simple to the explicit. In Mobile, Alabama, for example, the rules simply stated that "a paddle or a facsimile" may be used, but a strap was specifically forbidden.[33] Most states and school districts have left sizes and shapes of the paddle or ruler to the discretion of teachers and principals. Other districts, like New Mexico's Aztec School District, were more explicit:

Corporal punishment shall be administered with the use of a wooden paddle which is smoothly sanded and has no cracks or holes and which is in compliance with the dimensions described below: a) Round paddle—22″ long, 8″ diameter and ?″ [sic] thick or b) Straight paddle—30″ long × 4″ wide × ?″ [sic] thick. Acts such as slapping with a ruler, cuffing with the hand, or requiring a student to stand in a corner with his/her hands raised above their head constitute prohibited corporal punishment.[34]

Regardless of the description, these paddles were usually quite capable of causing serious injury if used carelessly. Hence most states and school districts also included restrictions on the manner of the administration, where it could take place, how many witnesses should be present, who could administer this punishment, and even suggestions about the emotional state of the person administering the punishment.

Because corporal punishment was often criticized as "cruel and unusual punishment," and schools were apprehensive of legal challenges, some districts explicitly warned administrators to consider carefully how harshly the practice was employed. For example, a school district in Alabama required:

The punishment must not be unusually cruel or excessive to the extent that it would break the skin, cause severe contusions to form on the body, or cause any lasting physical harm to the student. Corporal punishment

that causes pain is not necessarily unusual, cruel, or excessive. The causing of temporary pain is one of the results of corporal punishment. The
intent of corporal punishment, however, must not be to inflict lasting
physical harm on the student.[35]

In most cases, the number of swats delivered was not allowed to exceed
three. When the number was explicitly mentioned, we found no disciplinary protocols that allowed the student to be hit more times than this.
Usually, regulations stated that the paddle should be kept out of sight until
that time when it would be used to punish students. Often, specific regulations against having a child remove or drop his or her trousers, skirt, or
dress were included.[36] The student was usually hit upon the buttocks. If
students moved while being spanked and were hit in some place other than
the buttocks, school administrators were often required to report these incidents; this precaution was aimed at protecting the school and the administrator in the event that the child suggested that the school's protocol was
not followed. In most cases, parents had to be notified that children were
to be spanked, and if they objected, the child was often suspended as an alternative punishment.

Corporal punishment, in most cases, was not to take place in front of
other students. While some schools maintained separate rooms reserved
for such disciplinary actions, similar to those used for in-house suspensions, many simply allowed the punishment to take place in a school administrator's office or even the cloakroom used to store children's clothing
if the penalty was delivered by the child's teacher.

Rarely was the administration of corporal punishment allowed without
a witness. This was done as much for the protection of the administrator as
it was for the child. Usually, one witness sufficed and that person was often
a teacher or other professional staff member. The person authorized to administer the punishment differed from state to state and from district to
district. In Arkansas, only a school administrator could spank children.[37]
This regulation explicitly excluded teachers, bus drivers, and other school
personnel. In New Mexico, "corporal punishment shall be administered by
the principal, assistant principal, teacher in charge of the building in the
principal's absence or a professional staff member to whom authority has
been delegated, in writing or orally, for a specific instance of corporal punishment."[38] The last piece of this regulation precluded teacher-adminis-
tered spanking except in those particular cases when the teacher was au-

thorized to do so. Until corporal punishment was ended in Connecticut in 1990, the regulations on who could administer the punishment were fairly broad: "A parent, guardian, teacher or other person entrusted with the care and supervision of a minor may use reasonable force on the minor to maintain discipline."[39] Because of the fairly universal requirement for a professional staff person to witness the spanking, rarely were bus drivers or other supplemental school employees authorized to administer corporal punishment. In higher grades (7–12), regulations were almost unanimous in advocating that the person administering the punishment (or at least the witness) be of the same sex as the student being spanked.

Many handbooks regulating the use of corporal punishment discouraged its use and encouraged those who administered the punishment to be in control of their emotions before they administered it. Regulations were often careful to caution administrators not to spank children in a malicious or vengeful manner. Pennsylvania advised that "corporal punishment shall never be administered in the heat of anger."[40] Arkansas' Cave City School Board warned that "a teacher who continually resorts to corporal punishment endangers his/her professional status."[41] Ohio protocols stated that the penalty should "be resorted to only after serious consideration and never in anger or frustration."[42]

The relationship between corporal punishment and pro-school court climates was clear in the statistical analyses we conducted. First, we examined associations between prior court climate and the state-level average rate of corporal punishment in 1976, after accounting for a range of other state-level factors. Specifically, the effects of court climate were estimated net of state-level Republican Party influence, religious right presence, district-level bureaucratization, and the percentage of state residents who were college educated and African-American.[43] Pro-school court climates were associated with increased rates of corporal punishment for students in general and for both white and African-American students when considered separately. In states that had court climates characterized by only 47 percent of cases being decided in favor of schools—that is, significantly more pro-student than typical—corporal punishment of white students dropped to 1.6 percent and corporal punishment of African-American students was predicted at 2.5 percent. When a state's court climate was characterized by 79 percent of cases being decided in favor of schools, corporal punishment occurred at a rate of 4.0 percent for white students and 7.4 percent for African-American students.[44] It is important to remind readers that the effects of court climate identified both here and through-out the remainder of the chapter were conservatively estimated "direct effects" that have been calculated net of a wide range of other factors incorporated into our statistical modeling. The magnitude of the effects of court climate was significantly reduced by including other factors, such as a state's political culture, into our analysis, since many of these variables are associated both with court climate and school disciplinary practices. In particular, we found that the higher the percentage of a state's population that held membership in a denomination associated with the religious right, the higher the rate of corporal punishment used in a state's public schools—a 10 percent increase in membership in these religious denominations was associated with corporal punishment of white students increasing by 1.9 percent and a 3.4 percent increase amongst African-American students. In terms of standard deviations, the degree of religious right presence in a state was associated with about three times greater influence on the rates of corporal punishment than were the effects of variation in court climates.[45] Court climates, however, continue to matter *over and above* the effects of political culture and other influences that were controlled for in our modeling.

Alternative modeling strategies for examining the effects of court climates on the practice of corporal punishment in public schools yielded largely similar results. For example, we examined the association between *changes* in pro-school court climates and *changes* in the rate of corporal punishment from 1976–1992.[46] By 1992, public schools on average had reduced their rate of corporal punishment by about 60 percent. In states where courts became increasingly pro-school during this period, however, declines were significantly less pronounced—or actually completely absent in several Southern states that registered slightly increased rates of corporal punishment (Alabama, Arkansas, Louisiana, Mississippi). Again religious right presence in a state, here measured in terms of change over time, was associated with variation in the use of corporal punishment from 1976–1992. It is also worth commenting, given the Civil Rights context for changes in court climates and school discipline, that we could find little evidence suggesting court climates affected African-Americans differently than whites—effects of court climate were similar in magnitude regardless of whose rates of corporal punishment were examined.[47]

Figure 4.2 identifies the predicted likelihood that a state would end the use of corporal punishment in public schools from 1976 to 1992. We

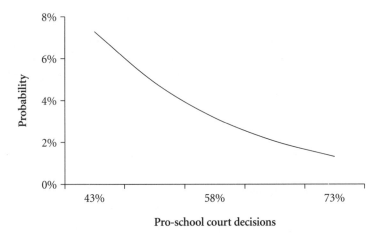

Figure 4.2 Effects of court climate on annual likelihood of state abandoning corporal punishment: 1976–1992 (based on Table 4.F, Model 2)

found in modeling state exits from corporal punishment that not only were court climates and state political culture implicated in these changes, but significant time period effects remained in our results even after considering these factors. That is, over time states were increasingly likely to have discontinued use of this practice in their public schools regardless of the countervailing influence of state-level court climates and political cultures that might have supported and upheld these traditional methods of school discipline.[48] We interpret these results to suggest that in the late 1980s and early 1990s, all states that were still continuing to use corporal punishment were under significant and increasing *institutional pressures* to curtail such practices. This pressure to abandon corporal punishment likely emerged from generalized normative pressures to conform with widely shared and diffuse notions of how school discipline *should* be structured. These "isomorphic pressures" would come from national associations of teachers and administrators, pedagogical approaches dominant in schools of education, and broadly based cultural commitments condemning physical punishment as "old-fashioned" and developmentally inappropriate.[49]

In addition to these broad time period effects, court climates also continued to matter. When court decisions were 73 percent pro-school, a state had less than a two percent annual likelihood of ending the practice; in a state with only 43 percent pro-school decisions, the state had a seven percent annual likelihood of ending the practice.[50] Even though courts in general have not been directly hostile to the practice of corporal punishment in schools, it was not surprising that educators still remained sensitive to their more general leanings. As the *St. Louis Post-Dispatch* commented on state legislative efforts to ban corporal punishment:

> something more practical may be driving the current trend: In states where paddling is still legal, teachers and administrators who use it are facing an increasing number of civil lawsuits and criminal cases charging physical abuse, and those have caused policy makers and educators alike to reassess their positions. Last year the Texas Elementary Principals and Supervisors Associations, which opposes a ban on spanking, nevertheless warned its members to discontinue the use of corporal punishment for their own protection.[51]

The court cases we examined in prior chapters only included cases that made it to the appellate level. Cases where teachers, administrators or schools faced judicial sanction or made legal settlements that were not contested in higher courts have not been thoroughly examined. Anecdotal evidence of the existence of these cases in newspaper accounts was fairly widespread. For example, there was a case in Aurora, Colorado, where a special education teacher actually served jail time for her administration of corporal punishment on elementary school students:

> Aurora special education teacher Sandra Asael served a short jail term for slapping, kicking and shoving several 5- to 7-year-olds in her class. In both of the local cases, teachers violated their district's rules and protocols. Aurora Public School's protocol allowed "application of a small paddle to a student's buttock in a controlled manner" and that was to be administered by a principal or other designated certified school employee. According to an Aurora Public Schools spokeswoman, a survey conducted last year found no one had used the protocol for three years.[52]

In this case and others like it, students were often injured in ways which drew angry attention and unwanted lawsuits upon not only the teacher, but the principal, the school, the school district, and in some cases even the state. In Washington, D.C. a teacher hit a second-grade student in the mouth for blowing bubbles; the force of the swat knocked a tooth through the child's lip. The case was settled out of court.[53] In California, a school district was sued because a 13-year-old child was required to stand in a masking-tape square in a classroom set aside for discipline for nearly two hours. The school was ordered to remove the squares and the practice ended.[54] In Ohio, a social studies teacher was charged with abuse for paddling a 10-year-old until the boy was black and blue. The teacher was acquitted.[55] In Arizona, a principal was charged with kidnapping and child abuse for allegedly forcing a female student to disrobe and then paddling her.[56] Cases like these, and the arguments that came out of them, likely fostered legislative or school district action against corporal punishment.

The effects of court climate on the likelihood that states would abandon the use of corporal punishment in public schools was particularly important given the way that institutional practices become firmly set once altered. Though courts in general have become more conservative, once corporal punishment and other disciplinary techniques were eliminated from public schools, they did not easily return—expanding legalization and extension of rights to youth was a process that once begun had a dynamic of its own. Sociologists studying organizations have found that organizational practices become institutionalized not just in laws, regulations, and guidelines, but as importantly in organizational cultures—in "taken for granted assumptions" about how things simply *must be.*[57] Once corporal punishment or other disciplinary practices were eliminated, any "reasonable" educator would be horrified by proposals to reintroduce the practice.

The closest any state has come to reversing its ban on corporal punishment was California in 1996. In January of that year, the state's Assembly Education Committee split along party lines in its vote to restore the practice.[58] The subcommittee, which had a Republican majority, passed the bill with a one-point margin on to the state's full Assembly, which also had a Republican majority. The bill, pushed by Orange County Republican Assemblyman Mickey Conroy, would have given school districts the right to define corporal punishment themselves rather than having the state Assembly do so. The bill to reintroduce the practice in schools was accompanied by a similar bill, also led by Conroy, to allow youth convicted of graffiti vandalism to be flogged, in open court, with a half-inch paddle (the latter bill apparently directly inspired by the controversy over the 1994 case of Michael Fay and his caning in Singapore). People weighed in on both sides of the corporal punishment argument. Conroy stated that "On almost every campus in the state, corporal punishment has been replaced with armed security and police [because teachers are not allowed to impose discipline]. By bringing back corporal punishment, we are telling California's youth that they will be held accountable for their actions."[59] Republican Assemblywoman Paula Boland, another supporter of returning corporal punishment to California public schools, questioned the logic of banning the practice. She challenged her audience: "Is there anyone here who thinks kids are better today because we outlawed spanking?"[60]

Opponents of the bill argued, however, not only that it was mean-spirited and counterproductive, but also that reintroducing corporal punishment was pedagogically *inconceivable.* The *San Francisco Chronicle,* for example, editorialized: "It seems incredible in this day and age that anyone should have to argue the case, yet again, against forms of physical punishment that most of the civilized world has abandoned on the self-evident grounds that violence begets violence."[61] The legislation was also challenged by State Superintendent of Public Schools Delaine Eastin, who explicitly referred to educators' vulnerability to adversarial legal challenges. Eastin's spokeswoman reported that she was "concerned about other people having the right to physically punish someone else's children . . . She's especially concerned about teachers having that sort of responsibility, let alone the liability. And she believes there are more constructive ways to discipline kids."[62] Democrats in the Assembly reported being "aghast at the testimony" and were unanimous in their opposition to the bill.[63] Republicans, who controlled the legislature, were split on the measure. Comments by the legislation's 68-year-old sponsor, Mickey Conroy, suggested the degree to which opposition to the bill from his colleagues was rooted in the "taken for granted assumptions" that had developed once public schools in the state had eliminated corporal punishment. Conroy noted that there was a generational split among Republicans "having white hair and not having white hair." According to Conroy, "Some young Republicans have never lived under anything but the psychobabble of touchy-feely, feel good . . . and all that. . . . They totally misunderstood what I was trying to say."[64] These moderate Republicans broke ranks from their more conservative—and perhaps older—colleagues and as a result, the bill was defeated. A similar 1997 bill in Montana died in committee.[65]

Challenges of state regulations banning corporal punishment were not always waged with the goal to overturn the ban statewide. Sometimes, as in the case of waiver challenges in Illinois in the mid 1990s, individual school districts requested the right to spank children without asking that this same authority be extended across the state to other districts.[66] Often these challenges came within a couple of years of the state's ban of the practice. In no case were the state legislatures convinced by their arguments.

The Southern region was a different story entirely: from Texas to Florida and from Louisiana north to Tennessee, most of the South has remained free to spank students. While large Southern cities like Atlanta and New Orleans have banned the practice, it is widely used across the South elsewhere without serious opposition. Rarely was corporal punishment's use challenged in Southern states. Even in the South, however, once the practice was eliminated in a local school district, it was difficult to restore. Efforts to bring spanking back in Florida's Manatee County public schools, for example, faced opposition similar to sentiments expressed in the California legislative debate. In support of the practice, a Manatee County parent argued that children weren't being beaten, as some suggested, but merely disciplined using a technique found in homes all across Florida; she complained that "what is being done now and for the past 10 years isn't working." Effective opposition to the reintroduction, however, came from both educators and other parents. The local paper reported, for example, that "Sandra Jordan, mother of two young girls, almost began crying as she repeated several times that 'spanking a child is wrong. *I'm shocked that it's even being discussed,*' she said. 'I'll pull my children out of public schools in a heartbeat' if it goes into effect."[67]

Even though a 1977 Supreme Court decision stated that the Eighth Amendment ban on cruel and unusual punishments did not apply to corporal punishment inflicted by school personnel on children, and that courts in general were relatively indifferent to the practice as compared to other forms of school punishment, over time the practice has been disappearing. The practice was most likely to be reduced and eliminated in states with court climates that were less pro-school, and once eliminated was unlikely to return, regardless of subsequent changes in the direction of court leanings.

Rules in Public Schools, 1980–1992

School rules are a way for school administrators to constrain student behavior and create order in schools. Rules can be thought of as a measure of school authority to regulate student behavior.

We modeled the effects of pro-school court climate on the number of rules that schools had in 1980 or 1990. The data sources we utilized surveyed school administrators about the rules in their schools. The surveys asked whether: 1) school grounds were closed at lunch; 2) hall passes were required; 3) smoking was prohibited; and 4) rules about student dress existed. Schools could also have no rules about any of these items, or a maximum of four rules. Clear patterns of *regional* variation emerge. In general, schools in Southern states reported having more rules: 53.6 percent of public schools in the South had adopted all four rules compared to only 31.4 percent in the West or 42.4 percent elsewhere.[68] If one examines state changes from 1980 to 1992, in almost all states the number of rules increased.[69]

Our statistical analysis suggests that schools tended to adopt more rules in states where pro-school court climates existed, even after controlling for a range of state, school, and individual factors. Figure 4.3 identifies the effect of court climates on the probability that an administrator reported a school's adoption of all four of the rules identified above. In a state with a 45 percent rate of pro-school court decisions—that is, significantly more pro-student than typical—a school had only a two percent likelihood of adopting all four rules. In a state with a 75 percent rate of pro-school decisions, 92 percent of schools were likely to adopt all four rules.

Educators tended to eliminate school rules when there was a perception that courts were hostile to the disciplining of students. In recounting the

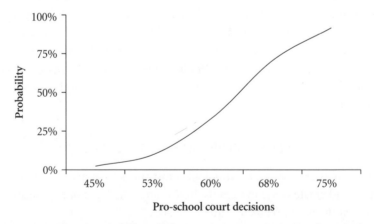

Figure 4.3 Predicted probability of administrator reports on adoption of school rules: 1980–1992 (based on Table 4.L)

history of a New York state high school, Gerald Grant described how during the height of pro-student court decisions, which were particularly pronounced in the Northeast, school rules were dramatically affected. Grant noted,

> Teachers joked that corporal punishment was a relic of the past—except for students who beat up on them. Not so much of a joke, however, was the school board's new regulation that stripped teachers of the power to keep students after school unless the pupil was allowed to call his parents: "If parents object to detaining their child after school hours, the pupil may not be kept after school." The school board lawyers cited the case of Pierce vs. The Society of Sisters, a 1925 Supreme Court Case which struck down the power of the state to prohibit private schooling, saying the state must not maintain a monopoly in education. It essentially gave parents the right to choose the form of schooling they wished for their child. But it had nothing to do with the age-old teacher's punishment of keeping children after school.[70]

We speculate that a public school operating during the early 1990s in a pro-school court climate would not have worried that school rules of this character were liable to legal challenge or would have had legal counsel remotely interested in this 1925 Supreme Court ruling.

Teacher Perceptions of Rule Enforcement

We have established the relationships between court climate and both administrator reports of the number of school rules and incidence of the use of corporal punishment in schools. School administrators and teachers would be the key players in the connection between the larger court climate and the disciplinary practices of the schools themselves. They were also the key agents in establishing moral authority in schools. We examined pooled data from the *School and Staffing Survey* (SASS) from 1990 and 1993 when teachers were asked about their perception of both the enforcement of school rules by fellow teachers and the level of support received from school principals in regards to disciplining students. On average, teachers reported higher levels of support and rule enforcement from principals than rule enforcement from their fellow teachers. Administrator support for discipline was critical to maintaining order, for without that support individual teachers typically feel severely constrained in dealing with student misbehavior. The Hollingsworth, Lufler, and Clune study of Wisconsin schools described how

> teachers pictured themselves as besieged, without allies, unsupported by administrators and parents, and facing an unruly crowd of students whom they characterized using unflattering terms . . . The teachers were also feuding with their principal. The principal had placed letters of reprimand in the files of several teachers for using too much physical force in handling altercations with students . . . Teachers also said they were not "supported" when they sent students to the office. One teacher's comments represented both points of view. "We send kids down. Nothing happens. The kids get a free day or two off, or maybe get a lecture, and they come back and start up right where they leave off. The Office could do a lot more to back up teachers. The principal should pressure downtown (the central system administration) to get more effective rules and disciplinary procedures. I think the administration is going down the wrong track on a number of things."[71]

Was there evidence that the court climate influenced rule enforcement and the support teachers felt they had from school administrators?

In 1990 and 1993, SASS specifically asked teachers to agree or disagree (on a scale of 1–4) with the following statement: "rules for student behavior are enforced by teachers." SASS also asked teachers to agree or disagree with the statement that the "principal enforces student conduct rules and supports me."[72] At a regional level, teachers in Southern states were particularly likely to report that fellow teachers enforced rules and that principals enforced rules and backed them up on matters of school discipline; teachers in the Northeast were likely to report less support and involvement in discipline.[73] Statistical analysis convinces us that court climates were partially responsible for these patterns. In states with more proschool court climates, principals in particular were more likely perceived as active in enforcing rules and willing to support teachers who disciplined students. These effects remained even after extensive controls at the individual level, school level, and for other state influences such as political culture (Republican Party and religious right influence), average education in the state, and size of educational bureaucracies. Again, this is not to suggest that these other factors did not also matter; rather, we were able to identify direct influence of court decisions in addition to other factors, such as the extent to which large schools had enforcement problems.[74]

Prior qualitative research on schools highlights the importance of such support for teachers, and shows what happens when this support is lack-ing. In Gerald Grant's history of a New York high school, he illustrates teacher frustration with the lack of administrative support with this anecdote:

> One of the most admired teachers in the English department, who came to the school in the mid-1970's, is quite liberal in her views. She told of the shock when she first pressed a case of cheating by a neurosurgeon's son: "The truth is I saw the kid cheating. I saw him with his open book on his lap during a test and the time I got back to him to get his paper the book was back on the floor. They wanted documentation. 'How can you prove it? How did he cheat?' I said I am telling you that he was cheating. But the question now is, 'We've heard John's side of the story, what's yours?' As much as I believe in giving due process to kids something grates when I hear, 'What's your side of the story?' Somehow it felt like I'm part of the crime . . . The issue is the boy's cheating and now two hours later I'm in the principal's office discussing due process. And that's not the only incident I've had."[75]

Sara Lawrence Lightfoot, in her portraiture of "good" high schools, ar-gued that principals' support for teachers' discipline was a critical factor in creating positive learning environments. Lightfoot noted,

> Teacher fearlessness not only comes from deep understandings of stu-dents, it also derives from an institutional authority that supports their individual encounters with students. The most explicit and visible signs of strong institutional authority are seen in the schools' responses to vio-lence and other disciplinary matters. In all the (good) schools I visited, there were clear codes of behavior and great attention paid to law and or-der. Acts of violence were quickly diluted and swiftly punished.[76]

The enforcement of rules by teachers and principals alike operates together in schools. When teachers feel supported from administrators, they in turn are more likely to enforce rules themselves. This suggests how school actors create different types of learning environments in response to variation in court climates around schools.

Student Perceptions of Strictness and Fairness

School disciplinary practices changed in response to court climates, but we have yet to demonstrate that these differences actually affected student per-

ceptions of school discipline. Student perceptions are critical, because ultimately it is their perception of school discipline that affects their behavior.
Large numbers of public high school sophomores were surveyed in 1980
and 1990 and asked whether discipline in their schools was strict and
whether it was fair.

The level of strictness that students viewed in their schools is an indicator of the degree to which schools were actively engaged in attempts to
control unwanted student behavior. The following excerpt from fieldwork
by Peter Clark in the 1970s shows student awareness of strictness, or the
lack of such strictness, in their schools: "Even though the students liked
their freedom, a poll showed widespread concern about the lack of safety
in the school. Students cited better discipline as one of the most-needed
improvements in the school. One of them told Clark: 'A few years ago, you
knew if you did something wrong, you'd get your ass busted; but now it
takes three, four, five times and they still don't throw anybody out.'"[77]

We would expect students in different schools, in different states or even
within the same school to vary in their perceptions of the strictness of
their schools. Was this variation in any way associated with court climates?

Student perceptions of strictness were taken from survey questions in
High School and Beyond (HSB) and the National Educational Longitudi-

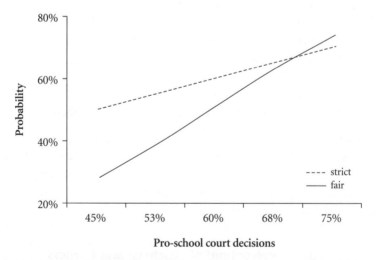

Figure 4.4 Predicted probability of student positive reports of strict and fair
school discipline (based on Table 4.L)

nal Study (NELS). In 1980 HSB asked students to rate their schools on the strictness of discipline, and in 1990 NELS asked students whether they agreed with the statement that "rules are strict."[78] In both cases, respondents had a choice of a four-point scale, with a higher number coded by us to indicate stricter. In terms of regional variation, we found that the South had the highest level of perceived strict discipline.[79] Our statistical analysis again found compelling evidence that students were more likely to report being in strict schools when their schools were located in states with more pro-school court climates. In states where courts have ruled more favorably for schools, students report that their schools were stricter than elsewhere (controlling for other factors including state-level "fixed-effects"). The probability of a student reporting his or her school as strict increased from 50 to 70 percent as one moved from court climates with 45 to those with 75 percent pro-school court decisions.[80] School personnel in these court climates probably felt at greater liberty to act vigilantly when confronting student misbehavior.

We were also interested in the level of fairness that students perceived in their schools. Fairness is an important indicator of the legitimacy of school authority. If school discipline was perceived as unfair, it lacked the moral authority to curtail disruptive behavior effectively. The importance of fairness in school discipline has been identified repeatedly in past research on schools. Within the same school, between schools, and across states, students may vary in their perceptions of how fair their schools were. The following excerpt notes some consensus on perceptions of fairness, but also that many disagreed:

> One high school junior said he felt students could expect teachers and guidance counselors to deal fairly with them and that rules (aside from the prohibition against card playing in lounge areas) were fair. Another, a student council leader, commented that, overall, teachers were open-minded and tried to communicate with students, treating them fairly: "I think most teachers try to understand us, and to be fair. You can talk to most of them pretty freely." Other students indicated that locker searches for drugs, detentions for throwing food, and other specific penalties were fair—if not always useful as deterrents. There is a substantial dissent from this majority position, however.[81]

Some questions we investigate are: How can we explain these differences in perceptions? Was the variation in perceptions of fairness related to court climate? And to what extent were student reports of strictness and fairness related?

High School and Beyond and the National Educational Longitudinal Survey asked students about how fair they felt their school's discipline was. HSB asked students to rate their school on the fairness of discipline (1–4); NELS asked students whether they agreed with the statement "discipline is fair at school."[82] In both cases, respondents had a choice of a four-point scale, with a higher number coded by us to indicate reports of fairer discipline. The extent to which fairness was a critical ingredient of successful school discipline has been suggested in past ethnographic research on schools. Mary Metz, for example, described the following student's conceptualization of the role of fairness in school discipline:

> He (the student) was very angry at his French teacher who treated different people committing the same offense in different ways. Asked what the relationship between strictness and fairness is, he explained it this way: "Like my French teacher . . . she gives me a bad time *and* she's unfair, you know. But other teachers they give everybody a bad time, you know, then that's fair. Like they give white, colored, Chinese, everybody gets a bad time, just mean teachers."[83]

One can contrast this situation with the way a fourth-grade student in Atlanta described her strict teacher's discipline as appropriate: "(Miss Clifton) disciplines us but that means that she loves us and it's the right thing for us to be."[84]

In our statistical analysis court climates significantly related to students' perceptions of fairness. After controlling for a wide range of individual, school, and state-level differences, we found that students in states with pro-school court climates were much more likely to find that their schools were fair. The likelihood that a student would report school discipline as fair increased from 28 to 74 percent as court climates moved from 45 to 75 percent pro-school in their decisions (see Figure 4.4). While pro-school court climates were associated with student perceptions of both more fairness and strictness, court decisions were particularly related to student perceptions of fairness. This is an important finding that is quite suggestive of the extent to which court challenges to school authority eroded not only school discipline, but more importantly also the legitimacy—that is, the perception of fairness—of school discipline. When courts were more pro-school, the legitimacy of school discipline was more "taken for granted" by students, and discipline was considered appropriate and fair. Gerald Grant commented on this phenomenon in describing the erosion of school discipline and its legitimacy:

> the effect of the increased legalization of the schools, at least in the short run, was neither to improve discipline nor to create a sense of greater justice . . . [Its] effect on students may have been to increase cynicism about the likelihood of justice being done and to encourage them to use the new rules to beat the system. After a decade of new due-process rules in public schools, a national survey asked students in both public and Catholic high schools about discipline . . . [When] asked whether discipline was fairly administered, students who supposedly had the benefit of new rules and procedures in the public schools were less likely than their Catholic counterparts (by a margin of 39 percent to 52 percent) to think it fair.[85]

Again, this is not to say that court climate was the only factor significantly affecting these attitudes. Rather, court decisions have direct effects on schools *over and above* the extent to which other social factors were associated with both court climate and school disciplinary practices.[86]

In terms of regional variation, it is important to identify differences in student perceptions of fairness in 1982 and 1992, because—unlike in the case of student perceptions of strictness and school rules—significant changes took place in the pattern of regional variation over the ten year period. Specifically, students in the South in 1982 were more likely to consider their schools as fair than did their peers in many other parts of the country. By 1992, however, students in the South were likely to report their schools as less fair than in many other states. Simultaneously, schools in the Northeast region changed from being some of the least fair to some of the fairest schools in the country on this measure.[87] To understand these anomalous changes requires considering not only the relationship between court climates and student perceptions of school discipline, but also the relationship between student reports of strictness and fairness in school discipline.

Figure 4.5 graphs the association between strictness and fairness in student responses. The graph displays the percentage of students who reported different levels of fairness as student reports moved from being least strict to most strict. The results identify what social scientists term curvilinear effects. Student perceptions of higher levels of strictness were

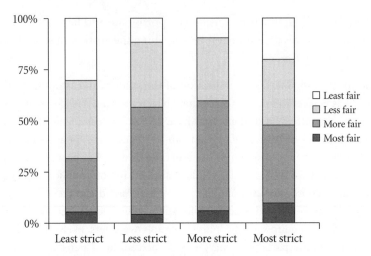

Figure 4.5 Relationship between perceptions of strictness and fairness

associated with higher levels of fairness only until a certain point, after which strictness was perceived as unfair. Too much school strictness could be viewed as authoritarian, arbitrary, and unfair. This is an important finding in identifying challenges to the moral authority of school discipline.

We believe that the regional historical pattern discussed above was likely related to the extent to which strictness and fairness were associated in a curvilinear fashion. Although all parts of the country showed increases in perceptions of fairness in the 1990s, the South made few improvements in this area relative to elsewhere.[88] The findings suggest what possibly happens when strictness has gone too far and becomes authoritarian, thus eroding the sense of fairness. In a sense, the South might have moved from an "optimal" level of strictness in the 1980s to at times an excessive and counterproductive level in the 1990s. Recall that earlier in this chapter we noted that schools in the Deep South not only maintained corporal punishment, but often increased its use during this period. In addition, students in the South during this decade may have received broader liberal cultural messages from media that were undergoing technological and organizational changes improving their capacity to target national youth audiences; exposure to these cultural influences probably further contributed to changing local adolescent judgments about the appropriateness and acceptability of traditional school disciplinary practices.

New England schools during this period adopted stricter school disciplinary practices than ones applied in 1980, which were probably so lenient that students also considered them illegitimate and unfair.[89] Twenty percent of students reporting the highest level of school discipline also reported the lowest level of fairness. Students reporting intermediate levels of school strictness were significantly less likely to report the lowest level of fairness than students who had reported either the highest or lowest level of strictness. Only 10 percent of students in the intermediate category reported the lowest response to the question of fairness of discipline.

Conclusion

Court climates affected both school practices and the perception of discipline by various school actors. To summarize, a pro-school court climate was associated with a greater prevalence and incidence of corporal punishment and an increased number of school rules. Students also perceived their schools as stricter and fairer in states with pro-school court climates. Schools that were strict were also considered to be fair, up to a certain point; if they became too strict, they were considered less fair by students. Our findings on teacher perceptions are particularly important. In pro-school court climates, teachers felt they had more classroom control and received greater rule enforcement and support from principals. These findings suggest that school actors, specifically principals and teachers, paid attention to court climates and altered their disciplinary practices accordingly.

Many social scientists have written on how the expansion of employee rights in the 1970s—an expansion also characterized by ambiguity and administrative fragmentation—transformed the workplace through promoting the growth of human resource departments and the formalization of personnel procedures; fewer researchers have written about the related expansion of rights to students and the subsequent transformation of the school.[90] It has been suggested that in the domain of corporate America, legalization of the workplace resulted in largely symbolic changes that were associated more with improving the institutional position of human resource specialists within firms than altering the conditions of employees in significant ways.[91] In schools, however, expanded legalization has clearly led to more than simply symbolic compliance: disciplinary practices have changed and more critically, the legitimacy of these practices has been undermined. Whereas firms pursuing profits only require employee compliance and not necessarily or typically a recognition of the institution's moral authority, in the case of schools, the organization is responsible for shaping and developing students as individuals, a task that does indeed require more than their simple compliance and acquiescence. Our findings demonstrate that pro-student court decisions eroded support for school discipline and contributed to undermining the moral authority of the institution.

5

School Discipline and Youth Socialization

With Sandra Way

> The same is true of punishment. Although it proceeds from an entirely mechanical reaction and from an access of passionate emotion, for the most part unthinking, it continues to play a useful role. But that role is not the one commonly perceived. It does not serve, or serves only very incidentally, to correct the guilty person or to scare off any possible imitators. From this dual viewpoint its effectiveness may rightly be questioned; in any case it is mediocre. Its real function is to maintain inviolate the cohesion of society by sustaining the common consciousness in all its vigour.
>
> —EMILE DURKHEIM, DIVISION OF LABOR
> IN SOCIETY (1893)

Conservative social critics have attributed many of the failures of public schools to lax disciplinary practices applied there. "Spare the rod, spoil the child," the refrain has it. Liberals usually fail to see any potential merits in this criticism and argue that public school failures were the result of too authoritarian and rigid disciplinary practices that produced student opposition and alienation. What both the typical conservative and liberal stances toward public school discipline have missed, however, is the degree to which effective discipline involves not just variation in strictness (that is, too much leniency or too much authoritarianism, depending on one's perspective), but *legitimacy* and *moral authority*. What gives school discipline its efficacy is the degree to which students internalize rules as fair and just. Both liberals and conservatives have been half right: school discipline that was perceived as either too lenient or too strict was also often perceived as unfair and thus not internalized by students. We demonstrate in this chapter that in order for discipline to be effective students must also perceive it as fair. We also show that factors associated with increased student attachment, commitment, and involvement in schools (such as smaller schools, reduced class size, and relevant curriculum) worked to improve some areas of student socialization and educational achievement.

Variation in court climates has been shown to affect the character of school disciplinary practices. Schools in court climates that favored school authority tended to have disciplinary practices that involved more rules, and more students perceived them as both strict and fair. Here we explore the extent to which these differences in school disciplinary climates and other factors (largely derived from Durkheim's work) were related to student socialization and academic performance. We find, not surprisingly, that student outcomes were indeed heavily influenced by such differences.

Despite all of the rhetoric surrounding school discipline, empirical analysis has been quite limited. Some evidence has been produced to support the contention that stricter disciplinary practices may be beneficial. Tom DiPrete and his colleagues, for example, found that schools with stricter discipline in tenth grade had lower rates of twelfth-grade misbehavior.[1] In related research, sociologist James Coleman and others argued that private schools obtained higher educational achievement than public schools partially because they had less disruptive peer climates.[2] Previous research suggested also that misbehaving students do not do well as measured by improvement in their grades and test scores.[3] Consistent with this position, some researchers have argued that stricter school disciplinary practices were associated with improved student behavior.[4] Others contended that school disorder was primarily related to individual student problems and that there existed "a large gap in schools' ability to successfully communicate and enforce rules and punishment."[5] Critics of traditional disciplinary measures also claim that strict, authoritarian school regimes were counterproductive in that they stifled individual creativity, produced student resistance, and were therefore detrimental to educational achievement.[6]

Contrary to the argument that increasing school leniency was itself to blame for increasing school disorder, our analysis suggests an alternative explanation. When courts ruled in favor of students and their parents, they indirectly eroded the disciplinary authority of school personnel. Not only were disciplinary sanctions reduced, but even more importantly, the rulings challenged the moral authority and legitimacy of the school personnel's right to exercise discipline. We suggest that school disorder was not simply due to more lenient disciplinary policies but was rather related more directly to a general decline in the moral authority of educators. Consequently, implementing extensive rules and harsher punishments without simultaneously addressing the issue of moral authority may be ineffective at best and counterproductive at worst.

Competing Pedagogical Logics

Conservative approaches to school discipline have tended to embrace authoritarian orientations derived philosophically from Hobbes and introduced into modern educational practice through the work of Skinner. On the other side, liberal and progressive educators following the work of Dewey, Piaget, and Kohlberg have tended to adopt orientations that have questioned the authoritative position of adults in the school and worked to empower and involve youth in creating their own systems of social order and regulation. This pedagogical practice has been widely embraced by schools of education and teacher training programs in the United States over the last several decades. A third approach towards guiding school disciplinary practices has been an orientation suggested by the work of Emile Durkheim. His sociological approach, however, has been largely overlooked by U.S. educators, who instead have embraced the more culturally familiar child-centered developmental theories of schooling advocated by educational psychologists. As James Davison Hunter has noted, the liberal pedagogy is more comfortable for U.S. educators, as it mirrors "a larger therapeutic moral order elucidated nearly everywhere else in the culture—in public discourse, the popular media, television talk shows, family advice and religious instruction."[7] Interestingly, Durkheim's insights into the role of school discipline in moral education, while largely ignored in educational theory and practice, have become (through the work of Travis Hirschi and others) the foundation of contemporary understandings of delinquency and criminal behavior. Before examining how, from a Durkheimian perspective, school discipline and other educational factors affect student outcomes, it is useful to discuss these three orientations in greater detail.

Authoritarian Approaches

Conservatives have often advocated "get tough" and "zero tolerance" policies derived from Hobbesian assumptions about maintaining social order. Hobbes argued that punishment was a necessary prerequisite to the creation and maintenance of social order, because fear of sanctions had the potential to deter would-be perpetrators when the costs of misbehavior outweighed the benefits and rewards associated with the activity. The individual or student was viewed as a rational actor who chose to obey rules because to do otherwise would extract a heavy penalty. Harsh punishments were thus commonly thought of as the most effective way of deterring misbehavior. Criminologists have outlined this premise more thoroughly in deterrence theory, pointing to severity, swiftness, and certainty of punishment as important elements to ensure effectiveness. According to the theory, punishment can deter misbehavior on the individual level—the person being punished will not do it again—and in the community, through the common knowledge of punishments others have received and hence heightened fear of individual consequences for misbehavior.

In pedagogical circles this approach has been most closely associated with work on behavior modification developed by B. F. Skinner and other educational psychologists. Skinner argued that students, like laboratory rats, could be trained to behave in desired ways based on external stimuli. Teachers can change student behaviors by modifying rewards and punishments: positive behavior is praised, negative behavior sanctioned: "by punishing behavior we wish to suppress, we arrange conditions under which acceptable behavior is strengthened."[8] While behavior modification approaches were meant to rely on positive stimuli as well as negative ones, the logic of the model largely equated increased punishment with greater effectiveness. For example, Skinner wrote:

> If punishment is used, it should be used effectively. Efforts to reduce its scope may actually extend it. The humane teacher often resorts to warning the student: "If you do that again, I will have to punish you." As a conditioned aversive stimulus, a warning is a mild punishment, but it is also a discriminative stimulus, and a student who is punished only after being warned will discriminate between occasions when behavior is and is not punished and will show the effects of the punishment only after the punishment has been given. Another mistake is to punish only gross instances of the unwanted behavior. The student is thus encouraged to go as far as he dares, and the effect on the teacher may lead to the construction of a program which actually strengthens the behavior to be suppressed. Punishing a student only occasionally can be even more harmful.[9]

Pedagogical approaches based largely on tenets associated with behavior modification have been widely disseminated in the form of various class-

room management models. For example, Rudolf Dreiker's Logical Consequence Model of classroom management advocated the replacement of the
arbitrary authoritarianism of the teacher with a socially engineered system
where aversive negative stimuli follow automatically as an inevitable, logical consequence of misbehavior.[10]

The support of stricter authoritarian forms of discipline has followed
a pressing demand to ensure student safety and restore classroom order.
Deterrence was not enough: when student misbehavior threatened the
safety of teachers or other students, it was necessary to stop it regardless of
pedagogical commitments. Other behavior, while perhaps not physically a
threat, has often been disruptive enough to make classroom instruction
impossible. In these instances, stricter discipline gives teachers and administrators the tools to remove students either temporarily through suspension or permanently through expulsion and transfer. Removal—related to
criminological theories of incapacitation—has directly attempted to reduce the number of students creating disorder and thus to allow teachers
and remaining students to focus on academic instruction. Expulsions have
become quite rare, however. A more common contemporary practice has
been to transfer students, but this procedure simply has concentrated misbehaving students in a few troubled schools or specially designated classrooms within schools.

Although arguments for stricter school discipline have some merit, we
believe that the relationship between school disorder and school discipline
is more complex than models of deterrence or incapacitation imply. According to the deterrence model, the appropriate solution to address increasing student disorder is simple: setting stricter rules and punishments
will reverse the problem and bring most misbehaving students into line.
Students who continue to misbehave may have to be "incapacitated" or
otherwise sacrificed for the good of the school. Our research suggests,
however, that increasing school rules and implementing harsher punishments will not necessarily address the nature of school disorder and could
potentially make the situation worse, as students often resist authoritarian
disciplinary policies that are perceived as unfair and illegitimate.

Child-Centered Approaches

Authoritarian approaches have assumed that teachers and administrators
as adults have a responsibility to define and enforce their conceptions of
proper school conduct and behavior, but liberals and progressives have

been less willing to accept this assumption. Instead, following the work of Dewey, they have argued that pedagogical practices should be so structured as to allow students to engage in lived experiences that incorporate their own interests, orientations, and capacities for self-government, and consequently facilitate moral development.

At the turn of the twentieth century, John Dewey forcefully argued against authoritarian pedagogical approaches that were then widespread in American schools. The notion that schools should work to instill certain student behaviors (such as "punctuality, obedience and silence") as pedagogical ends unto themselves appeared ludicrous to Dewey. Instead, a definition of appropriate student behavior and its regulation should emerge out of the intrinsic social life of the school—a life "in which all participate, in which all have a cooperative share."[11] Dewey suggested the possibility of encouraging student growth through increasing student involvement and engagement in school activities. In *Democracy and Education,* he wrote that "since a democratic society repudiates the principle of external authority, it must find a substitute in voluntary disposition and interest," and schools should thus increase the "number of individuals who participate in an interest so that each has to refer his own action to that of others."[12] Dewey specifically advocated that teachers refrain from utilizing authoritarian forms of discipline: "the discipline of the school should proceed from the life of the school as a whole and not directly from the teacher."[13]

The pedagogical belief that school discipline should not be imposed by adults was later advanced and greatly extended by the work of educational psychologist Jean Piaget in the 1930s. Piaget not only rejected authoritarian forms of school discipline, but also explicitly challenged sociologist Emile Durkheim's conception that proper socialization required adults in schools taking responsibility for defining and imposing their own standards of morality on students. Rather than support the imposition of adult-defined standards on youth, Piaget criticized Durkheim for ignoring "the existence of spontaneously formed children's societies, and of the facts relating to mutual respect."[14] The Swiss psychologist believed that "the child ties himself down to all sorts of rules in every sphere of his activity, and especially in that of play" and thus advocated a system of school discipline "called *self-government,* which is at the opposite pole from the Durkheimian pedagogy."[15] While Dewey advocated structuring school activities in a way that would encourage student involvement in social life and therefore limit the need for punitive discipline, Piaget advocated a much more radical position: adult authority in schools should be reconstituted to incorporate students directly into democratic forms of governance and self-regulation.[16] According to Piaget, "children are capable of democracy" and the only "true discipline" was one "that the children themselves have willed and consented to."[17]

In the decades following Piaget's influential book *The Moral Judgment of the Child*, many progressive educators interested in moral development embraced Piaget's contention that since children created their own rules in games and play, they must therefore also be capable of creating and enforcing rules in schools and classrooms. Carl Rodgers, for example, encouraged teachers to see themselves as facilitators of the process of students becoming and developing through their own autonomous efforts.[18] In the 1960s and early 1970s, Lawrence Kohlberg critiqued Durkheimian reliance on "collective responsibility, collective punishment and reward," terming these pedagogical techniques "horrifying innovations in the hidden curriculum."[19] Kohlberg emphasized how both Piaget and his own conception of moral education stressed the formation of "ethical principles" in students based on processes of abstract cognitive reasoning, rather than through Durkheimian socialization and internalization of social norms and values. Kohlberg, like Piaget, called for an expanded role of students and a diminished role of adults in controlling and regulating youth behavior in schools. Kohlberg advocated "governance of the classroom and the school as a just community or participatory democracy."[20] The school, according to Kohlberg, should provide "the adolescent with direct power and responsibility for governance in a society that is small and personal, like the family, but that is complex, rule-governed, and democratic."[21]

The difficulty inherent in assuming that given the instruments of self-government, adolescents will actually use such power to regulate themselves appropriately was illustrated well in Kohlberg's own description of his involvement in an experiment in student self-governance at an alternative public high school in Scarsdale, an affluent suburb of New York City. Kohlberg advised the school to "become rigorously democratic with all rules and disciplines being formulated by the whole community—one person, one vote."[22] Kohlberg described a meeting where rules and enforcement were to be discussed prohibiting the use of drugs and alcohol during an upcoming school retreat:

> The students agreed not to use dope on the retreat. The staff urged that
> students, as well as staff, have responsibility for enforcing the rule, not

just for obeying it. After much discussion, the students voted that in the abstract, they had the responsibility to enforce the rule, they should enforce it, but that in practice they couldn't be expected to police their friends, that while they *should* enforce the rule they wouldn't vote that they *would* enforce the rule.

After the retreat I raised the question as to whether students had observed the rule they voted on. A mild discipline was agreed upon in case anyone wished to admit violations. Soon, 20 students spoke up admitting that they had violated the rule. Their attitudes ranged from the feeling that they were civilly disobedient heroes of individual rights to penitence at letting down the community. Some of the upright students castigated the sinners; other upright students castigated the moralists for hurting the feelings of the sinners. In the end, the dominant feeling was that everyone, saint and sinner, cared about one another and the community.[23]

Regardless of whether students ultimately "cared about one another and the community" and setting aside one's beliefs about the permissibility of adolescent drug and alcohol use, it is hard to imagine that students would come to learn to embrace higher abstract "ethical principles" from such school interactions. Kohlberg's report of a subsequent schoolwide meeting where students debated whether coming high to school was any different from "picking one's nose" in class offers little comfort. Although students from places like Scarsdale were not likely to face serious consequences from the school's inability to provide adequate socialization (if need be, their families could afford to hire adequate legal counsel), the consequences of similar educational experiences and tolerance toward illegal activities for disadvantaged students could lead to life-long devastating consequences.

As James Davison Hunter pointed out in a review of these pedagogical developments, "the net effect is that established structures of authority recede in social significance; the moral authority of the social order is demystified and deconstructed."[24] It is worth noting that much of the theoretical development of these pedagogical approaches occurred prior to the extension of due process rights to students in the mid-1970s. Ironically, the expansion of youth rights furthered the development of the ideas advocated by these writers—since democracy today, as Michael Schudson has noted,[25] often has involved the exercise of individual rights in judicial settings more than the exercise of the franchise at the ballot box—but undermined the conditions allowing for these approaches to flourish fully. If school administrators felt constrained and uncertain that courts would support their disciplinary decisions, they would be certainly unwilling to subject disciplinary actions and proceedings to even greater court scrutiny by involving students more fully in these processes.

Sociological Approaches

The examination of the relationship between obedience and authority is not new. Emile Durkheim and Max Weber focused on these issues more than a century ago. More recently, Christopher Hurn argued that authority relationships in schools have changed as a result of a variety of social factors, including changes in cultural norms as well as specific court challenges to traditional school disciplinary practices. "Decreasing agreement among educators both as to their appropriate prescriptive rights and the grounds on which those rights were exercised, weakened student motivation," Hurn wrote. He added that these disagreements have undermined taken-for-granted assumptions about school practices and thus have led to "an increase in such perceptions as unfairness and injustice."[26]

Sociologists have examined how normative commitments to authority influenced obedience to law more generally. Although this research has not often been applied to schools, information about why laws have been obeyed more generally may help us understand why students misbehave in schools and classrooms. According to a normative perspective, people obey the law because of personal morality or the legitimacy of the regulatory agency. When people base compliance on personal morality, they obey the law because they feel the law is just. When people base compliance on legitimacy, they obey the law because they feel the enforcing authority has the responsibility and right to regulate behavior in such a manner. Perceptions of fairness play an important role in both compliance and legitimacy.[27] Hollingsworth, Luffler, and Clune's earlier research on several Wisconsin public schools has suggested that the greater the extent to which students thought administrators and teachers were fair, the less likely they were to skip class or receive direct disciplinary sanction.[28]

While Max Weber identified how authority could be based on charisma, tradition, or bureaucratic order, Emile Durkheim related authority specifically to morality and developed the concept of moral authority specifically in the context of formal schooling. According to Durkheim, one of the most important tasks for the school was the socialization of children. Schools should not only teach socially appropriate behavior but must also inculcate a general respect and obligation toward social rules. Durkheim referred to this social authority of rules as moral authority; because moral authority was internalized, self-control was generated. For Durkheim, a successful school was one that did not need to enforce rules and dole out heavy punishment because students had internalized school rules and thus did not challenge authority in the first place. When infractions occurred, sanctions served not so much as an individual deterrent, but rather as an instrument that prevented the erosion of moral authority threatened by the public violation of social norms: "What matters is not that the child suffers, but rather that his behavior be vigorously censored. It is the disapproval leveled against the given conduct that alone makes for reparation ... Thus, severity of treatment is justified only to the extent that it is necessary to make disapproval of the act utterly unequivocal."[29]

As a primary agent of socialization, the teacher must be able to instill respect for impersonal law. The work of socialization can be accomplished with the help of discipline. As educational psychologist Philip Jackson has suggested,

> One of the earliest lessons a child must learn is how to comply with the wishes of others. Soon after he becomes aware of the world he is in, the newborn infant becomes conscious of one of the main features of that world: adult authority. As he moves from home to school the authority of parents is gradually supplemented by control from teachers, the second most important set of adults in his life.[30]

Durkheimian discipline only has moral value, however, if it is perceived as just and legitimate. If the teacher's moral authority is doubted, then respect for social values and obligation to obey may fail to develop within the child, an outcome which is important not only for school order but ultimately for the general social order as well. Hence, while the internalization of moral authority may be the ultimate goal and the most efficient mechanism of social order, the legitimization of teacher authority is the necessary first step. Without teacher authority, socialization is less than effective. Durkheim argued that "If the teacher permits a lapse in this (student) respect without intervening, such leniency bears witness—or seems to, which amounts to the same thing—that he no longer deems it so worthy of respect. The hesitation, the doubts, the weakening of conviction which betray his attitude are necessarily communicated to the children."[31]

Contemporary court climates hostile to school authority have contributed to eroding both student and school personnel confidence in the legitimate right of a teacher or administrator to exercise discipline. It is this hesitation, doubt, and weakening of conviction—which we have partially attributed to hostile court decisions—that has undermined the effectiveness of school discipline.

The insights of Emile Durkheim's work on youth socialization were extended into the field of contemporary criminology through the influential research of Travis Hirschi. His *Causes of Delinquency* laid the foundation for the advancement of social control theory in criminology. Hirschi specified different mechanisms whereby an individual's bond to society could be strengthened and delinquency reduced. Specifically, he identified attachment, involvement, commitment, and belief as important elements of ensuring desirable conduct and behavior. Elsewhere we have elaborated on this perspective and identified the extent to which certain educational experiences in high school can affect the likelihood that a student will become attached, involved, and committed to conventional activity.[32] Student integration to school activities is plausibly encouraged by more intimate educational settings[33] (smaller school and class size); in addition, student engagement is likely enhanced by curriculum differentiation—students who can choose either vocational or college preparatory curriculum will be more attached, involved, and committed to their studies than youth experiencing general curricular programs that have neither a college nor labor market focus.

Measuring Student Outcomes

Our analysis of the effects of school disciplinary practices in this chapter seeks to identify not simply student outcomes associated with school rules and their perceptions that disciplinary practices were strict, but, more importantly, student perceptions of fairness and legitimacy of discipline. Specifically, we were interested in how moral authority associated with school discipline influenced student behavior, attitudes, and academic achievement. Since the legitimacy and moral authority of school personnel exist at the level of student perceptions, we focused largely on student assessments of school disciplinary practices. In addition we looked for effects of smaller school and classroom size as well as curricular differentiation on student outcomes.

Again we use the two national student data sets, High School and Beyond and the National Educational Longitudinal Study. Instead of analyzing student perceptions of discipline as a product of court climates and other social factors, we now identify the role these perceptions play in school effectiveness. Specifically, we demonstrate how perceptions of discipline and other school factors related to student engagement concretely influenced student attitudes, behavior, and educational achievement.

Recent academic, political, and popular discourse has measured school effectiveness largely in terms of standardized test scores—and subsequently focused reform efforts on proposals tied to increased standardized testing. We believe that such a narrow focus has been misguided and limited. Along with teaching academic curriculum, schools are important arenas for the socialization of youth; settings where children learn socially appropriate behavior, values, and interpersonal skills from teachers, principals, and fellow students. The long hours children spend in schools make it obvious that these institutions are critical in the contemporary process of youth socialization. Regardless of whether the explicit goal of schools is to instill specific moral values, teachers and administrators do teach important implicit lessons through their policies and behaviors. As Philip Jackson argued in *The Moral Life of Schools:*

> To anyone who takes a close look at what goes on in classrooms it becomes quickly apparent that our schools do much more than pass along requisite knowledge to the students attending them (or fail to do so, as the case may be). They also influence the way those students look upon themselves and others. They affect the way learning is valued and sought after and lay the foundations of lifelong habits of thought and action. They shape opinion and develop taste, helping to form likes and aversions. They contribute to the growth of character and, in some instances, they may even be a factor in its corruption. Schools in the aggregate do all this and more to and for the students they serve. Moreover, and here is the important point, they do much of it without the full awareness and thoughtful engagement of those in charge.[34]

This moral subtext of school life has often been disparaged as the "hidden curriculum" of schooling. Neo-Marxists have equated the socialization that occurs with individuals learning obedience, compliance, and docility through a process designed solely to serve the functional needs of a larger capitalist system.[35] Such critiques have been overly simplistic, however, and failed to recognize a legitimate role of schools in socializing youth for productive roles in a democratic society—an educational goal, incidentally, that working-class parents have long embraced.[36]

In modern societies, schools have an increasing responsibility for youth socialization. More and more parents work away from the home, and the school is the primary nonfamilial social institution (other than perhaps organized religion) that embodies the principles, structures, and rules of a larger society. One could argue that the well-being of a society depends on the degree to which schools have instilled respect for morality and legitimate societal rules, as much as the extent to which they have succeeded in providing academic skills measured by standardized test results.

On the surface, the question of how school discipline influences student outcomes might appear straightforward. One could simply measure whether schools with stricter disciplinary policies produced better-behaved and academically more successful students, after taking into account other differences among schools that might also have influenced behavior and achievement (such as the composition of the student body). Similarly, to determine whether discipline had a positive effect on individuals, one could measure student outcomes after accounting for other characteristics of the individual (such as their family background and prior test scores) that would have increased or decreased the probability of the student exhibiting a certain behavior. Given our theoretical framework, which emphasizes the centrality of moral authority and legitimacy in school discipline, such an analysis would have missed the underlying mechanisms explaining the nature of disorder in our schools today. We focused instead on how normative evaluations of the authority of rules and legitimacy—that is, how disciplinary practices were interpreted and understood by students—influenced the internalization of rules and thus their effectiveness. After all, individuals react to a situation based on their perceptions of it, not as a consequence of some "objective" reality such as the number and type of school rules or punishments. If social actors believe something to be true, it often has social significance and measurable consequences regardless of the objective validity of the original perception. Therefore, our analysis focused on student perceptions of school discipline—particularly the extent to which students found their schools strict and fair.[37] The extent to which students with different characteristics attached varying meanings to concepts such as strictness and fairness could be partially adjusted for in our modeling by including covariates to account for such differences.[38]

Overall, since fairness always was a positive normative response, one would expect that it would have a positive influence on academic achievement and spill over into other positive attitudes and behaviors toward school. While perceptions of fairness were usually associated with positive effects, perceptions of strictness were more complex. We can assume that most students interpreted the term "strict" to mean stringent or rigorous application of rules and punishments. Their assessments of the desirability of such strict discipline, however, would vary. For some, the presence of strict rules was positive, while for others it was negative. Initially, one might think the more prevalent opinion would be that stricter rules were bad. After all, has not freedom from restriction been a common battle cry amongst high school age adolescents for decades? This was not true for everyone, however. Students in chaotic learning environments have often advocated increasing the strictness of school discipline, as they also have been the most vulnerable to uncertainty and risks produced by chaotic learning environments.[39] In the last chapter we also show how strictness has a curvilinear relationship with fairness (that is, increased strictness was associated with greater reports of fairness only up to a level of moderate strictness); in addition, when courts supported school authority, students reported that discipline was both stricter and fairer. It is particularly interesting that students viewed such schools as fairer than schools that had fewer rules and less discipline. In our analysis, we considered student reports of strictness and fairness independently as well as in conjunction. By combining the two perceptions we developed a new measure that reflected rigorous school discipline that incorporated moral authority. Individuals who viewed discipline as both strict and fair would look positively upon regulations imposed by schools and show respect for rules and authority.

The main discussion here is additionally amplified (in the notes and tables) by several other measures of school discipline associated with student outcomes: administrative reports of the number of school rules;[40] student reports of school safety; and aggregate school-level measures of student perceptions of strictness and fairness of discipline. We measured aggregate school-level strictness and fairness because individual perceptions of fairness and strictness potentially could come together within a school to create student climates. Individual schools have climates that can be thought of as particular institutional personalities or cultures. Since individuals do not develop their reactions in isolation, we considered in the analysis what other students in the school thought about school discipline.[41] We also identified the distinct effects of more or fewer school rules on student outcomes in our modeling.[42] In addition, guided by Durkheimian aspects of social control theory, we explored the extent to which more intimate schools and classrooms as well as more focused ones (smaller school and class size, and more specialized curricular programs) positively affected a school's capacity to socialize youth.

Our supplementary analyses also examined student perceptions of school safety as an additional factor affecting outcomes.[43] Although perceptions of safety are not necessarily a school discipline variable, we incorporated them because the physical security of students in school has been an important goal in its own right, and because such perceptions, regardless of whether students have ever been threatened, may also have various implications for the process of socialization. If students did not feel secure in their schools, this may have eroded the authority of school personnel. If they felt that school personnel could not protect them, then why respect the officials' authority? In unsafe settings, students may also have believed that the only way to address their own safety was to take matters into their own hands, fighting and disobeying rules simply to protect themselves. An alternative reaction to fear of victimization may simply have been staying home from school, which also would have prevented students from concentrating on activities related to school performance.[44]

We measured administrator and student reports of school discipline in the tenth grade and their effects on outcomes at the end of the twelfth grade.[45] We incorporated this time lag in our analysis to test the assumption that school discipline affected subsequent student outcomes.[46] We statistically controlled for a range of other factors at the individual and school level that may have influenced whether individuals misbehaved, held certain attitudes towards school, or succeeded academically.[47] By including tenth-grade test scores in the analysis, prior performance was statistically held constant for all respondents, compensating as best we could for any effects it may have produced.[48] Individual factors controlled for were characteristics related to a particular individual such as race, socioeconomic status, gender, and family background. School-level variables were characteristics of the school that might have influenced outcomes through directly affecting the learning environment or indirectly influencing the social-psychological orientations of individuals.[49] Many of the variables included as statistical "controls"—for example, race, gender, social background, and aggregate school-level measures of student composition—were interesting influences on student outcome in their own right and have been studied as such in prior research. Results from our analysis could be utilized to address questions such as: Did students from two-parent families have better academic and behavioral outcomes than students who did not?[50] How was student race and immigration status related to these outcomes?[51] To what extent was gender related to student achievement and socialization?[52] Since this project focuses on school discipline, however, the primary purpose of these variables in our analyses was simply to help us isolate the influence of perceptions of school discipline and a select number of other educational variables related to a Durkheimian sociological orientation toward schooling; we therefore have left out of the main text the identification and discussion of the effects of these covariates.

We assessed the effectiveness of school discipline and related factors on diverse important student outcomes. Although test scores provide some indication of academic mastery, these performance-based measures fail to capture other elements of school success. In addition to test scores, we examined student grades and likelihood of graduation from high school. Grades reflect not only what knowledge a child was able to demonstrate on a particular test, but also provide teacher assessments that incorporate elements such as effort, compliance, and perseverance—factors associated with successful socialization and more broadly defined long-term success. Graduation from high school was important in its own right, as a credential that would bring long-term labor market benefits to individuals.

We also looked at school commitment and attitudes about obeying school rules. Students were asked how often they had completed their homework, forgot supplies, were absent, tardy, and cut class. Disregard for basic school activities often precedes more general school failure that may then result in nonconformity to social norms. Another question was whether students thought it was acceptable to disobey school rules. Finally, to address our interest in student misbehavior, we included measures of fighting, arrests, and disruptive behavior. Students were asked how often they got into fights in school and whether or not they had ever been arrested; an additional measure of disruptive classroom behavior was based on teacher assessment, rather than student self-reports.[53]

School Discipline and Other Factors Affecting Youth Socialization

Figure 5.1 identifies the degree to which tenth-grade student reports of strictness and fairness were associated with the concurrent belief that school was a safe setting. This figure—as well as subsequent illustrations of results in this chapter—identifies analytical results for both strictness and

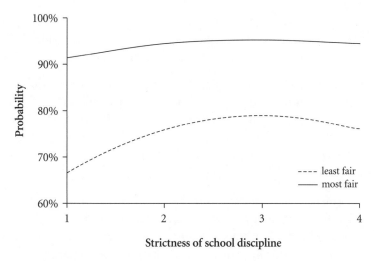

Figure 5.1 Effects of strictness and fairness of school discipline on school safety (based on Table 5.C, Model 3)

fairness. This graphing technique allows one to identify the relative magnitude of the independent influence of student perceptions of strictness and fairness on the outcome examined, as well as the degree to which strictness and fairness interact to codetermine results. The solid line in the figure identifies predicted outcomes when students reported the fairest school discipline; the dotted line identifies results for reports of the most unfair school discipline. As one moves from left to right across the x-axis, the effects of different levels of strictness are identified. The gaps between the solid and dotted lines thus identify the extent to which fairness was related to the outcome examined; the slope (or steepness) of the lines identify the extent to which various levels of strictness were associated with the outcome.[54]

Figure 5.1 thus illustrates the degree to which student perceptions of fairness of school discipline were closely associated with beliefs about school safety. Students who report that their schools had discipline that was neither strict nor fair had only a 67 percent probability of reporting a safe school setting, as compared to a 94 percent probability if school discipline was considered both fair and strict. Variation in student perceptions of fairness was associated with school safety at almost twice the level as the association between strictness and safety. Recall, however, that court decisions hostile to school authority have led students to perceive schools as both less strict and less fair. The extent to which these court challenges might directly relate to school safety has been described vividly in John Devine's description of an incident in a New York City public high school:

> A meeting in the principal's office broke up fast when word arrived that a "female teacher had just been beaten up by a female student." The police had to come into the building. The teacher had to be taken to the health clinic and then to the hospital. The fight got so vicious that the male security guards would not break it up: "We're not touchin' females . . . unless they are starting to kill us; the lawyers would have a field day."[55]

Court challenges have undermined the ability of school personnel to assume that interventions even to maintain safety and order were necessarily legally defensible.[56] The results in Figure 5.1 also suggest some small curvilinear effects of strictness: when schools moved past a moderate level of perceived strictness, they were associated with slightly lower levels of reported safety. In our analysis, we also found—concurrent with prior research—evidence that students felt safer in smaller schools. After controlling for confounding factors such as whether a school was located in a rural or urban setting and the average economic background of the student body, students in schools with 2,000 students were approximately 1.13 times more likely to report that they felt unsafe in school than individuals in schools with 1,000 students.[57]

We also examined associations between perceptions of school discipline and a composite measure of students' commitment to the educational process. As noted above, we created this measure based on student responses to several questions about tardiness, homework completed, forgotten supplies, absences, and cutting classes. Such a measure captures the extent to which schools successfully encouraged conventional academically oriented behavior. When schools were perceived as fairer and stricter, students had greater educational commitment. Similar to associations with school safety, variation in student perceptions of fairness was associated with about twice the variation in educational commitment compared to differences in reports of strictness. In our modeling of this behavioral outcome, we also found significant associations with both school size and curricular program differentiation: students in smaller schools and students in academic and vocational tracks reported greater educational commitment than did students in general programs.[58]

The extent to which student perceptions of fairness and strictness of school discipline were often interdependent factors codetermining outcomes was clear in our statistical analysis of association between perceptions of school discipline and student grades. When schools were fairest, increased strictness had positive effects on improving student grades. When schools were least fair, a student was likely to report slightly lower grades as the strictness of discipline increased. The traditional liberal critique of increased discipline being counterproductive and alienating students from the educational process did indeed have some merit in settings where school discipline was perceived as unfair. In schools with the fairest discipline, however, variation from least strict to most strict was associated with movement upward of a little less than a quarter of a letter grade from about a C+ to a B−.[59]

A recent study of students in urban public schools identified similar results of authoritarian discipline being perceived as unfair and leading to decreased school performance. Bruce Wilson and H. Dickson Corbett recorded the following conversation between an interviewer (I) and a student (S), who was attempting to account for receiving a low grade in a particular class:

I: Why [are you getting a low grade in Math]?
S: The teacher mostly.
I: What do you mean?
S: Like the kids talk, and if one talks, he blame the whole class. He screams at us. He threw a desk.
I: Why did you get a C?
S: He did not explain it, and I do poorly on the test.
I: Describe a day in the class.
S: You don't learn nothing. It's boring. He always suspending kids; that's how he wastes his time.[60]

High school grades were also positively influenced by other school factors associated with Durkheimian elements of social control theory. Specifically, students had higher grades when their coursework was more specialized (in either vocational or academic areas). Likewise, students reported higher grades in more intimate settings; both smaller schools and classroom size affected this outcome.[61] It is worth noting that this was the only time in our modeling that we were able to identify positive effects of smaller student/teacher ratios on improving student behavioral and academic outcomes.

When high school graduation is examined in Figure 5.2, the effects of strictness and fairness on student outcomes were similar to the previously identified effects on student grades. When discipline was perceived as most fair, strictness of discipline moderately improved the odds of high school graduation. When school discipline was perceived as unfair, however, increasing discipline produced a significantly lower likelihood of graduation. The probability of high school graduation in schools reported as least fair decreased from 87 percent to 74 percent as perceptions of strictness increased; students reporting their schools as most fair only marginally improved the likelihood of high school graduation from 84 percent to 85 percent as reports of strictness increased. The likelihood of high school graduation was also improved significantly by student enrollment in college preparatory or vocational programs as well as enrollment in smaller school settings. Students in vocational programs were 2.4 times less likely to drop out and students in college preparatory programs were 3.7 times less likely to drop out than their peers in the general track. Students in schools with 1,000 students were 1.3 times less likely to drop out than students in schools with twice that number of students.[62]

Figure 5.3 examines the effects of perceptions of school discipline on student test scores. In terms of standard deviations, little variation in test

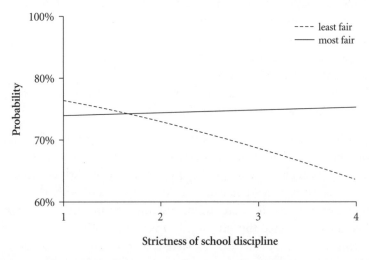

Figure 5.2 Effects of strictness and fairness of school discipline on high school graduation (based on Table 5.F, Model 4)

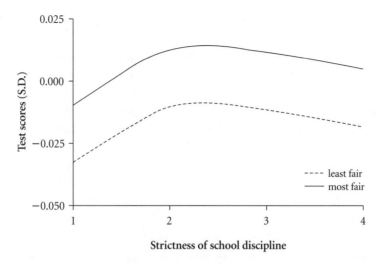

Figure 5.3 Effects of strictness and fairness of school discipline on student test scores (based on Table 5.G, Model 3)

score was associated with school disciplinary practices, as our analysis of twelfth-grade test scores controlled for tenth-grade performance, and test results in high school were relatively stable across grades. Nevertheless, the results suggest that test scores were marginally higher where discipline was perceived as fairer; modest improvements in performance were also associated with increases in strictness of school discipline if schools were perceived as especially lax in disciplinary enforcement. Differences between moderate and higher levels of strictness, however, were associated with slight decreases in test scores.

Educational reforms directed at improving student test score results have received great attention in recent years, and policy analysts in particular have focused on the gap between white and African-American student performance.[63] Many of these analysts would like to know whether and to what degree the "black-white test gap" has been related to differences in perceptions of school discipline. Our analysis suggests that variation in these perceptions was indeed significantly related to the test score gap in at least two ways. First, African-American students were affected more strongly by variation in school strictness than were white students. Second, these racial differences in the association between school discipline and test score results have increased significance owing to related racial differences in reports of the level of strictness of school discipline. Specifically, African-American students were more likely than white students to experience school settings that were either the most lenient or the strictest—settings often perceived as unfair and thus poorly designed for cognitive development.[64] At the same time, African-American test scores were lowest in settings perceived as overly lenient or excessively strict. When African-American students perceived their schools as least strict, their test scores were significantly below the national average (.49 standard deviations); they rose when their schools were perceived to have moderate levels of strictness (.32 standard deviations below) and were again higher when schools were reported as strictest (.45 standard deviations below).

Figure 5.4 demonstrates the relationship between perceptions of school strictness and test score performance in even more dramatic fashion. Here we show results on twelfth-grade scores of the effects of race by variation in student reports of fairness and strictness, utilizing models that control for a range of factors including tenth-grade test performance. The x-axis in this figure (unlike other figures in this chapter) represents variation in perceptions of strictness and fairness considered simultaneously, with the far right side of the graph identifying results for students who report disci-

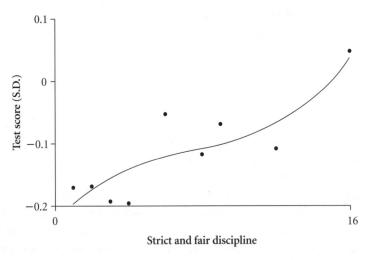

Figure 5.4 African-Americans' twelfth-grade test score performance relative to that of whites, by disciplinary perception

pline in their schools was both strict *and* fair. The effects of student perceptions on the predicted black-white test score gap were dramatic and remarkable. In school settings that as a whole were considered both unfair and lenient, African-American students performed considerably worse than white students on their twelfth-grade test even after considering their prior tenth-grade test performance and other environmental factors. However, when students reported that their schools were both strict and fair, there were no negative effects of race on twelfth-grade test score performance.[65] School discipline has been a central element of differences in black-white test score performance.

The extent to which the effectiveness of strict discipline was related to the perception of fairness was illustrated again in our modeling of student reports of willingness to disobey rules (see Figure 5.5). Perceived strictness of discipline had varying effects on outcomes when discipline was considered more or less fair. When students perceived their school's discipline to be unfair, increased strictness was associated with a greater expressed willingness to disobey rules; where discipline was considered fairest, increased strictness led to slightly greater rule compliance. Mary Metz's work on "principled conflict" in schools illustrates the social-psychological aspects

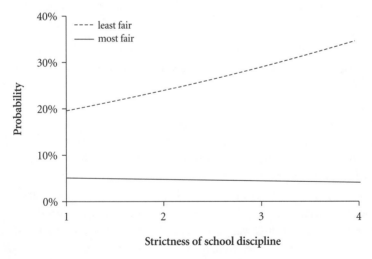

Figure 5.5 Effects of strictness and fairness of school discipline on students' expressed willingness to disobey rules (based on Table 5.H, Model 4)

of this process well. Metz describes an incident in which a high school student offered "ferocious resistance" to a teacher's sanctioning because he considered the discipline unfair:

> [The students were working at their desks.] Miss Brown looked up and said to Stillman, "All right, go back in the corner without your books." There had only been a very quiet murmur in the room. I don't know whether Stillman was the source of it or not.
>
> Stillman asked very quietly, almost in a mumble, what he had done. Miss Brown simply told him to go on, without his books. Stillman asked, this time clearly audibly, what he had done. Miss Brown said, "Don't talk back, Stillman. Go on back in the corner." Stillman said he was not talking back, he was simply asking what he had done. Why should he have to go back there?
>
> Miss Brown said, "Because I'm telling you to." She looked down to her work again. Stillman just sat there. She looked up again and he mumbled that he wanted to know what he had done. Miss Brown said, "we'll discuss it later." Stillman still insisted that he must know what he did. Miss Brown picked up the pad of referral notices and told him warningly to go on back. He kept his ground silently and she said, "All right," and put down her pad. She told him to go out in the hall without his books and wait until she brought him the referral notice. "Go on, hurry up." Slowly and reluctantly but without pausing, he went.[66]

Metz interpreted the student's willingness to disobey authority and suffer the consequences of greater punishment as a result of his perception that the sanction was applied unfairly. We found support for this argument in our quantitative analysis. When students perceived discipline as strict and unfair, they had a 35 percent likelihood of expressing a willingness to disobey rules; when students perceived school discipline as most fair, their likelihood of expressing a willingness to disobey was five percent or less, regardless of perceptions of strictness.

Sociological research on schools has repeatedly demonstrated that school authority that was not perceived as legitimate often produced student resistance and thus was counterproductive. Resistance to school authority has been well documented, with populations as diverse as white male working-class students in England and African-American students in California.[67] Whether the behavior has been labeled "principled conflict," "oppositional," or simply "resistance" is less important than the realization that authority exercised without legitimacy will usually be counterproductive.

The importance of fairness in the effectiveness of school discipline is highlighted again in our analysis of associations between perceived strictness and fairness of school discipline and teacher reports of student disruption. While the level of strictness again had no significant effects, student beliefs about the fairness of school discipline were indeed strongly related to student disruption. School discipline that was perceived as fair was associated with significantly lower rates of disruptive behavior.[68] Again, we believe that in expanding student rights, court decisions have undermined the extent to which the legitimacy of school discipline was simply a taken-for-granted assumption of students, parents, and school personnel. The degree of erosion was captured well in recent ethnographies of U.S. public schools. For example, as a New York City school administrator reported to John Devine in describing how immigrant families adjusted to the U.S. setting:

> The other difficulty in adjusting comes from kids who come from places like Barbados where you don't open your mouth in class. And if the teacher comes down on you for something and a parent finds out about it, you get double, because your parent gives it to you also. And they [the parents] don't even ask if you were right or wrong. Then they come into a system where they suddenly find they have rights . . . A kid goes home and starts talking about rights to the parent and the parent looks at the kid like, are you crazy?[69]

Courts have weakened the sense that school discipline must by its very nature and source be recognized by individuals as fair and legitimate. Traditional assumptions that teachers and principals' authority could be exercised largely without challenge have been undermined.

Fairness of disciplinary practices also was strongly implicated in whether strict discipline was associated with more or less student fighting in school. Educational researcher Pedro Noguera reported the following comments from a male high school student in an urban school where students had respect for school personnel's ability and willingness to exercise disciplinary authority:

The campus monitors at our school are really tough. If anyone wants to fight somebody they usually get caught right away by one of these guys. And they are really big. You'd have to be crazy to think that you could get away with fighting at this school, and if you tried to get someone after school, the principal or somebody will get you the next day, and kids who fight usually get suspended. You can't get away with any fighting around here, not even play fighting.[70]

Figure 5.6 suggests that when school discipline was considered fair, strict discipline was indeed related to decreased levels of student fighting; when discipline was considered unfair, stricter discipline was actually associated with higher rates of fighting. In school settings that were perceived as unfair and lenient, 11 percent of students reported being involved in fighting, compared to 20 percent when these schools were strict. In school settings that were considered fair, however, strict discipline lowered rates of fighting from 11 to 7 percent.

Figure 5.7 identifies results from our final analysis of student outcomes when unsuccessful socialization was modeled most extremely, in the form of criminal arrest. In this case we again found that fairness of discipline was essential in increasing the positive effects of strictness of school disci-

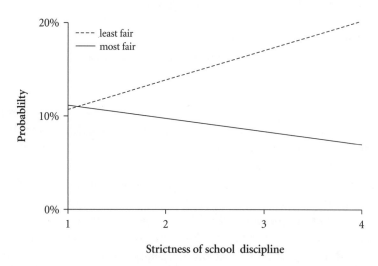

Figure 5.6 Effects of strictness and fairness of school discipline on fighting in school (based on Table 5.J, Model 4)

Figure 5.7 Effects of strictness and fairness of school discipline on individual arrest (based on Table 5.K, Model 4)

pline. When students perceived school discipline as being fair, stricter discipline led dramatically to reduced rates of individual arrest. In schools that were perceived as being the most fair, the probability of individual arrest decreased from six percent to two percent as perceptions of school strictness increased. In schools that were perceived as least fair, student perceptions of strictness had less significant effects. Again, the importance of legitimacy in promoting the efficacy of stricter disciplinary climates was highlighted.

Conclusion

Pro-student court rulings of the early 1960s granted students important individual rights, particularly in the area of free expression and due process. One result of protecting individual rights, however, was the weakening of the historical *in loco parentis* authority given to school personnel. While limiting school authority may have curtailed certain abuses, it also had the unintended consequence of reducing the power teachers had to shape the classroom and school environment in a positive manner. School personnel had less discretion over the application of school discipline, and in the context of legal ambiguity, teachers began to fear the consequences of using any remaining *in loco parentis* authority. Consequently, a shift of authority occurred: educational instruction became the primary task of the teacher while student discipline became the job of school personnel who specialized in its legally tolerated administration. At the same time that teachers have understandably pulled away from their role as disciplinarians, we have seen a change in how students viewed school discipline.

The relatively recent popularity of standardized testing has helped to reinforce the belief that the primary role of the teacher and the school is to impart cognitive skills. Mastering course material, however, is only one aspect of schooling. Too often ignored is the equally important role of socialization. According to Durkheim, at the same time that teacher discipline helps control the learning environment and thus facilitates instruction, it also serves an important role in socialization more generally. The moral authority of school discipline is critical in fostering students' ability to learn socially appropriate behaviors and values so they can become healthy individuals and productive citizens. In order to socialize youth effectively, however, schools must have the capacity to exercise reasonable discipline free from external efforts to undermine the legitimacy of the practices. As Durkheim suggested, "School discipline can produce the useful results that it should only by confining itself within certain limits . . . It has a moral character and moral value only if the penalty is regarded as just by those subjected to it, which implies that the authority which punishes is itself recognized as legitimate."[71]

Critics of *in loco parentis* have argued that culturally rigid socialization can disproportionately favor some groups over others and stifle individuality. Although these criticisms have some validity, the adopted remedies have reduced the positive exercise of the moral authority of schooling for all students, including, ironically, the most socially vulnerable students— those segregated and concentrated in impoverished urban public schools.

The popularity of standardized testing and an increased focus on the acquisition of cognitive skills in schooling has not eliminated the importance of school discipline for socialization. School safety and discipline have been leading concerns of parents, educators, and lawmakers. While some reformers have called for an increase in teacher authority and involvement in classroom discipline, more often attention has turned to increasing security with metal detectors, armed guards, and tougher rules and harsher zero-tolerance policies. This deterrence approach to discipline does not address the issue of moral authority or the importance that student perceptions may have for the success or failure of school policy. The results of our analysis suggest that tougher school discipline policies and practices do not necessarily deter students from misbehaving. Authoritarian discipline is not a credible solution for ameliorating school disorder. If anything, our research suggests that tougher discipline without increases in student perceptions of fairness could stifle educational development and proper socialization. Students who perceive discipline as moderately strict tend to have better outcomes than those who thought discipline was either too lenient or overly strict. School climates can be either excessively permissive or obtrusively harsh.

Students who perceived school discipline as fair, however, were consistently better behaved, more committed to school, less likely to countenance disobeying rules, and had higher test scores and grades than those who perceived school discipline as unfair. These findings lend support to claims in the law literature that fairness is an important element of compliance. Fairness is a function of legitimacy and moral authority. When individuals believe that the creator or enforcer of a rule has the authority to enforce it, they are more likely to view the regulation as fair. Our results indicate that student perceptions of both strictness and fairness in school discipline have the highest behavioral and achievement payoffs for students. Additional features of educational experience related to improving student attachment and engagement in school—particularly smaller school size and curricular program specialization—can also improve student behavioral and academic outcomes.

6

Restoring Moral Authority
in American Schools

It is not enough to point out that the school is a despotism. It is a
despotism in a state of perilous equilibrium. It is a despotism
threatened from within and exposed to regulation and interference from without. It is a despotism capable of being overturned
in a moment, exposed to the instant loss of its stability and its
prestige. It is a despotism demanded by the community of parents, but specially limited by them as to the techniques which it
may use for the maintenance of a stable social order. It is a despotism resting upon children, at once the most tractable and the
most unstable members of the community.

—WILLARD WALLER, *THE SOCIOLOGY OF
TEACHING* (1932)

American public school life, once described as "a despotism in a state of
perilous equilibrium," now often resembles more a chaotic environment
undermined by chronic organizational instability. In a manner that Waller
theoretically predicted but whose dimensions could hardly have been
imagined in the 1930s, the social order of public schools has been significantly "threatened from within and exposed to regulation and interference from without" over the past several decades. This state of disequilib-
rium, related to a crisis in moral authority, has led to widespread loss of
public school institutional prestige. Court decisions challenging the administrative discretion of school personnel have undermined the effectiveness of school discipline and have threatened the ability of public schools
to socialize youth for productive roles in society. Schools are in a crisis not
simply because they have become chaotic settings where violent incidents
have too often occurred, but because a public school system that is widely
perceived to lack the capacity of properly socializing youth will face in-

creased political challenges that threaten its organizational existence. Rather than confront this serious and complex problem, educational reformers have preferred to focus attention on more peripheral educational issues, such as the promotion of schemes intended to improve standardized test scores.

Failed Liberal Educational Reforms

When liberal reformers have discussed the problem of school discipline, they often have done so in a narrow and self-contradictory manner. Rather than appreciate the degree to which legal constraints have limited the actions of school personnel, or the extent to which successful external challenges have reduced the legitimacy and moral authority of school discipline, the liberal educational establishment has viewed the current legal environment as an evolutionary political advance as well as a desirable social given; at the same time, it held school personnel accountable for addressing deteriorating public school climates associated with these changes. For example, the Carnegie Foundation for the Advancement of Teaching, in a 1983 report of over three hundred pages, devoted only one paragraph to school discipline. The report, midway through, simply noted: "At a minimum, every school should have a fair, clearly stated, widely understood code of conduct. In addition, principals and other administrators have an obligation to see that standards of discipline are consistently and fairly enforced throughout the school, that disruptive students are promptly removed from the classroom, and that teachers are supported in the maintenance of discipline."[1] The Carnegie report—a good summary of liberal educational sentiment of the time—not only underemphasized the problem of discipline and disorder found in American schools, but incorrectly assigned responsibility for addressing the current situation primarily to teachers, principals, and other administrators. The authors failed to recognize or discuss how courts in the previous decade had seriously limited school administrators' ability both to remove disruptive students promptly from the classroom and to support teachers effectively in the maintenance of discipline.

Recent accounts of inner-city public education in the United States have described in vivid detail the extent to which a large number of schools today lack the capacity to maintain even a semblance of order. John Devine, for example, comments as follows:

As I became acquainted with lower-tier schools, I began to think of this phenomenon as the "marshmallow effect" of the New York City high school system—wherever students pushed a rule, the system, like a marshmallow, gave way. Personal stereos, beepers, hats, bandannas, hoods, and jewelry are all officially forbidden but unofficially tolerated. If students were challenged, they usually cast scornful looks at the challenger and strolled on, continuing with exactly the same behavior . . . The frightening message for the newcomer is that the adults have handed over the school not to some democratic process (e.g., a student senate) but to the aimless, anarchic, and often unpredictable whims of the adolescent peer group. The peer group now essentially controls the inner-city school but is itself essentially out of control.[2]

Some liberal commentators have attempted to dismiss such disturbing descriptions of contemporary student disorder, arguing that public schools have always been sites for adolescent misbehavior.[3]

The contention that nothing is new about public school disorder or seriously amiss with public school discipline is wrong on at least two counts. First, though some degree of student and adolescent misbehavior should be assumed as culturally normative in our society, the pervasiveness and form this disorder takes has been historically variable. In 1956, 95 percent of teachers surveyed by the National Educational Association reported that their students were either "exceptionally well behaved" or "reasonably well behaved."[4]

In recent decades the situation has changed significantly. Today, with few limits on its expression, student disorder often has assumed a violent character. In 1997 more than one quarter of public school secondary students reported the presence of street gangs in their schools, 13 percent reported knowing someone who had brought a gun to school, and eight percent reported being threatened or injured with a weapon on school property in the past twelve months.[5] Teachers also have experienced high rates of physical threats and acts of violence: in 1993, 15 percent of teachers in central city public schools had been threatened with injury by students, and about six percent reported having been physically assaulted by students.[6] Violence has become a common presence in many public schools. John Devine again has captured well the character of this reality:

Yesterday I went to . . . school at lunchtime. I chatted with Mrs. S [our coordinator] and, at first, she said everything was going well. But as I hung around, several things emerged. The principal came to the lunchroom, looking very preoccupied, not smiling at anyone. Mrs. S then told me that there had been a slashing that morning—one student cut another's face with a knife; and this was on top of the knifing that took place last Friday . . . Then, before leaving, R, a Haitian teacher, told me of how another teacher had been punched in the face by a student that week (his nose is broken) and is swearing he will not return to the school. Finally, a paraprofessional was injured when attacked by some students whom she surprised when they were in a classroom by themselves, gambling. R said that in this school, things get covered up as fast as they happen; no one wants to talk about it.[7]

Some liberal commentators and defenders of public education prefer neither to acknowledge nor "to talk about" this situation. Yet the level of violence and disorder in public secondary schools in the past several decades has clearly climbed higher than at any earlier time in American history.

Second, subsequent to the 1969–1976 student rights contestation period, youth in public schools were for the first time afforded a set of legal protections from school discipline, and thus school personnel faced significant external legal regulation and constraints on their discretionary authority. Some legal commentators have attempted to dismiss the significance of this unprecedented challenge by arguing that courts have always been actively involved in regulating school discipline. Hartwig and Ruesch, for example, cited a nineteenth-century Wisconsin case that occurred as a result of a dispute between a parent and teacher over whether a sick child should be required to carry wood into a classroom after recess. The authors identified the case to argue that "it is not surprising that now, as in 1885, parents and advocates believe that the courts need to be involved in establishing benchmarks for appropriate school disciplinary practices."[8] That case, however, was quite unusual and anomalous; the dispute also centered not on student rights as such, but—like most early historical cases—on adjudicating between parental and school authority in regulating children's behavior.[9] Identifying obscure nineteenth-century cases simply obfuscates the extent to which schools today operate under a unique legal climate that has generated unprecedented constraints on school administrators' disciplinary discretion. As sociologist James Coleman and his colleagues have argued:

> The growth of student rights constitutes a fundamental change in the relation of the school to the student, which had been that of trustee for parental authority. This had been replaced by a relation in which the stu-

dent in a high school is regarded as having full civil rights (in particular the right of due process), undiminished by the student's status as a minor. The institution of due process rights for students, and the general reduction in the school's authority over the student, means that the public schools are not only constrained in the exercise of authority, they are also increasingly involved in litigation brought on behalf of the student.[10]

Liberal public school advocates who care about education in America must have the courage to put aside ideological predispositions and face the reality of this situation. The level of disorder in public schools was not an inevitable product of change in cultural mores or a simple reflection of demographic change. Institutional factors—specifically, changes in the legal environment—were empirically implicated in recent public school failures in this area.

Limits to Proposed Conservative School Reforms

When conservative commentators discuss the problem of discipline in public schools, they correctly bring attention to this critical area; too often, however, their focus and proposed remedies are narrow and miss the point. Specifically, they have suggested addressing the issue through three primary policy reforms: providing voucher subsidies to remove students altogether from public school authority; introducing curriculum with explicit moral content (sex education focused on the promotion of sexual abstinence, or the reintroduction of formal education in character and virtue); and increasing authoritative discipline through "get-tough" zero-tolerance policies.

Conservative school reformers have advocated voucher initiatives as an "institutional panacea" for failing public school performance.[11] Since John Chubb and Terry Moe's influential study, these efforts have been explicitly linked to the argument that public school inefficiencies and inadequacies have been produced by over-regulation of schools and their "subordination to public authority."[12] Chubb and Moe insightfully identified the extent to which the external institutional environment has been responsible for the structure and character of public schooling in this country, but they incorrectly emphasized the degree to which contemporary school environments were primarily based on political (that is, legislative and administrative)—as opposed to legal and judicial—institutional coercive regulation.[13]

Chubb and Moe have asserted that school "agendas are set by politicians, administrators, and the various democratic constituencies that hold the keys to political power," and that "bureaucracy arises naturally and inevitably out of these efforts at democratic control."[14] In many matters of contemporary public school practice, however, legal advocacy groups working through courts—and not political, bureaucratic, or democratic control more generally—have had the greatest influence in shaping public education. The implications related to this distinction are critical. While private schools that have not received public funding are generally exempt from the application of particular statutory and case law affecting school discipline and related educational matters, private schools that receive public funding in the future will likely no longer be largely immune from legal challenges and civil prosecution. Ironically, if conservative educational reformers are successful in getting widespread public funding for private elementary and secondary schools, they will most likely succeed in spreading the government regulation and legal constraints that they abhor to the private sector that they cherish.

Conservative efforts to improve the climate in public schools through the infusion of explicit moral messages in the curriculum have also, unfortunately, shared similar unsuccessful effects. Sociologist James Davison Hunter has provided the best description of these developments and their inherent limitations. He described contemporary approaches to character education and the extent to which they have embraced universality in moral orientations. Given this level of moral generality, however, the curriculum content has failed to engage individual students' lived experiences. Hunter has noted that "moral matters simply cannot be addressed without getting into the particularities of moral commitment and the traditions and communities that ground those commitments." Neo-classical approaches toward moral education advanced by William Bennett and others have tended to "champion the 'Tao' or the 'Judeo-Christian ethic.'" Hunter has suggested that while principles at this level of generality have been hard to oppose politically, "they champion an ethic that never existed in reality and now only exists as an ethical abstraction or political slogan."[15] The introduction of programs based on culturally neutral principles into the public schools often has taken the form of "virtue-of-the-month programs, word-of-the-week programs, citizen-of-the-month programs," rather than a "comprehensive approach to character education."[16] Regardless of their depth, these programs lack the capacity to address the current situation. We are pessimistic about the utility of these programs, not just because empirical evidence suggests that they have been ineffective (the evidence appears overwhelming on this assessment), or on grounds of their ineffectual universality, but more centrally because we believe that moral education occurs primarily through students' lived experiences (meaning, students' interaction with school authority). This, rather than the moral content of formal curriculum, is the primary mechanism involved in such a pedagogical developmental task.[17] Moreover, even if the explicit moral content of formal curriculum was able to affect youth attitudes and behaviors, it would be impossible to isolate students from the world of technological changes in communication that have made generalized youth culture with quite contrary messages widely available and virtually impossible to limit. The introduction of moral content directly into curriculum materials in opposition to the contemporary cultural experiences of many young people would be unlikely to improve student socialization significantly and would fail to address the core problem of redefining relationships between students and school authority.

Likewise, draconian "zero-tolerance" policies that conservatives have sometimes advocated and introduced in the last decade have also failed to produce positive changes in school climate. Implicit in these policies has been a strong undercurrent of blaming school personnel's leniency for contributing to this problem. The criminologist Jackson Toby, for example, astutely recognizing that courts have undermined possibilities for effective school discipline, has also argued for school-based "get tough" approaches to address teacher culpability: "In short, teachers' reluctance to show disapproval of misbehaving students may be partly the *cause* of the high level of disorder in some schools as well as its effects . . . the primary peace keepers in schools have to be the teachers."[18] If only teachers and administrators would try harder, the argument often has gone, the situation could be corrected.

Ironically, liberals have also blamed school personnel for problems related to enforcement of these zero-tolerance policies. For example, the Advancement Project, organized by a Washington-based legal advocacy group and the Civil Rights Project at Harvard University, has highlighted several examples of students inappropriately and excessively punished systematically for minor disciplinary infractions. These two organizations also have criticized the application of zero-tolerance policies in Miami-Dade County public schools, noting that "although schools may be subject to the same district-wide disciplinary code, the philosophy of the principal in many in-stances determines how these policies are actually applied."[19] Liberal cri-tiques thus have been clear in their condemnation of the application of ex-cessive sanctions, but less articulate and persuasive—they have rejected "discretionary provisions of the student code of conduct" as well as any at-tempt to impose formal limits on such discretion—in identifying desirable structuring of the disciplinary processes advocated.

Whether admonished for disciplinary leniency or urged to action by well-meaning conservative policy makers, school officials often have re-sorted to authoritarian "get tough" practices in an effort to restore order. Schools that adopt "zero-tolerance" policies have at times increased the presence of uniformed security guards or invited police directly onto cam-pus to handcuff and temporarily detain misbehaving students. These prac-tices have been more prone to produce negative than positive outcomes. Strict discipline, as we have demonstrated in Chapters 4 and 5, has been as-sociated with lowered student perceptions of fairness as well as less favor-able student behavioral outcomes if the legitimacy of school practices has been challenged.

Zero-tolerance practices have likely been generally ineffective or coun-terproductive because they have failed to address the central problem of a decline in *moral authority* and *legitimacy* of school discipline. In fact, these programs, like the pro-student court decisions, themselves challenge and undermine school personnel discretion in these matters. Get-tough poli-cies have coincided with recent changes limiting trial judge's sentencing discretion—institutional challenges to professional judgment and author-ity thus have come back to haunt even the judicial system. The externally imposed policies have communicated to students and the larger school community a very clear message: teachers and school administrators—or trial judges in the case of criminal sentencing—have been incapable of ap-plying appropriate and adequate sanctions when left to their own devices. Such a message cannot help but further undermine the moral authority and legitimacy of these actors.

Reducing Disorder at the School Level

School personnel can and should act to reduce violence and disorder. Re-sorting to authoritarian disciplinary practices at the school level—particu-larly in the current cultural climate—will almost certainly lead to a further erosion in the moral authority of schools and thus produce undesirable outcomes. Yet there are many concrete positive steps that schools can take to address the crisis. We will identify school-level measures that we believe could moderately improve the current situation; measures to address the general crisis of moral authority, however, must be taken at a larger societal level.

Guiding our recommendations about reforming school-level practices is an orientation closely informed by Durkheimian approaches to understanding youth socialization and the role of sanctions in maintaining social order. Specifically, our understanding of the role of schools in youth socialization includes not only an appreciation for the role of school discipline, but also extensions of Durkheim's work to both social control and "broken windows" theories advanced in criminology. The criminologist Travis Hirschi has suggested that insofar as the school "is able to command his attachment, involvement, and commitment, the adolescent is presumably able to move from childhood to adulthood with a minimum of delinquent acts."[20] We have hypothesized here and elsewhere that schools can enhance student "attachment, involvement and commitment"[21] by making educational experiences more intimate (smaller schools and classrooms), as well as more relevant (curriculum differentiation). In addition, Durkheim's insights have been extended to "broken windows" models of neighborhood policing and school discipline—approaches that have emphasized attention to enforcing violations of *minor* infractions that contribute to perceptions of social disorder.

At the school-level, educational researchers have long identified the importance of familiarity and personal contact of students and teachers through reducing school and classroom sizes. Smaller schools—or large schools restructured into smaller units or "schools within schools"—can help students get involved with educational activities and increase the ability of school personnel to monitor and address student misbehavior.[22] As Harvard educational researcher and sociologist Pedro Noguera noted, "anonymity increases the vulnerability of schools to outbreaks of violence because it limits the possibility that a responsible adult will know when a student is in distress and in need of help."[23] Sociologists and criminologists have long appreciated how inadequate social integration of individuals has been related to negative behavioral outcomes, and how greater intergenerational connections in communities has facilitated greater identification, monitoring, and adherence to social norms.[24] Recent research on school characteristics associated with student behavioral outcomes, as well as our modeling of student outcomes in Chapter 5, has suggested that reforms of this character—particularly those related to reduced school size—might result in small improvements in student outcomes.

Along with noting the advantages of decreasing the size of the basic secondary school organizational unit, Noguera and others have suggested the importance of applying lessons learned from the "broken windows" hypothesis to schools. Criminologists have argued that when communities were characterized by visible signs of disorder produced from the sum of minor infractions, perceptions of heightened disorder produced a greater willingness on the part of individuals to engage in further and more serious criminal behavior: "if a window in a building is broken *and is left unrepaired,* all the rest of the windows will soon be broken."[25] This argument has suggested the symbolic importance attached to addressing minor disciplinary infractions quickly. Noguera, whose credentials as a progressive educator included chairing the Berkeley Public School Board and leading numerous University of California student groups, has suggested that

> When schools respond rapidly, effectively and consistently to offenses that are often treated as minor infractions (such as cutting class, sexual harassment, vandalism, graffiti, and hateful and disrespectful language), it will be less likely that major offenses will occur. This is because responding to minor offenses sends the strong message that any attempt to undermine the values of a school-community will be addressed immediately.[26]

Such arguments are, of course, quite consistent with Durkheim's contention that "it is not punishment that gives discipline its authority; but it is punishment that prevents discipline from losing this authority, which infractions, if they went unpunished, would progressively erode."[27]

Bernard Harcourt in recent work on the topic has highlighted the degree to which such "order-maintenance" approaches have "privileged regulation and minimized sanction." As Harcourt has noted, "Rather than punish severely to deter, broken windows policing seeks to enforce, in part, order or rules of civilian conduct that are geared toward producing a more harmonious social environment with strong moral bonds."[28] Although he has appreciated the Durkheimian roots of "broken window" policing, his account has questioned the merits of both the approach and its application. Harcourt has questioned whether drops in crime rates associated with such policing may have been spuriously produced by other factors, such as economic prosperity in urban areas where the policies were adopted. In addition, Harcourt has embraced orientations suggested by the work of Pierre Bourdieu, Michel Foucault, and David Garland to question the initial social construction of the category of disorderly behavior and thus the entire theoretical foundation and rationale for these approaches.[29]

While Harcourt might be correct in raising theoretical questions about whether public urination, solicitation of or by prostitutes, and other such targets were socially constructed categories "arbitrarily" subjected to enforcement (whereas minor tax evasion, fraud, and police brutality were excluded from attention and prosecution).[30] Perceived distinctions between these arbitrarily drawn categories have real meanings to social actors exposed to either their environmental tolerance or suppression. Indeed, school rules about appropriate dress, appearance (like the "Beatle haircut"), and comportment are also by definition arbitrarily drawn distinctions. When school officials set rules to regulate student behaviors that are widely seen as disruptive of a proper learning environment—rules that focus on comportment rather than styles of appearance—then enforcement of these social norms can promote greater internalization of respect for the rulemakers' moral authority and reduce the likelihood that individuals will subsequently engage in more serious infractions. This is so regardless of whether the categories of "proper" behavior are (by definition) arbitrarily and socially constructed; authorities must carefully choose the minor infractions that are recognized as legitimate targets (cutting class or verbally threatening teachers, for example), and drop infractions in areas where no clear consensus exists (boys displaying facial hair or girls wearing pants). Administrators could encourage parents and other members of a larger school community to become actively involved in drawing these distinctions. Educational researchers have widely advocated that schools should clearly articulate and communicate a set of agreed-upon rules of conduct and sanction violation of those rules consistently, swiftly, and thoroughly.

Schools also can reduce disciplinary problems by designing curricula to engage student interest better and more directly. Disorder in classrooms (although not necessarily elsewhere in the school) has been associated with inappropriate and ineffective curriculum and instruction.[31] In particular, curriculum design should take into account the variety of motivations, inclinations, and interests that students bring with them into the classroom.

This advice, long ago articulated by progressive educators such as John Dewey, receives too little attention in contemporary reforms. Rather than making education more relevant, recent policies have promoted a deliberate narrowing of the curriculum to focus almost exclusively on traditional academic coursework. This reflects the reformers' long-term goal of preparing all students for four-year college training, but the reality is that the vast majority of students in many schools do not have much of a chance of achieving such aspirations.[32]

Educational reformers pushing the ideal of preparing all students for higher education have ignored the fact that most students today fail to complete even a single year of postsecondary education, and that many socially valuable and essential jobs in our society continue to be found in traditional skilled, manual, and clerical occupations. In the short run, recent educational reforms have also been justified on the basis of improving cognitive standardized test scores. Narrowing the curriculum to achieve such ends, however, has potentially aggravated existing disciplinary problems. The distortion of curricular design has reached the point where the work of students in one high school typing class can be to spend the class period typing up multiple choice standardized test questions.[33] It is likely that such narrowing of the curriculum has only led to greater student alienation, misbehavior, and disorder. In a recent National Research Council panel report organized by Robert Hauser and Jay Heubert, the authors have worried that "high stake testing" could indeed inadvertently and significantly increase student dropout rates.[34]

Realigning and differentiating the curriculum by supporting programs that have suffered a history of neglect might better address student needs and interests and thereby reduce the tendency for students to "drift" into misbehavior at school through lack of engagement with the instructional program.[35] Whether for budgetary or ideological reasons, many courses with such a focus (vocational education, music, the arts) have been decimated in public schools over the past two decades. Granted, these programs often have "failed the test" when their existence has been made dependent on students' demonstrated measurable improvement in English or math performance. Yet such classes have been able to motivate youth, integrate students into conventional school activities, and facilitate successful socialization.

Vocational education was introduced into high schools in the United States during the Progressive Era, with the explicit intention of increasing the relevance of curriculum to young people who were unlikely to finish secondary school and at high risk for adolescent delinquency. These programs were systematically dismantled once federal funding was curtailed after 1980. Vocational education programs were attacked for being expensive and ineffective in preparing young people for the labor market. Reports from blue-ribbon panels doubted "the value of traditional vocational education" and argued for "eliminating the vocational track" because twelve years of education was thought insufficient to prepare students for work.[36] Vocational education was criticized in particular for failing to improve high school graduates' earnings significantly. What the critics missed, however, was the original purpose of these programs. They did not aim at the narrow goal of improving labor market outcomes as German occupationally focused programs did, but were developed with the specific intention of positively affecting attitudes and dispositions of otherwise disaffected youth. Vocational education in the United States—which comparatively was always broader and less occupationally focused than elsewhere—has been more about socialization than occupational training. John Dewey argued in favor of occupational coursework a century ago, not because such training would prepare students for the labor market, but because it would provide students with *discipline* no longer learned in the household or neighborhood. "Out of the occupation, out of doing things that are to produce results . . . there is born a discipline of its own kind and type," Dewey maintained.[37] Our own findings and those of researchers in the past have suggested that a focused curriculum under proper conditions—either vocational or academic in character—can have positive effects on improving student outcomes.[38]

Restoring School Moral Authority at the Societal Level

Schools can only partially address the problem of student disorder by taking measures such as making schools more intimate in the scale of instructional organization, more responsive and proactive in their disciplinary regulation, and more relevant through curricular differentiation. If one appreciates the extent to which the problem has not simply been lax discipline, but school discipline that has suffered from diminished moral authority and legitimacy, remedies must be sought more fundamentally in the organizational environment of schools. Specifically, the damage that institutionally sponsored legal challenges and court decisions have wreaked on the moral authority of schools must be redressed.

Fundamental judicial review by courts and a rethinking of the appropriateness of adversarial legal challenge by student advocacy lawyers are necessary and warranted in this area. We categorically reject conservative assertions that court intervention in public schools uniformly produced excessive bureaucracy, inefficiency, and detrimental outcomes; in the specific area of regulating school discipline, however, court intervention has indeed been particularly unsettling and damaging. Again, the problem is not simply that school personnel reduced the level of discipline in the face of legal uncertainty. It is that the legitimacy and moral authority of school discipline has been seriously undermined. Expansion of individual legal rights in the area of school discipline, unlike in other areas of educational or employment law more broadly, has not simply led to expanded legalization within institutions or reduced inequitable organizational practices; it has undermined schools' legitimacy and capacity for carrying out the socialization of adolescents. Legal advocates interested in advancing student interests should resist what David Kirp, immediately following *Goss v. Lopez,* termed the "allure of due process"—expanding such rights in schools through aggressive legal challenges that proved destructive of school moral authority yet failed to ameliorate racial and socioeconomic disparities in disciplinary outcomes.[39] Just as conservatives have been wrong to disparage all legal challenges to public school practices, liberals have been equally mistaken when they equate the expansion of individual rights unreflexively with social progress.

Conservatives have argued that adversarial legalism in general has been detrimental to public education. We believe that using our research to support such broadly framed political claims is illegitimate. An appreciation for the limitations of educational law reform's effectiveness and a careful consideration of unintended consequences in adversarial challenges to public schools is indeed warranted, not simply by our results, but also from the historic record of legal challenges in this area. Legal challenges to public school financing, for example, when successful, often increased equity across public schools within a state, but simultaneously engendered political dynamics that threatened to lower overall public school expenditures.[40] Litigation supporting racial school integration significantly contributed to ending *de jure* racial school segregation, but also produced white flight from public schools, decreased support for public education, and left *de facto* racial school segregation in its place.[41] Advocacy for disabled and handicapped students brought greater access for individuals, but simultaneously contributed to distorting educational budgets, along with labeling and warehousing of disproportionate numbers of minority students in special education programs with diminished educational horizons.[42] To acknowledge that legal challenges of schools have been ineffective or counterproductive is, again, not meant to suggest that public interest lawyers should refrain from challenging public school practices. Rather, appreciating the complexity of how law affects school organization should lead advocacy lawyers to consider their targets carefully and strategically. In some areas of litigation—for example, racial integration and school finance equity cases—the moral and legal principles involved are perhaps sufficiently great that such cases should be pursued regardless of their ultimate organizational effects.

Similarly, it is inappropriate to interpret our findings to suggest that since federally sponsored OEO litigation concerning school discipline produced detrimental changes in school practices, federal involvement in public education itself should be limited. It was rather the peculiar institutional form of federal involvement that created many of the problems identified. In democratic societies where public education is more centrally administered, national educational ministries have been able to introduce reforms (such as expanding legalization of school disciplinary practices) bureaucratically and internally within the system. Since the U.S. federal government has lacked this option, reformers have resorted to influencing local school practices indirectly through legal challenges. It is quite likely, however, that bureaucratically introduced reforms imposed hierarchically within an educational system would produce less resistance, less organizational uncertainty, and fewer detrimental effects on individual perceptions of moral authority of disciplinary practices than was the case when these reforms were forced on schools through adversarial litigation. Indeed, absent externally imposed challenges to school moral authority, internal adoption of due process procedures could well have led to greater legitimacy of school disciplinary practices. It is the adversarial and ambiguous external legal climate, not the internal organizational features of due process practices, that has undermined school moral authority.

Given the unique institutional governance structure in the United States, it is worth considering, in the context of the current crisis of school moral authority, a range of hypothetical alternatives that could emerge from potential judicial case review. One possible judicial action would be the adoption of new case law that would *eliminate all due process rights* previously extended to youth in public schools in the 1960s and 1970s. One could read the evidence presented in this book as suggesting the overall failure of the experiment of extending to children in public schools legal rights previously afforded only to adults. This reading would be unwarranted and likely detrimental and counterproductive as well. The expansion of legal protections for students in certain instances was likely beneficial and desirable even if it also partially threatened the moral authority of school personnel. Specifically, we believe that long-term exclusion of students from public schooling is a serious matter, and individuals should be afforded full due process consideration in these instances. Application of due process rights in these cases does not necessarily undermine a school's moral authority, because the extension of legal guarantees and due process can symbolically serve to communicate society's belief in the importance of access to schooling: in sociological terms, formal school hearings in these matters could be understood in part as *rituals* that could be explicitly designed to communicate to the community that public school participation is *sacred* and will not be corrupted nor profaned by egregious student misbehavior.

Furthermore, in a democratic society students' rights to political expression should be afforded special due process protections. If we are to encourage the development of a future generation of active democratic citizens, public schools as representatives of larger state authority should be limited in their efforts to control explicit political expression. It is worth reminding readers that the majority of early appellate court cases dealing with school discipline involved just these matters (student protest and free expression). Seminal Supreme Court cases also concerned these issues: in the *Tinker* case students wore armbands to protest the Vietnam War; in *Goss v. Lopez* students protested the absence of African-American school curriculum. Since 1976 only eight percent of appellate cases have dealt with issues of politics and free expression.

Lastly, eliminating all due process guarantees that students gained in the 1960s and 1970s would likely be counterproductive. Once rights are extended to individuals, they are understood as entitlements. Students as well as citizens more generally would not respond well to a significant loss of legal rights in this area. Rather than increase the moral authority of schools, such changes would be termed draconian and might further undermine the legitimacy of school personnel and societal institutions more generally. Once individuals have widely embraced perceptions of legal entitlements, assumptions of what is considered acceptable shift in a manner that prohibits returning to an original state.

We believe a more reasonable and productive judicial alternative presents itself in *redefining and limiting the scope of previously granted student due process rights.* These rights should not apply in situations when discipline simply involves minor sanctioning of students for general misbehavior, violence, and drugs. Rather than being liberally extended to minors in public schools under overly broad judicial readings of the Fourteenth Amendment, due process rights should be limited to cases when students face long-term exclusion from schools, or when student infractions have an explicit political character (that is, in cases when student behavior deserves special protections related to First Amendment rights of freedom of speech, press, and peaceful assembly).

For rethinking the issues involved in due process and to clarify our recommendations for judicial review of these matters, let us revisit the *Goss v. Lopez* decision. Beginning in the 1960s, public school students facing long-term suspension or expulsion had begun to enjoy due process protections as a result of several lower court decisions.[43] Although the Supreme Court in a 1967 decision had ruled to extend due process protections under the Fourteenth Amendment to youth in juvenile courts,[44] prior to *Goss v. Lopez* (1975) the Court had not ruled on how or whether due process should be applied in public schools. *Goss v. Lopez* extended "rudimentary" due process guarantees—such as notification of charges, a description of the evidentiary basis of accusations, and an informal hearing—to students facing even short-term suspensions (less than ten days). "More formal procedures" respecting constitutional due process rights were required for students facing longer-term suspensions or expulsions.

Several points Justice Powell made in his dissent are worth reconsidering. First, he argued that extending due process rights to youth in public school settings

> ignores the experience of mankind, as well as the long history of our law, recognizing that there *are* differences which must be accommodated in determining the rights and duties of children as compared with those of adults . . . Until today and except in the special context of the First Amendment issue in *Tinker,* the educational rights of children and teenagers in the elementary and secondary schools have not been analogous to the rights of adults or to those accorded college students.

Second, Powell pointed out the importance of considering not only the rights of student facing discipline, but also the rights of other students to an environment conducive to learning.

The State's interest, broadly put, is in the proper functioning of its public school system for the benefit of *all* pupils and the public generally. Few rulings would interfere more extensively in the daily functioning of schools than subjecting routine discipline to formalities and judicial oversight of due process. Suspensions are one of the traditional means—ranging from keeping a student after class to permanent expulsion—used to maintain discipline in the schools. It is common knowledge that maintaining order and reasonable decorum in school buildings and classrooms is a major educational problem, and one which has increased significantly in magnitude in recent years. Often the teacher, in protecting the rights of other children to an education (if not his or their safety), is compelled to rely on the power to suspend.

Lastly, Powell worried about the effects of extending due process rights to students facing even minor disciplinary sanctions such as short-term suspensions. He closed his dissent with the warning:

Some half dozen years ago, the Court extended First Amendment rights under limited circumstances to public school pupils. Mr. Justice Black, dissenting, viewed the decision as ushering in "an entirely new era in which the power to control pupils by the elected 'officials of state supported public schools' . . . is in ultimate effect transferred to the Supreme Court." *Tinker v. Des Moines School Dist.*, 393 U.S. 503, 515 (1969). There were some who thought Mr. Justice Black was unduly concerned. But his prophecy is now being fulfilled. In the few years since *Tinker* there have been literally hundreds of cases by schoolchildren alleging violation of their constitutional rights. This flood of litigation, between pupils and school authorities, was triggered by a narrowly written First Amendment opinion which I could well have joined on its facts. One can only speculate as to the extent to which public education will be disrupted by giving every schoolchild the power to contest *in court* any decision made by his teacher which arguably infringes the state-conferred right to education.[45]

From the perspective of a quarter century of history, we can see that Powell's apprehensions were quite well founded. Following the *Goss v. Lopez* decision, advocacy organizations worked to broaden and extend these protections to mundane and minor school disciplinary practices such as lowering students' grades, barring them from participation in extra-curricular activities, and excluding them from transportation on school buses.

We believe that it is difficult (if not impossible) for schools to socialize youth successfully when student due process protections have been extended so broadly. Such diffusion of these guarantees is difficult to reconcile with the Supreme Court's *Ingraham* decision, two years after the *Goss v. Lopez* decision, which supported the use of corporal punishment in schools:

> imposing a constitutional requirement of prior notice and a hearing would significantly burden the use of corporal punishment as a disciplinary measure and would entail a significant intrusion into an area of primary educational responsibility, whereas the risk of error that might result in violation of a student's substantive rights could only be regarded as minimal, in view of the low incidence of abuse of corporal punishment by school authorities, the openness of the public schools, and the common law safeguards.[46]

The logic of Supreme Court's decision in the *Ingraham* corporal punishment case suggests that student due process guarantees should be more limited and invoked only in cases when students face long-term suspension, permanent expulsion from schools, or when student infractions have an explicit political character related to First Amendment rights.[47] The legal positions that schools face can be altered through citizens encouraging legislative, administrative, and judicial action. Specifically, Attorney Generals' offices could enter existing cases as friends of the court, arguing in favor of expanded school discretionary authority. In addition, legislators could pass new laws that might also stimulate judicial review of earlier case law decisions.

West Virginia, for example, recently passed the Productive and Safe Schools Act to address problems related to school discipline. This law, although encouraged and welcomed by the American Federation of Teachers, has flaws that limit its capacity to address the situation fundamentally. One of its limitations is that it imposes "zero tolerance" disciplinary procedures with mandatory severe sanctions imposed on student misbehavior involving guns, violence, and drugs. Such policies are misguided because they assume that student disorder can be successfully addressed simply by requiring that schools impose stricter sanctions. Our research suggests, however, that stricter discipline without concurrent increase in legitimacy can be counterproductive. The West Virginia legislation does not address the core problem of reduced moral authority of school personnel: instead, it grants local school officials even less discretionary authority than they had before the legislation. The fact that administrators must respond to certain infractions without being able to consider particular details and extenuating circumstances produces discipline that can appear quite authoritarian, arbitrary, and unfair. Consider the hypothetical case of a model student who confesses possessing drugs that are widespread but unacknowledged on a high school campus; local administrators would feel compelled to expel the student. Though appeals to administrative review are technically possible under many zero-tolerance policies, administrative reversals of decisions are rare, as the programs are explicitly designed to substitute authoritarian consistency for administrative and teacher discretion. Moral authority in school discipline will not be restored by reducing the disciplinary discretion of school personnel even further.

The American Federation of Teachers also worked on the passage of the Texas Safe Schools Act in 1995. This legislation is better designed to reduce school disorder, but has features that resemble the West Virginia legislation. For example, it requires local districts to adopt student codes of conduct with clear sanctions attached to infractions, and to provide alternative education programs for students removed from regular classrooms. More productively, however, the legislation also grants teachers the explicit legal authority to send students to the principal's office and to remove chronically disruptive students from class. Unfortunately, a survey of Texas teachers the year following the passage of the legislation found that only 34 percent of teachers reported implementation of the act in their school district.[48]

Challenges to Reestablishing Moral Authority in Public Schools

In advocating the removal of due process legal protections from students facing school discipline that does not involve long-term exclusion or violation of First Amendment rights, we have a moral and ethical responsibility to consider negative outcomes potentially associated with this remedy. Would these proposed changes in the relationship between law and education lead to an increase in arbitrary and authoritarian school discipline? Given the history of racial inequality in our society, would such changes produce an increase in racially discriminatory discipline?

Although policy makers must be attentive to these issues and follow any reforms with careful monitoring of subsequent changes in school practices, we are confident that these negative outcomes would fail to materialize in a manner that liberal legal advocates might suggest. Reducing due process guarantees as we have recommended would not result in a dramatic increase in arbitrary, authoritarian, or racist disciplinary practices.

To begin with, the changes we advocate are primarily of symbolic significance, since public school students have quite limited "rudimentary" rights in these areas in the first place. Contrary to the perception of many students, teachers, and school administrators, due process guarantees provide little formal protection from inappropriately exercised discipline in cases that do not involve long-term suspension or expulsion. Principals (whether fairly or unjustly) who seek to suspend a student for less than ten days have simply been required to have informal meetings with the student to identify the cause and basis of the suspension, and to hear the student's side of the story. Such rights offer no real protection from administrators who act in arbitrary, authoritarian, or discriminatory fashion. The fact of the matter is that students have not actually been granted many formal legal rights in this area; what students have gained, however, is the widespread *perception*—shared by teachers, administrators, and parents—that school discipline even for minor sanctions has been subjected to judicial, not simply administrative, oversight. The perception that a student can potentially invoke constitutional due process rights virtually anywhere and at any time has led not necessarily to greater protection for individuals, but to the legalization of school practices, the intimidation of school personnel faced with an ambiguous legal terrain, and an undermining of the school's moral authority.[49]

Second, concern that inappropriate school discipline will expand is unfounded, because school practices are strongly shaped by other institutions surrounding schools. Institutional practices paralleling or exceeding the limited "rudimentary" due process requirements demanded by *Goss v. Lopez* already existed in many public schools prior to the court decision. As Justice White noted in the *Goss v. Lopez* decision: "we have imposed requirements which are, if anything, less than a fair-minded school principal would impose upon himself in order to avoid unfair suspensions."[50] Neo-institutional researchers who have examined the diffusion of organizational practices have argued that coercive government regulation is only one limited mechanism that shapes institutional behaviors. Effective and appropriate behaviors have also been structured, identified, and defined by other institutions in school environments.[51] In particular, we would remind legal advocates that schools are institutions inhabited by professionals. Teachers and administrators are subject to significant professional normative pressures that encourage them to embrace—or "impose upon" themselves—a reasonable set of school disciplinary practices.

Public school teachers and administrators have been trained and socialized in colleges and graduate schools of education to treat students equally, fairly, and reasonably. States have come to require all public school teachers to possess not only a college education, but an additional year of professional training. Today, over 99 percent of public school teachers are college graduates, and 47 percent have received a further degree at the Master's level or higher; 98 percent of public school principals have attained the equivalent of at least a Master's degree.[52] The vast majority of educators also belong to professional associations, such as the National Educational Association, which encourage normative compliance and define "reasonable" organizational practices. State and local school districts also require educators to undergo extensive and continuous in-service training that seeks to produce appropriate educational practices and behaviors.

Other institutional pressures in the organizational environment of schools—such as democratically elected school boards, state and local educational regulatory agencies, as well as voluntary associations (such as local Parent Teacher Associations and various other community organizations interested in public education)—would also work to ensure that school personnel avoided arbitrary, authoritarian, or discriminatory disciplinary practices. In fact, practices would likely be less authoritarian if administrators did not need to rely on zero-tolerance policies. As it is, schools already generally embrace institutional cultures characterized by legalization. As the sociologist John Meyer has noted: "even though the actors in the system are not routinely conscious of it, the whole institutionalized structure itself is embedded in legal rules."[53] Even without externally imposed constitutional due process rights, one would expect a public school to maintain internal practices quite similar to those now mandated by the court. These internally adopted practices would work to produce greater legitimacy and moral authority in discipline, unlike external legal challenges, which have produced the opposite effect. In the face of these myriad social pressures, only the most arrogant and ideologically motivated legal advocate would suggest that reducing due process guarantees in the limited way we have suggested would inevitably produce widespread irresponsible disciplinary abuses.

Given the particular concern that we have for reducing racial inequality in our society, it is also appropriate to consider racial dimensions of the question in greater detail. Our research confirms that African-Americans are subjected to school discipline at higher rates than white students. We have not attempted to examine the extent to which these disciplinary sanctions were related to social background factors (such as differences in class or family structure) or to social environment (such as concentration of poor African-American students in troubled schools that serve as catalysts for youthful misbehavior). Differences in social background and environmental influences probably account for a great deal of existing racial disparities in school discipline, as these patterns emerge also in school districts where superintendents, school board members, principals, and teachers are generally nonwhite.

It is worth emphasizing that in spite of the political, racially charged rhetoric around these issues, we found very few appellate court cases that referenced the race of the student or alleged racial discrimination in the application of school discipline. Our analysis suggests that African-American youth are by and large not the population benefiting from the expansion of due process rights to students in public schools: many of these students and their families—unlike middle-class whites—are not in a position to sustain serious legal challenges or pursue legal remedies related to the application of school disciplinary procedures without significant institutional support. Rather, African-American and other nonwhite students have suffered disparate impact associated with both the collapse of moral authority and the related ineffectiveness of school discipline. Our research in Chapter 5 identifies, for example, that black and white differences in student test scores were significantly related to differences in student perceptions of disciplinary climates. More African-American students were in schools where discipline was perceived as unfair and either too lenient or too authoritative. In addition, while the media often presents reports of racially disparate disciplinary rates in the context of an assumption of racially integrated schooling, such assumptions are clearly and increasingly erroneous today. In many areas of the country, African-American and other nonwhite students are concentrated in *de facto* racially segregated high-poverty settings. Approximately 60 percent of African-American public school students in New York, Illinois, and Michigan attend schools with between 90 and 100 percent nonwhite student enrollments . The majority of students in 87 percent of these schools live in impoverished families. African-American students on average attend schools with more than twice the percentage of their fellow students in conditions of poverty than do white students.[54] Students in settings of concentrated poverty are likely to be the most sensitive to changes in school disciplinary climates. Ethnographic descriptions such as John Devine's account above, attest to the degree that behavioral problems are endemic in these school settings. It is politically and morally irresponsible to discuss racially disparate disciplinary rates without also acknowledging how the collapse of school discipline has taken its highest toll on nonwhite students segregated in poor urban neighborhoods.

The extent to which the extension of rudimentary due process guarantees has done little to address the potential for racist or arbitrary school discipline is suggested in considering the recent controversy involving civil rights leader Jesse Jackson's protest of student discipline in Decatur, Illinois. Six students involved in a fight at a school football game faced long-term exclusion from school under a zero-tolerance policy. Jackson and others contended that school enforcement of the zero-tolerance policy violated student due process rights and was authoritarian, excessive, and racist. Jackson noted that the school's discipline involved "racial profiling," that 83 percent of expelled Decatur students were African-American (compared to only 42 percent of the student body), and that nationwide "African Americans and other minorities are disproportionately impacted by school disciplinary rules."[55] Jackson protested the exclusions and supported the students' challenge of the school's action in courts. We are in no position to assess the details discussed in the matter (whether the students were largely truant "third year freshmen" involved in a "gang-related melee" or just ordinary kids unfairly punished for involvement in a "simple fistfight").[56] But even in this situation, when the students had the right under the *Goss v. Lopez* decision to "more formal" and extensive due process procedures for expulsion than would be the case for short-term suspensions, the courts were not sympathetic. U.S. District Judge Michael McCuskey found that the school district "did not act illegally, improperly or deny the students their constitutional rights."[57] While existing student due process rights thus have often done little to protect African-American students from discipline that some might characterize as racist and unfair, it would be wrong to assume that they have had no effect at all. In the case of the Decatur suit, for example, the school district assumed legal costs estimated at $100,000.[58]

More significant in our opinion is the extent to which challenges to school discipline have encouraged the sense of widespread legal ambiguity and the impression that due process rights were generally available to students. In the Decatur case we are in agreement with Jesse Jackson's opposition to counterproductive zero-tolerance policies and support the right of students to raise legal due process issues when facing long-term public school exclusion, but we are also quite cognizant of the damage to school moral authority that occurs in such situations. Kenneth Arndt, the Superintendent of Decatur Public School, reported: "In some of our elementary schools, we now have students, warned about minor infractions, telling us, 'I'm going to call Jesse Jackson.'"[59] Given the social (and financial) costs associated with such legal challenges to school discipline, we believe legal challenges should be reserved and judicially tolerated only for situations involving long-term exclusion or suppression of student First Amendment rights.

Pragmatism and Public Policy

The design of effective public policy in this area requires an appreciation of how individual perceptions and collective understandings of situations are formed. Narrow readings of case law have failed to recognize how decisions are socially understood—that is, how legal ambiguity interacts with "bounded rationality" of public school personnel to create particular institutional outcomes. Teachers and administrators' implementation of school practices related to due process is informed by their uncertain knowledge of case law; their contradictory, convoluted, and confused prior experiences of due process applications; and the unpredictability of reactions of students, parents, and colleagues. In such situations, attempts to lecture school personnel on procedural details related to due process legal requirements can only have limited positive effects if done well; otherwise, they are likely to do more harm than good. School personnel's lived experience of the way legal experts present the minutiae and ambiguity present in court rulings would be likely—regardless of the intent—simply to heighten overall apprehension and diminish individual willingness to act decisively.

Appreciation for how individual perceptions and bounded rationality work should be explicitly considered in attempting to alter public opinion about current due process rights afforded to students. Though students today enjoy only quite rudimentary due process rights (when the case does not involve long-term exclusion), and courts since the mid-1970s have become generally unsympathetic to students, the courts' application of due process rights in cases where students experience minor disciplinary sanction has created the general impression that legal challenges might occur in virtually any disciplinary situation, including even when teachers are simply attempting physically to break up a student fight. Legislation and case law review are required to remove the legal ambiguity that was created by extending rudimentary due process protections for minor discipline that does not involve long-term student expulsion or First Amendment rights. Because in reality students enjoy only very limited rights in these areas, the changes in formal law would be largely symbolic. The changes would, however, signal and communicate faith in public educators' discretionary judgment and a commitment to restoring their moral authority. Most likely, school disciplinary procedures would remain remarkably the same. The important point is that individuals' perceptions of these disciplinary practices would be altered; as it is, students in settings with more limited due process rights (such as private schools or public schools in states with pro-school court climates) often perceive school discipline as actually being fairer and more legitimate.

We believe that at a pedagogical level it is possible to incorporate constructively two aspects of discipline into school practices: Emile Durkheim's notion of moral authority, and John Dewey's appreciation for discipline's connection to relevant curriculum design. Both Dewey and Durkheim appreciated the extent to which school practices must be designed to guide yet conform with the lived experience and consciousness of students. While pedagogically such reforms are possible, political and practical institutional obstacles appear as significant constraints. Politically, it is difficult to make changes that affect individual perceptions of legal entitlements when profound skepticism exists as to the intention of political actors. If conservatives want their voices heard and respected on these issues, they will likely first have to demonstrate political good faith by curtailing outspoken advocacy of schemes designed to dismantle the American public education system. Needless to say, institutional obstacles to altering case law in the manner that we have suggested are also quite formidable.

We remain hopeful, however, because the alternative of doing nothing to correct this situation—that is, simply accepting the dysfunctional character of public schools as an unavoidable price paid for the general expansion of individual rights—is clearly unacceptable and untenable in the long run. In the United States 90 percent of youth attend public schools; to ensure the development of future generations of productive citizenry, we will ultimately be forced collectively to attend to conflicts between the logic of expanding legalization in our society and the necessity of school and family's ability to socialize youth. Effective school discipline does not require zero-tolerance; it requires moral authority. School discipline, Durkheim commented a century ago, "has a moral character and moral value only if the penalty is regarded as just by those subjected to it, which implies that the authority which punishes is itself recognized as legitimate."[60] This today is what has been brought into question.

Appendix: Tables

Table 2.A Means on all variables identified through content-coding state and federal appellate court cases, 1960–1992

	Public school cases only	All cases
Direction of court decision		
Pro-school	0.652	0.726
Time period		
1960–1968 (pre-contestation)	0.058	0.060
1969–1975 (contestation)	0.391	0.376
1976–1992 (post-contestation)	0.550	0.564
Case origin		
Mid-Atlantic region	0.154	0.166
Midwest region	0.304	0.292
Western region	0.105	0.096
Southern region	0.241	0.227
Mountain region	0.047	0.047
Northeast region	0.149	0.172
Court level		
State lower courts	0.337	0.342
State high courts	0.105	0.108
Federal appellate courts	0.194	0.200
Federal district courts	0.350	0.337
Federal Supreme Court	0.014	0.012
School and student characteristics		
Elementary level	0.039	0.039
Student nonwhite	0.092	0.096
Student handicapped	0.043	0.044
Form of school discipline		
Suspension	0.517	0.507
Expulsion	0.266	0.294
Corporal punishment	0.069	0.066
School transfer	0.029	0.027
Other	0.252	0.238

Table 2.A (continued)

	Public school cases only	All cases
Type of student misbehavior		
Drugs	0.130	0.124
Alcohol	0.050	0.049
Violence/weapons	0.159	0.149
Political protest	0.134	0.137
Free expression	0.158	0.145
General misbehavior	0.392	0.419

Public school cases only, $N = 1,081$; all cases, $N = 1,204$.

Table 2.B Description of variable coding of school disciplinary court cases

	Direction of court decision
Pro-school	Dummy variable (coded 1) for court cases favoring schools.
Time period	
1960–1968	Dummy variable (coded 1) for court cases occurring in the precontestation period of 1960–1968.
1969–1975	Dummy variable (coded 1) for court cases occurring in the contestation period of 1969–1975.
1976–1992	Dummy variable (coded 1) for court cases occurring in the postcontestation period of 1976–1992.
Case location	
Western region	Dummy variable (coded 1) for court cases in western region. Includes circuit 9.
Midwest region	Dummy variable (coded 1) for court cases in midwest region. Includes circuits 6, 7, 8.
Mid-Atlantic region	Dummy variable (coded 1) for court cases in mid-Atlantic region. Includes circuits 3, 4, and Washington, D.C.
Southern region	Dummy variable (coded 1) for court cases in southern region. Includes circuits 5, 11.
Mountain region	Dummy variable (coded 1) for court cases in mountain region. Includes circuit 10.
Northeast region	Dummy variable (coded 1) for court cases in western region. Includes circuits 1, 2.
Court level	
State lower court	Dummy variable (coded 1) for court cases tried in lower state-level court.
State high court	Dummy variable (coded 1) for court cases tried in higher state-level court.
Federal district court	Dummy variable (coded 1) for court cases tried in federal district courts.
Federal appellate court	Dummy variable (coded 1) for court cases tried in federal district or appellate court.
Federal Supreme Court	Dummy variable (coded 1) for court cases tried in federal Supreme Court.
School and student characteristics	
Private	Dummy variable (coded 1) for court cases involving private school.
Elementary/early childhood	Educational level of the school/student involved in suit. Dummy variable (coded 1) for court cases involving elementary or early childhood schools.

Table 2.B (continued)

	Direction of court decision
Student nonwhite	Identification of nonwhite race of student(s) involved in litigation. Dummy variable (coded 1) if African-American, Hispanic, Asian, Native American, or multiple nonwhite racial classification mentioned.
Student handicapped	Dummy variable (coded 1) for identification of handicapped/disability status of student.
Disciplinary issue of litigation	
Suspension	Dummy variable (coded 1) if case substantively involves student suspension.
Expulsion	Dummy variable (coded 1) if case substantively involves student expulsion.
Corporal punishment	Dummy variable (coded 1) if case substantively involves corporal punishment.
School transfer	Dummy variable (coded 1) if case substantively involves school transfer.
Other discipline	Dummy variable (coded 1) if case substantively involves other school discipline.
Type of student misbehavior	
Drugs	Dummy variable (coded 1) for court cases involving student distribution, use, or possession of drugs.
Alcohol	Dummy variable (coded 1) for court cases involving student distribution, use, or possession of alcohol.
Violence/weapons	Dummy variable (coded 1) for court cases involving student violence or use/possession of weapon.
Political protest	Dummy variable (coded 1) for student participation in activity explicitly involving political protest.
Free expression	Dummy variable (coded 1) for student activity related to freedom of expression.
General misbehavior	Dummy variable (coded 1) for all other general types of student misbehavior.

Note: Cases were identified via a Lexis-Nexis search string: "student w/p discip! or expulsion or expel! or suspen! or punish." A case is considered relevant if it involves a conflict between a school and a student over the school's attempt to discipline the student or the school's attempt to otherwise maintain school order and safety. Cases involving conflicts between schools and teachers (e.g., teacher dismissal cases), schools and non-student outsiders (e.g., drug and weapon free zone cases), and students' rights cases focused exclusively on free speech issues (i.e., without being also combined with the school's use of suspension, expulsion, corporal punishment, transfer, etc.) are excluded. Cases involving the use of state agents (such as the police), who are acting on behalf of the school in the vicinity of school grounds to deal with students, are included.

Table 3.A Logistic regression of factors affecting pro-student school discipline court case decisions, 1960–1992 (public schools only)

	Model 1	Model 2
Intercept	−0.626***	−0.485*
	(0.236)	(0.248)
Time period		
1960–1968 (pre-contestation)	0.041	0.016
	(0.287)	(0.303)
1969–1975 (contestation)	0.330**	0.251
	(0.145)	(0.161)
Case origin		
Mid-Atlantic region	−0.612**	−0.606**
	(0.239)	(0.242)
Midwest region	−0.483**	−0.569***
	(0.211)	(0.215)
Western region	−0.235	−0.276
	(0.268)	(0.273)
Southern region	−0.511**	−0.559**
	(0.216)	(0.220)
Mountain region	−1.154***	−1.299***
	(0.392)	(0.401)
Court level		
State lower courts	0.106	0.146
	(0.172)	(0.176)
State high courts	0.401*	0.443*
	(0.233)	(0.241)
Federal appellate courts	0.062	0.046
	(0.187)	(0.189)
Federal Supreme Court	−0.415	−0.328
	(0.586)	(0.594)
School and student characteristics		
Elementary level	0.540	0.447
	(0.346)	(0.350)
Student nonwhite	0.611***	0.722***
	(0.222)	(0.228)
Student handicapped		0.233
		(0.324)

Table 3.A (continued)

	Model 1	Model 2
Form of school discipline		
Suspension	0.091	0.034
	(0.144)	(0.150)
Expulsion	0.300**	0.365**
	(0.150)	(0.154)
Corporal punishment	−0.200	−0.213
	(0.292)	(0.297)
School transfer	0.455	0.393
	(0.381)	(0.386)
Type of student misbehavior		
Drugs		−0.500**
		(0.224)
Alcohol		0.210
		(0.305)
Violence/weapons		−0.310
		(0.195)
Political protest		−0.345
		(0.237)
Free expression		0.376*
		(0.218)

*$p < .10$. **$p < .05$. ***$p < .01$. $N = 1,081$. See Tables 2.A and 2.B for description of data.

Table 3.B Logistic regression of interacting factors affecting pro-student school discipline court case decisions, 1960–1992 (public schools only)

	Model 1	Model 2	Model 3
Intercept	−0.489**	−0.018	−0.465*
	(0.248)	(0.276)	(0.245)
Time period			
1960–1968 (pre-contestation)	0.215	−0.005	0.000
	(0.320)	(0.303)	(0.304)
1969–1975 (contestation)	0.236	0.265	0.239
	(0.162)	(0.162)	(0.162)
Interactions			
Free expression*1960–1968	−1.431^{a}		
	(0.900)		
Politics*federal courts		1.334*	
		(0.681)	
Race*expulsion*federal high court			2.340**
			(1.096)
Case origin			
Mid-Atlantic region	−0.616**	−0.566**	−0.602**
	(0.242)	(0.237)	(0.238)
Midwest region	−0.584***	−0.537***	−0.550***
	(0.215)	(0.208)	(0.208)
Western region	−0.260	−0.232	−0.264
	(0.274)	(0.269)	(0.269)
Southern region	−0.557**	−0.545**	−0.543**
	(0.221)	(0.216)	(0.215)
Mountain region	−1.315***	−1.289***	−1.288***
	(0.402)	(0.398)	(0.402)
Court level[b]			
State lower courts	0.141	−0.288	0.135
	(0.177)	(0.240)	(0.176)
State high courts	0.421*		0.446*
	(0.242)		(0.241)
Federal appellate courts	0.036		
	(0.189)		
Federal Supreme Court	−0.324		
	(0.594)		
Federal courts (all)		−0.509**	
		(0.236)	
Federal high courts			-0.062
			(0.188)

Table 3.B (continued)

	Model 1	Model 2	Model 3
School and student characteristics			
Elementary level	0.515	0.442	0.417
	(0.352)	(0.350)	(0.354)
Student nonwhite	0.709***	0.730***	0.560**
	(0.229)	(0.228)	(0.239)
Student handicapped	0.241	0.237	0.260
	(0.325)	(0.324)	(0.323)
Form of school discipline			
Suspension	0.036	−0.005	0.036
	(0.150)	(0.151)	(0.150)
Expulsion	0.382**	0.355**	0.296*
	(0.154)	(0.154)	(0.156)
Corporal punishment	−0.222	−0.217	−0.182
	(0.298)	(0.297)	(0.297)
School transfer	0.391	0.417	0.366
	(0.386)	(0.385)	(0.391)
Type of student misbehavior			
Drugs	−0.493**	−0.516**	−0.487**
	(0.224)	(0.224)	(0.224)
Alcohol	0.223	0.196	0.197
	(0.305)	(0.304)	(0.304)
Violence/weapons	−0.302	−0.315	−0.293
	(0.195)	(0.195)	(0.196)
Political protest	−0.362	−1.482**	−0.319
	(0.238)	(0.650)	(0.239)
Free expression	0.453**	0.411*	0.393*
	(0.223)	(0.219)	(0.219)

$*p < .10, **p < .05, ***p < .01$ N = 1,081. See Tables 2.A and 2.B for description of data.

a. This interaction coefficient is significant at the $p < .12$ level. We include it here because our substantive reading of the cases suggests that the outcomes of free expression cases in this earlier time period were more school-favored than in the later time periods. Further, our significance test for interaction terms is somewhat hypothetical, given that our sample includes the entire population of school discipline court cases. Thus we include this term here because we are convinced that it represents an important relationship in the effect of time period and the type of student misbehavior.

b. We include different specifications of court level in different models because interactions with various combinations of court level are significant in our models. There are five different court levels: lower state courts, high state courts, United States district courts, United States courts of appeals, and the Supreme Court. Omitted categories differ between the various models.

Table 3.C Logistic regression of factors affecting pro-student school discipline court case decisions, 1960–1992 (public and private schools)

	Model 1	Model 2
Intercept	−0.779***	−0.650***
	(0.225)	(0.236)
Time period		
1960–1968 (pre-contestation)	0.125	0.087
	(0.266)	(0.281)
1969–1975 (contestation)	0.341**	0.245
	(0.139)	(0.153)
Case origin		
Mid-Atlantic region	−0.453**	−0.445**
	(0.217)	(0.219)
Midwest region	−0.344*	−0.420**
	(0.198)	(0.201)
Western region	−0.095	−0.137
	(0.258)	(0.263)
Southern region	−0.331	−0.376*
	(0.203)	(0.206)
Mountain region	−1.002***	−1.134***
	(0.371)	(0.379)
Court level		
State lower courts	0.168	0.218
	(0.164)	(0.168)
State high courts	0.521**	0.584**
	(0.219)	(0.227)
Federal appellate courts	0.061	0.053
	(0.179)	(0.181)
Federal Supreme Court	−0.230	−0.130
	(0.582)	(0.587)
School and student characteristics		
Private school	−0.328	−0.384*
	(0.223)	(0.228)
Elementary level	0.631*	0.535
	(0.326)	(0.330)
Student nonwhite	0.530**	0.618***
	(0.207)	(0.212)
Student handicapped		0.097
		(0.307)

Table 3.C (continued)

	Model 1	Model 2
Form of school discipline		
Suspension	0.069	0.014
	(0.138)	(0.143)
Expulsion	0.253*	0.306**
	(0.143)	(0.145)
Corporal punishment	−0.193	−0.188
	(0.281)	(0.285)
School transfer	0.567	0.533
	(0.374)	(0.378)
Type of student misbehavior		
Drugs		−0.486**
		(0.216)
Alcohol		0.071
		(0.294)
Violence/weapons		−0.292
		(0.190)
Political protest		−0.262
		(0.222)
Free expression		0.428**
		(0.210)

*$p < .10$. **$p < .05$. ***$p < .01$. $N = 1{,}204$. See Tables 2.A and 2.B for description of data.

Table 4.A Description of variable coding on all variables used in analysis of Office of Civil Rights (OCR) data, 1976–1992

School disciplinary practices (dependent variables)

1976 corporal punishment rate—all students	OCR report of corporal punishment for all students divided by OCR enrollments for all students.
1976 corporal punishment rate—white students	OCR report of corporal punishment for white students divided by OCR enrollments for white students.
1976 corporal punishment rate—black students	OCR report of corporal punishment for black students divided by OCR enrollments for black students.
1976–1992 change in corporal punishment—all students	1992 corporal punishment rate divided by 1976 corporal punishment rate—all students
1976–1992 change in corporal punishment—white students	1992 corporal punishment rate divided by 1976 corporal punishment rate—white students.
1976–1992 change in corporal punishment—blacks	1992 corporal punishment rate divided by 1976 corporal punishment rate—black students.
State exit from use of corporal punishment	1976–1992 observation of discontinued identification of state schools using corporal punishment.
1992 corporal punishment rate (district level)	1992 district-level measure of corporal punishment rate.

State legal environment

Pro-school court climate	Average of all prior court decisions from courts with direct jurisdiction over state schools—that is, state, regional federal appellate, regional federal district, and federal Supreme. All decisions weighted equally and coded −1 for pro-student, 0 for ambiguous, and 1 for pro-school.
Increase in pro-school court climate	1992 pro-student court climate measure minus 1976 pro-student court climate.

State political culture

Republican Party influence	Percentage of three state government institutions (governor's office, upper legislative house, and lower legislative house) controlled by Republican Party.
Increase in Republican Party influence	1992 measure minus 1976 measure.
Religious right influence	Percentage membership in religious right denominations within state (see Bernstein 1997, Heatwole 1978).
Increase in religious right influence	1992 measure minus 1976 measure.

Table 4.A (continued)

Other factors

College educated (percent)	Percentage of adults with college degrees in state (Statistical Abstracts) for state-level analysis; or in neighborhood for district-level analysis (Common Core of Data).
Increase in college educated	1992 measure minus 1976 measure.
African-American students	African-American students divided by all enrollments (OCR state and district-level data).
Increase in African-Americans	1992 measure minus 1976 measure (OCR state-level data).
District administration	Number of district administrators to students (state-level measure is square root and taken from NCES data published in *Digest of Education Statistics*; district-level measure is natural log and derived from Common Core of Data).
Increase in district administration	1992 measure minus 1976 measure.
Hispanic students	Hispanic students divided by all enrollments (OCR state- and district-level data).
African-American teachers	Percentage African-American teachers in district (Common Core of Data).
Hispanic teachers	Percentage Hispanic teachers in district (Common Core of Data).
Students enrolled	Log number of students enrolled in district (Common Core of Data).

Note: NCES (National Center for Education Statistics) Common Core of Data, School Years 1988–89 through 1993–94 (NCES 96-316 computer disk); *Statistical Abstracts of the United States* (Washington, D.C.: Government Printing Office), volumes from 1976–1994 in series used.

Table 4.B Descriptive statistics on state-level variables used in analysis of Office of Civil Rights data, 1976–1992

	State level (N = 50)	State-year observation (N = 410)	District-level (N = 4,621)
Disciplinary practices			
1976 corporal punishment rate—all students	0.031 (0.035)		
1976 corporal punishment rate—white students	0.028 (0.031)		
1976 corporal punishment rate—black students	0.049 (0.057)		
1976–1992 change in corporal punishment—all students	−0.701 (0.487)		
1976–1992 change in corporal punishment—white students	−0.714 (0.465)		
1976–1992 change in corporal punishment—black students	−0.654 (0.475)		
State exit from use of corporal punishment		0.063 (0.244)	
1992 corporal punishment rate (district level)			0.019 (0.053)
State legal environment			
Pro-school court climate	0.038 (0.094)	0.153 (0.152)	0.242 (0.146)
Increase in pro-school court climate	0.213 (0.107)		
State political culture			
Republican Party influence	0.387 (0.255)	0.392 (0.306)	0.372 (0.309)
Increase in Republican Party influence	0.007 (0.297)		
Religious right influence	0.109 (0.101)	0.125 (0.103)	0.112 (0.101)
Increase in religious right influence	0.001 (0.007)		

Table 4.B (continued)

	State level (N = 50)	State-year observation (N = 410)	District-level (N = 4,621)
Other factors			
College educated	0.138	0.169	0.178
	(0.025)	(0.039)	(0.120)
Increase in college educated	0.061		
	(0.022)		
African-American students	0.164	0.180	0.087
	(0.143)	(0.145)	(0.181)
Increase in African-American	−0.002		
	(0.028)		
District administration	2.573	3.161	6.642
	(4.292)	(3.123)	(0.893)
Increased in district administration	1.613		
	(2.804)		
Hispanic students		0.059	0.058
		(0.097)	(0.139)
African-American teachers			0.068
			(0.089)
Hispanic teachers			0.020
			(0.043)
Students enrolled			7.183
			(1.796)

Note: State-year observations identify state-level characteristics for each year of observation when the state is at risk for ending the use of corporal punishment in pubic schools—that is, the state has not yet abandoned the practice by the prior year (1976–1992).

Table 4.C Descriptive statistics and coding of all variables used for modeling factors related to secondary public school teacher perceptions that teachers enforce rules and that principals enforce rules and back teachers up, 1990 and 1993 pooled data

	Teachers ($N = 53,565$)	
State legal environment		
Pro-school court climate	0.275 (0.162)	Average of all prior court decisions from courts with direct jurisdiction over state schools—that is, state, regional federal appellate, regional federal district, and federal Supreme. All decisions weighted equally and coded -1 for pro-student, 0 for ambiguous, and 1 for pro-school.
State political culture		
Republican Party influence	0.376 (0.298)	Percentage of three state government institutions (governor's office, upper legislative house, and lower legislative house) controlled by Republican Party.
Religious right influence	0.122 (0.106)	Percentage membership in religious right denominations (see Bernstein 1997, Heatwole 1978).
State factors (other)		
College educated (percent)	0.198 (0.038)	Percentage of adults with college degrees in state (Statistical Abstract).
District administration	3.213 (3.894)	Square root of number of students per district administrator (NCES data).
School characteristics		
Rural location	0.550 (0.497)	Dummy variable coded 1 for rural school location.
Urban location	0.210 (0.407)	Dummy variable coded 1 for urban school location.
School size	6.374 (0.971)	Log of number of enrolled students.
Nonwhite students (percent)	0.249 (0.288)	Percentage of students in school nonwhite.
Nonwhite teachers (percent)	0.105 (0.174)	Percentage of teachers in school nonwhite.

Table 4.C (continued)

	Teachers ($N = 53{,}565$)	
Individual characteristics		
Male	0.453	Dummy variable coded 1 for male teacher.
	(0.498)	
African-American	0.056	Dummy variable coded 1 for African-
	(0.229)	American teacher.
Hispanic	0.027	Dummy variable coded 1 for Hispanic
	(0.161)	teacher.
Age (years)	42.627	Age of teacher in years.
	(9.382)	
Teaching experience	15.052	Teaching experience in years.
(years)	(9.012)	
B.A. degree	0.538	Dummy variable coded 1 for B.A. degree as
	(0.499)	highest education.
M.A. degree (or higher)	0.405	Dummy variable coded 1 for M.A. degree
	(0.491)	or greater as highest education.

Table 4.D Ordinary least square regression of the rate of corporal punishment in a state's public schools on pro-school court climate and other variables, 1976

	All (1)	White (2)	Black (3)
Intercept	0.034	0.033	0.068
	(0.026)	(0.023)	(0.050)
State legal environment			
Pro-school court climate	0.062*	0.065**	0.131*
	(0.036)	(0.032)	(0.069)
State political culture			
Republican Party influence	−0.007	−0.007	−0.020
	(0.012)	(0.011)	(0.023)
Religious right influence	0.222***	0.194***	0.341***
	(0.044)	(0.039)	(0.084)
State factors (other)			
College educated (percent)	−0.211	−0.194	−0.344
	(0.161)	(0.142)	(0.308)
African-American (percent)	0.013	0.004	−0.037
	(0.025)	(0.022)	(0.048)
District administration	0.001	0.001	0.001
	(0.001)	(0.001)	(0.001)
R^2	0.693	0.689	0.571

$*p < .10$. $**p < .05$. $***p < .01$. $N = 50$. For details on data, see Tables 4.A and 4.B.

Table 4.E Ordinary least-square regression of change in the rate of corporal punishment in a state's public schools on change in pro-school court climate and other variables, 1976–1992

	All (1)	White (2)	Black (3)
Intercept	−1.280***	−1.300***	−1.199***
	(0.242)	(0.227)	(0.233)
State legal environment			
Increase in pro-school court	1.268*	1.276**	1.468**
climate	(0.635)	(0.595)	(0.611)
State political culture			
Increase in Republican Party	−0.090	−0.056	−0.228
influence	(0.227)	(0.213)	(0.218)
Increase in religious right	17.796*	19.376**	13.647
influence	(8.962)	(8.402)	(8.622)
State factors (other)			
Increase in college educated	4.390	4.399	2.832
	(3.019)	(2.831)	(2.905)
Increase in African-Americans	2.046	1.382	1.877
	(2.513)	(2.356)	(2.418)
Increase in district administration	0.022	0.023	0.035
	(0.024)	(0.022)	(0.023)
R^2	0.235	0.263	0.257

*$p < .10$. **$p < .05$. ***$p < .01$. $N = 50$. For details on data, see Tables 4.A and 4.B.
Note: Dependent variable constrained to 1 (affecting one state).

Table 4.F Event history analysis of the likelihood of state schools ending the
practice of corporal punishment, 1976–1992

	Model (1)	Model (2)
Intercept	−3.140***	−1.713
	(0.343)	(1.412)
Time (in years) squared	0.009***	0.012***
	(0.002)	(0.002)
State legal environment		
Pro-school court climate	−5.130***	−3.045*
	(1.683)	(1.689)
State political culture		
Republican Party influence		−2.153**
		(0.837)
Religious right influence		−27.019***
		(8.358)
State factors (other)		
College educated (percent)		8.103
		(6.610)
African-American (percent)		−5.726*
		(2.470)
Hispanic (percent)		−1.309
		(2.847)
District administration		−0.021
		(0.063)

*$p < .10$. **$p < .05$. ***$p < .01$. $N = 410$, State-Year observations (in risk set). For details on data, see Tables 4.A and 4.B.

Table 4.G Tobit analysis of the rate of public school corporal punishment in districts surveyed by the Office of Civil Rights, 1992

	All Surveyed Districts (1)	At-Risk[a] Districts (2)
Intercept	−1.654***	−1.464***
	(0.316)	(0.316)
Sigma	1.100	1.024
	(0.024)	(0.025)
State legal environment		
Pro-school court climate	−0.716**	−1.172***
	(0.333)	(0.350)
State political culture		
Republican Party influence	−0.991***	−0.419**
	(0.141)	(0.182)
Religious right influence	6.199***	4.800***
	(0.438)	(0.524)
Demographics		
College educated in neighborhood	−5.408***	−5.032***
	(0.510)	(0.527)
African-American students (percent)	1.215***	1.122***
	(0.183)	(0.181)
Hispanic students (percent)	0.684***	0.880***
	(0.264)	(0.285)
African-American teachers (percent)	−0.031	−0.001
	(0.327)	(0.321)
Hispanic teachers (percent)	−1.415	−1.713*
	(0.962)	(0.958)
Institutional structure		
District administration	−0.128**	-0.076
	(0.052)	(0.055)
Students enrolled (logged)	0.137***	−0.153***
	(0.039)	(0.042)

*$p < .10$. ** $p < .05$, ***$p < .01$. $N = 4,621$ (model 1); $N = 1,327$ (model 2). For details on data, see Tables 4.A and 4.B.

Note: Means substitution for missing data on teachers' race and college education; dummy variables for substitution not reported.

a. At risk districts are restricted to districts in states with some corporal punishment.

Table 4.H Descriptive statistics on number of school rules (1982 and 1992 pooled data), secondary public school teacher perceptions that teachers enforce rules and that principals enforce rules and back teachers up (1990 and 1993 pooled data), student perceptions of strictness and fairness of school discipline (1982 and 1992 data), by region (in percent)

Region	All rules adopted (1)	Teacher enforcement (2)	Principal support (3)	Strict discipline (4)	1982 fair discipline (5)	1992 fair discipline (6)
Northeast	42.0	50.7	80.1	55.2	40.1	70.3
Midwest	42.8	57.0	82.2	56.2	38.5	68.2
South	53.6	59.0	85.0	59.7	42.0	68.4
West	31.4%	54.9%	81.8%	53.6%	43.6%	73.3%
Sample size	1,888	53,565	53,565	28,879	20,858	12,315

Note: Column 1 is percentage of schools reporting four out of four rules; columns 2–6 are the percent of individuals reporting highest two out of four response categories; data for columns 1 and 4 are pooled reports from High School and Beyond and National Educational Longitudinal Survey data; columns 2 and 3 are reports from School and Staffing Survey; column 5 is High School and Beyond data; column 6 is National Educational Longitudinal Survey data. For details on coding, see Tables 4.C, 5.A, and 5.B.

Table 4.1 Hierarchical linear modeling of number of public school rules on pro-
school court climate and other variables, 1982 and 1992 pooled data

	Model (1)	Model (2)
Intercept	2.512***	1.340***
	(0.242)	(0.420)
State legal environment		
Pro-school court climate	1.366***	0.932**
	(0.346)	(0.368)
State political culture		
Republican Party influence		−0.018
		(0.204)
Religious right influence		1.557**
		(0.728)
State factors (other)		
College educated (percent)		6.296***
		(1.680)
District administration		−0.006
		(0.011)
School characteristics		
Rural location	−0.102**	−0.103**
	(0.049)	(0.049)
Urban location	−0.103**	−0.102**
	(0.051)	(0.051)
School size	0.119***	0.111***
	(0.035)	(0.035)
School student/teacher ratio	−0.108***	−0.100***
	(0.034)	(0.034)
African-American students (percent)	−0.232*	−0.252*
	(0.133)	(0.134)
Hispanic students (percent)	−0.224	−0.255*
	(0.148)	(0.148)
Poor students (percent)	0.188*	0.197*
	(0.111)	(0.111)
Dropout rate (percent)	−0.150	−0.124
	(0.201)	(0.204)

	Model (1)	Model (2)
African-American teachers (percent)	0.051	0.084
	(0.207)	(0.211)
Hispanic teachers (percent)	−0.354	−0.353
	(0.263)	(0.263)

$^*p < .10.$ $^{**}p < .05.$ $^{***}p < .01.$ $N = 1,872$ schools. For details on data, see Tables 5.A and 5.B.

Note: Means substitution for missing data on school characteristics; dummy variables for substitution not reported.

Table 4.J Hierarchical linear modeling of secondary public school teacher perceptions that teachers enforce rules and principals enforce rules and back teachers up on pro-school court climate and other variables, 1990 and 1993 pooled data.

	Teachers (1)	Teachers (2)	Principals (3)	Principals (4)
Intercept	3.430***	3.392***	3.370***	3.405***
	(0.056)	(0.128)	(0.051)	(0.104)
State legal environment				
Pro-school court	0.187*	0.067	0.246***	0.141*
climate	(0.109)	(0.105)	(0.088)	(0.083)
State political culture				
Republican Party		0.069		0.011
influence		(0.063)		(0.050)
Religious right		0.774***		0.611***
influence		(0.209)		(0.166)
State factors (other)				
College educated		−0.301		−0.403
(percent)		(0.497)		(0.394)
District administration		0.005*		0.001
		(0.003)		(0.002)
School characteristics				
Rural location	−0.052***	−0.053***	−0.041***	−0.043***
	(0.011)	(0.011)	(0.010)	(0.010)
Urban location	−0.012	−0.011	−0.036***	−0.036***
	(0.012)	(0.012)	(0.012)	(0.012)
School size	−0.169***	−0.169***	−0.033***	−0.033***
	(0.005)	(0.005)	(0.005)	(0.005)
Nonwhite students	−0.156***	−0.154***	−0.174***	−0.174***
(percent)	(0.023)	(0.023)	(0.022)	(0.022)
Nonwhite teachers	−0.232***	−0.248***	−0.156***	−0.162***
(percent)	(0.038)	(0.038)	(0.036)	(0.037)

	Teachers (1)	Teachers (2)	Principals (3)	Principals (4)
Individual characteristics				
Male	−0.007	−0.007	−0.016**	−0.015**
	(0.008)	(0.008)	(0.008)	(0.008)
African-American	0.336***	0.334***	0.121***	0.117***
	(0.019)	(0.019)	(0.018)	(0.018)
Hispanic	0.122***	0.125***	0.055**	0.057**
	(0.025)	(0.025)	(0.024)	(0.024)
Age (years)	0.006***	0.006***	0.003***	0.003***
	(0.001)	(0.001)	(0.001)	(0.001)
Teaching experience	−0.004***	−0.004***	−0.005***	−0.005***
(years)	(0.001)	(0.001)	(0.001)	(0.001)
B.A. degree	0.027	0.026	0.048***	0.047***
	(0.018)	(0.018)	(0.017)	(0.017)
M.A. degree (or higher)	−0.007	−0.008	0.033**	0.033*
	(0.018)	(0.018)	(0.017)	(0.017)

$^*p < .10.$ $^{**}p < .05.$ $^{***}p < .01$ $N = 53,565$ teachers. For details on data see Table 4.C.

Note: Means substitution for missing data on school characteristics; dummy variables for substitution not reported.

Table 4.K Hierarchical linear modeling of student perceptions of school discipline as being "strict" and "fair" on pro-school court climate and other variables, 1982 and 1992 pooled data

	Strict (1)	Strict (2)	Fair (3)	Fair (4)	Strict*Fair (5)	Strict*Fair (6)
Intercept	2.375***	2.136***	2.196***	1.731***	5.266***	3.694***
	(0.065)	(0.104)	(0.066)	(0.118)	(0.246)	(0.456)
State legal environment						
Pro-school court climate	0.297***	0.146*	0.332***	0.218**	1.411***	0.822**
	(0.084)	(0.087)	(0.104)	(0.104)	(0.389)	(0.405)
State political culture						
Republican Party influence		0.006		−0.022		0.079
		(0.048)		(0.058)		(0.226)
Religious right influence		0.705***		0.378*		2.515***
		(0.173)		(0.209)		(0.815)
State factors (other)						
College educated (percent)		1.058**		2.297***		7.388***
		(0.405)		(0.487)		(1.902)
District administration		−0.001		0.006*		0.012
		(0.003)		(0.003)		(0.012)
School characteristics						
Rural location	0.010	0.010	0.014	0.016	0.056	0.060
	(0.012)	(0.012)	(0.012)	(0.012)	(0.044)	(0.044)
Urban location	−0.059***	−0.056***	0.043***	0.043***	−0.017	−0.013
	(0.014)	(0.014)	(0.013)	(0.013)	(0.050)	(0.050)

	Strict (1)	Strict (2)	Fair (3)	Fair (4)	Strict*Fair (5)	Strict*Fair (6)
School size	0.026***	0.026***	0.018**	0.018**	0.099***	0.099***
	(0.009)	(0.009)	(0.009)	(0.009)	(0.034)	(0.034)
School student/teacher ratio	0.000	0.000	0.006	0.007	0.019	0.020
	(0.008)	(0.008)	(0.008)	(0.008)	(0.031)	(0.031)
African-American students (percent)	−0.091**	−0.098**	0.015	0.011	−0.137	−0.153
	(0.039)	(0.039)	(0.038)	(0.038)	(0.145)	(0.145)
Hispanic students (percent)	−0.007	−0.009	0.086**	0.078**	0.219	0.205
	(0.040)	(0.040)	(0.039)	(0.039)	(0.149)	(0.149)
Poor students (percent)	0.094***	0.092***	0.017	0.015	0.283**	0.267**
	(0.030)	(0.030)	(0.029)	(0.030)	(0.111)	(0.111)
Average Student SES	0.026***	0.026***	0.024***	0.022***	0.109***	0.105***
	(0.007)	(0.007)	(0.007)	(0.007)	(0.026)	(0.026)
Dropout rate (percent)	−0.176***	−0.187***	−0.022	−0.020	−0.550***	−0.572***
	(0.054)	(0.054)	(0.053)	(0.053)	(0.200)	(0.201)
African-American teachers (percent)	0.069	0.063	−0.050	−0.044	0.029	0.038
	(0.058)	(0.059)	(0.057)	(0.058)	(0.216)	(0.218)
Hispanic teachers (percent)	−0.087	−0.087	0.082	0.082	0.003	0.007
	(0.069)	(0.069)	(0.068)	(0.068)	(0.256)	(0.256)
Individual characteristics						
Male	0.033***	0.033***	−0.033***	−0.034***	−0.018	−0.020
	(0.009)	(0.009)	(0.009)	(0.009)	(0.032)	(0.032)

Table 4.K (continued)

	Strict (1)	Strict (2)	Fair (3)	Fair (4)	Strict*Fair (5)	Strict*Fair (6)
Hispanic	0.028*	0.029*	0.002	0.003	0.102*	0.105*
	(0.015)	(0.015)	(0.015)	(0.015)	(0.057)	(0.057)
African-American	0.078***	0.078***	−0.038**	−0.038**	0.080	0.080
	(0.017)	(0.017)	(0.017)	(0.017)	(0.064)	(0.064)
Two-parent family	−0.004	−0.003	0.051***	0.051***	0.144***	0.146***
	(0.011)	(0.011)	(0.011)	(0.011)	(0.040)	(0.040)
Academic track	−0.004	−0.003	0.142***	0.143***	0.373***	0.378***
	(0.010)	(0.010)	(0.010)	(0.010)	(0.038)	(0.038)
Vocational track	0.042***	0.043***	0.013	0.014	0.139***	0.146***
	(0.012)	(0.012)	(0.012)	(0.012)	(0.045)	(0.045)
Siblings	0.004	0.004*	−0.004	−0.004	0.001	0.001
	(0.002)	(0.002)	(0.002)	(0.002)	(0.009)	(0.009)
Student SES	−0.009*	−0.009*	0.021***	0.021***	0.046**	0.046**
	(0.005)	(0.005)	(0.005)	(0.005)	(0.019)	(0.019)
Non-English home	−0.004	−0.005	0.057***	0.056***	0.140*	0.137*
	(0.020)	(0.020)	(0.019)	(0.019)	(0.072)	(0.072)

$*p < .10.$ $**p < .05.$ $***p < .01.$ $N = 32,508.$ For details on data, see Tables 5.A and 5.B.

Note: Means substitution for missing data on school and student characteristics; dummy variables for substitution not reported.

Table 4.L Ordered logit modeling of administrative reports of school rules and student reports of perceptions of strictness and fairness of school discipline on pro-school
court climate and other variables, 1982 and 1992 pooled data (with state-level fixed
effects and robust state-clustered standard errors)

	School Rules (1)	Strictness (2)	Fairness (3)	Strict*Fair (4)
State legal environment				
Pro-school court climate	10.332**	1.446**	3.361**	2.912**
	(2.105)	(0.381)	(0.620)	(0.575)
School characteristics				
Rural location	−0.202	0.002	0.036	0.023
	(0.170)	(0.045)	(0.061)	(0.053)
Urban location	−0.103	−0.124**	0.127**	0.034
	(0.157)	(0.047)	(0.040)	(0.050)
School size	0.319**	0.063	−0.001	0.052
	(0.089)	(0.040)	(0.044)	(0.041)
School student/teacher ratio	−0.471**	−0.017	−0.005	−0.029
	(0.126)	(0.033)	(0.032)	(0.031)
African-American students	−1.106*	−0.332*	0.024	−0.169
(percent)	(0.427)	(0.156)	(0.138)	(0.161)
Hispanic students (percent)	−0.402	0.209	0.554**	0.482**
	(0.307)	(0.148)	(0.119)	(0.108)
Poor students (percent)	1.179**	0.217	0.438**	0.467**
	(0.328)	(0.119)	(0.104)	(0.126)
Average student SES	−0.290**	0.101**	0.106**	0.114**
	(0.084)	(0.030)	(0.031)	(0.028)
Dropout rate (percent)	−0.535	−0.335	−0.027	−0.177
	(0.489)	(0.208)	(0.187)	(0.195)
African-American teachers	0.396	0.280	−0.195	−0.218
(percent)	(0.556)	(0.245)	(0.222)	(0.263)
Hispanic teachers (percent)	−1.341*	0.031	−0.106	0.011
	(0.660)	(0.245)	(0.170)	(0.145)
Individual characteristics				
Male		0.072*	−0.026	0.003
		(0.036)	(0.026)	(0.033)
Hispanic		0.074	−0.001	0.015
		(0.089)	(0.050)	(0.072)
African-American		−0.096*	−0.094	−0.121*
		(0.049)	(0.053)	(0.054)

Table 4.L (continued)

	School Rules (1)	Strictness (2)	Fairness (3)	Strict*Fair (4)
Two-parent family		0.001	0.171**	0.091*
		(0.037)	(0.038)	(0.037)
Test score tenth grade		−0.159**	0.096**	−0.015
		(0.024)	(0.019)	(0.020)
Academic track		0.132**	0.236**	0.256**
		(0.032)	(0.036)	(0.030)
Vocational track		0.034	−0.068	−0.006
		(0.045)	(0.035)	(0.050)
Siblings		0.005	−0.014	−0.010
		(0.008)	(0.009)	(0.009)
Student S.E.S.		0.003	0.011	0.018
		(0.013)	(0.022)	(0.018)
Non-English home		0.082	0.220*	0.200*
		(0.055)	(0.096)	(0.083)
Adjacent logit cut points				
First cut	−3.073	−1.557	−1.064	−2.784
	(0.793)	(0.280)	(0.305)	(0.252)
Second cut	−0.871	0.685	0.682	−1.239
	(0.756)	(0.284)	(0.302)	(0.250)
Third cut	0.974	2.920	3.643	−0.635
	(0.734)	(0.277)	(0.307)	(0.250)
Fourth cut	2.707			0.244
	(0.743)			(0.253)
Fifth cut				1.614
				(0.255)
Sixth cut				1.865
				(0.255)
Seventh cut				3.491
				(0.249)
Eighth cut				5.511
				(0.254)
Pseudo R^2	0.111	0.013	0.032	0.016
N	1,878	27,264	29,571	26,043

$*p < .05$. $**p < .01$. For details on data, see Tables 5.A and 5.B.

Note: Means substitution for missing data on school characteristics; dummy variables for substitution and state-level fixed effects not reported. Standard errors adjusted for clustering at state level.

Table 5.A Description of variable coding for multi-level analysis utilizing data on public high schools and students from *High School and Beyond* (1982) and *National Educational Longitudinal Study* (1992)

State-level organizational environment

Pro-school court climate — Average of all prior court decisions from courts with direct jurisdiction over state schools—that is, state, regional federal appellate, regional federal district and federal supreme. All decisions weighted equally and coded − 1 for pro-student, 0 for ambiguous, and 1 for pro-school. Measures based on cases from 1960 to year prior to relevant dependent variable.

School discipline measures

School rules — Administrator reports of the presence of school rules in the following four areas: hall passes, smoking, open campus, dress code (coded 0–4).

Strictness perception — Self-reported perception of whether a student's high school followed strict school disciplinary practices (coded 1–4, with higher indicating greater belief in strictness at student level; school-level measure is average of student reports z-scored).

Fairness perception — Self-reported perception of whether a student's high school applied disciplinary practices fairly (coded 1–4, with higher values indicating greater belief in fairness at student level; school-level measure is average of student reports z-scored).

Youth socialization and school climate measures

Safe school — Self-reported perception of safe school (coded 1 for safe, 0 otherwise).

Educational commitment — Composite measure of the sum of the following z-scored measures on self-reported tardiness, homework completion, forgotten classroom materials, absences, and cutting class (higher numbers indicating greater student educational commitment).

Student grades — Z-scored measure of high school grades as senior.

High school graduation — Student graduated from high school (coded 1 for graduated, 0 otherwise).

Test score (twelfth grade) — Z-scored measure of twelfth-grade test score on battery of English and math exams.

Table 5.A (continued)

Willing to disobey rules	Student self-reported willingness to disobey school rules (NELS only; coded 1–4, with higher numbers indicating greater willingness to disobey).
Student disruptive behavior	Teacher reported disruptive behavior of student (NELS only; coded 1–5, with higher numbers indicating greater amounts of disruptive behavior).
Student fighting	Student self-reported in-school fighting (NELS only; coded 0–2 with higher numbers indicating more fighting).
Student arrest	Student self-reported arrest (coded 1 for arrest, 0 otherwise).
Individual-level covariates	
Male	Dummy variable (coded 1) for males.
African-American	Dummy variable (coded 1) for African-Americans.
Hispanic	Dummy variable (coded 1) for Hispanic-Americans.
Two-parent family	Dummy variable (coded 1) for individuals living with male and female adults in household.
Test score (tenth grade)	Z-scored measure of tenth-grade test score on battery of English and Math exams.
Vocational track	Dummy variable (coded 1) for participation in vocational high school program. Self-report of current or last attended high school program.
Academic track	Dummy variable (coded 1) for participation in academic high school program (track). Self-report of current or last attended high school program.
Siblings	Number of siblings.
Non-English home	Dummy variable (coded 1) for individuals who primarily speak a non-English language in the home.
Student SES	Composite measure of student socioeconomic status based on student reports of father's years of education, mother's years of education, highest parental occupation and family income (logged). Variables z-scored and then summed. Final composite variable is standardized.

School-level covariates

Urban location	Dummy variable (coded 1) for high school in urban area (suburban omitted).
Rural location	Dummy variable (coded 1) for high school in rural area (suburban omitted).
Suburban location	Dummy variable (coded 1) for high school in suburban area (omitted category).
Dropout rate (%)	Percentage of tenth graders who drop out of high school (administrator reports).
Poor students (%)	Percentage of economically disadvantaged students at the school. Based on percentage of students who receive free or reduced school lunch (administrator reports).
African-American students (%)	Percentage of African American students at the school (administrator reports).
Hispanic students (%)	Percentage of Hispanic students at the school (administrator reports).
School student/teacher ratio	Number of students at school divided by number of teachers at school based on school administrator reports. Square root of measure used to deal with outliers.
African-American teachers (%)	Percentage of full-time regular teachers in school who are classified as African-American (administrator reports).
Hispanic teachers (%)	Percentage of full-time regular teachers in school who are classified as Hispanic (administrator reports)
School size	Total number of students in the school (logged).
Average student SES	The average socioeconomic status of the school. Based on within-school aggregation of the composite student SES scores, which are based on self-reports from individual student questionnaires.

Table 5.B Description of variable coding for multilevel analysis utilizing data on public high schools and students from *High School and Beyond (1982)* and *National Educational Longitudinal Study (1992)*

	N	Mean	S.D.
State-level organizational environment			
Pro-school court climate	35,793	0.196	0.151
School discipline measures			
School rules	33,667	2.946	0.954
Strictness perception	32,508	2.637	0.796
Fairness perception	33,077	2.421	0.820
Youth socialization and school climate measures			
Safe school	34,163	0.889	0.314
Educational commitment	31,923	0.255	2.851
Student grades	30,215	0.000	1.000
High school graduation	23,104	0.827	1.000
Test score (twelfth grade)	29,069	0.000	1.000
Willing to disobey rules	11,877	1.582	0.764
Student disruptive behavior	6,097	1.426	0.740
Student fighting	10,790	0.139	0.414
Student arrest	34,802	0.041	0.216
Individual-level covariates			
Male	35,793	0.499	0.500
African-American	35,793	0.141	0.346
Hispanic	35,793	0.150	0.327
Two-parent family	35,793	0.703	0.455
Test score (tenth grade)	32,296	0.000	1.000
Vocational	35,793	0.258	0.414
Academic	35,793	0.387	0.456
Siblings	35,793	2.818	1.784
Non-English home	35,793	0.086	0.211
Student SES	35,793	0.000	1.000

	N	Mean	S.D.
School-level covariates			
Urban location	35,793	0.220	0.414
Rural location	35,793	0.331	0.470
Dropout rate (%)	35,793	0.084	0.091
Poor students (%)	35,793	0.193	0.198
African-American students (%)	35,793	0.141	0.223
Hispanic students (%)	35,793	0.074	0.165
Student/teacher ratio	35,793	4.287	0.653
African-American teachers (%)	35,793	0.076	0.133
Hispanic teachers (%)	35,793	0.021	0.064
School size	35,793	6.987	0.698
Average student SES	35,793	0.000	1.000

Table 5.C Logistic regression of student reported safe school on school rules, student perceptions of school discipline, and other variables, 1982 and 1992 pooled data

	(1)	(2)	(3)	(4)
Intercept	−3.751**	−2.274**	−1.435**	−2.615**
	(0.379)	(0.386)	(0.419)	(0.439)
Discipline—school level				
School Rules	0.041	−0.008	−0.008	−0.006
	(0.033)	(0.034)	(0.034)	(0.034)
Strictness perception (average)	0.060	0.036	0.039	0.035
	(0.033)	(0.034)	(0.034)	(0.034)
Fairness perception (average)	0.235**	0.117**	0.115**	0.117**
	(0.032)	(0.033)	(0.033)	(0.033)
Discipline—student level				
Strictness perception		0.143**	0.939**	0.009
		(0.037)	(0.157)	(0.092)
Fairness perception		0.540**	0.513**	0.365**
		(0.039)	(0.038)	(0.116)
Strictness perception (squared)			−0.158**	
			(0.031)	
Strictness*fairness perception				0.068
				(0.042)
School characteristics				
Rural location	−0.035	−0.044	−0.046	−0.043
	(0.073)	(0.073)	(0.074)	(0.073)
Urban location	−0.002	−0.030	−0.035	−0.028
	(0.093)	(0.094)	(0.095)	(0.094)
School size	−0.176**	−0.181**	−0.182**	−0.182**
	(0.058)	(0.058)	(0.059)	(0.058)
School student/teacher ratio	0.020	0.038	0.042	0.038
	(0.052)	(0.053)	(0.053)	(0.053)
African-American students (percent)	−0.497*	−0.500*	−0.473	−0.501*
	(0.249)	(0.253)	(0.255)	(0.254)
Hispanic students (%)	−0.380	−0.510	−0.510	−0.514
	(0.325)	(0.321)	(0.321)	(0.320)
Poor students (%)	−0.324	−0.415*	−0.414*	−0.419*
	(0.180)	(0.185)	(0.188)	(0.185)
Average student SES	−0.044	−0.061	−0.061	−0.059
	(0.050)	(0.051)	(0.051)	(0.051)

	(1)	(2)	(3)	(4)
Dropout rate (%)	−0.415	−0.493	−0.499	−0.489
	(0.405)	(0.421)	(0.422)	(0.421)
African-American teachers (%)	−0.612	−0.608	−0.601	−0.607
	(0.365)	(0.377)	(0.378)	(0.379)
Hispanic teachers (%)	−0.126	−0.087	−0.071	−0.082
	(0.570)	(0.567)	(0.560)	(0.565)
Individual characteristics				
Male	−0.309**	−0.309**	−0.302**	−0.308**
	(0.058)	(0.058)	(0.058)	(0.058)
Hispanic	−0.062	−0.018	−0.020	−0.021
	(0.096)	(0.096)	(0.096)	(0.096)
African-American	0.122	0.126	0.127	0.127
	(0.120)	(0.120)	(0.121)	(0.120)
Two-parent family	0.026	−0.001	−0.004	−0.002
	(0.067)	(0.067)	(0.067)	(0.067)
Test score (tenth grade)	0.373**	0.366**	0.362**	0.367**
	(0.037)	(0.036)	(0.036)	(0.036)
Academic track	0.129	0.081	0.079	0.081
	(0.073)	(0.073)	(0.074)	(0.073)
Vocational track	−0.068	−0.049	−0.044	−0.049
	(0.070)	(0.070)	(0.070)	(0.069)
Siblings	0.016	0.018	0.019	0.018
	(0.017)	(0.017)	(0.017)	(0.017)
Student SES	0.030	0.029	0.028	0.028
	(0.033)	(0.034)	(0.034)	(0.034)
Non-English home	−0.061	−0.116	−0.121	−0.113
	(0.149)	(0.150)	(0.151)	(0.150)
Pseudo R^2	0.052	0.077	0.079	0.077

*$p < .05$. **$p < .01$. $N = 23,907$. For details on data, see Tables 5.A and 5.B.

Note: Means substitution for missing data on school and student characteristics; dummy variables for substitution not reported. Robust standard errors with clustering at school-level.

Table 5.D Hierarchical linear modeling of student educational commitment on school rules, student perceptions of school discipline, and other variables, 1982 and 1992 pooled data

	(1)	(2)	(3)	(4)	(5)
Intercept	0.889**	0.029	0.065	0.256	−0.121
	(0.334)	(0.343)	(0.367)	(0.375)	(0.348)
Discipline—school level					
School rules	0.033	0.005	0.005	0.006	0.005
	(0.029)	(0.029)	(0.029)	(0.029)	(0.029)
Strictness perception (average)	0.077**	0.066*	0.066*	0.065*	0.065*
	(0.028)	(0.029)	(0.029)	(0.029)	(0.029)
Fairness perception (average)	0.109**	0.041	0.041	0.041	0.039
	(0.024)	(0.025)	(0.025)	(0.025)	(0.025)
Discipline—student level					
Strictness perception		0.067**	0.034	−0.021	0.065**
		(0.023)	(0.118)	(0.063)	(0.023)
Fairness perception		0.308**	0.309**	0.208**	0.301**
		(0.023)	(0.024)	(0.071)	(0.024)
Strictness perception (squared)			0.006		
			(0.022)		
Strictness*fairness perception				0.038	
				(0.025)	
Safe school (perception)					0.169**
					(0.064)
School characteristics					
Rural location	0.142*	0.134	0.134*	0.135*	0.134
	(0.068)	(0.068)	(0.068)	(0.068)	(0.068)

	(1)	(2)	(3)	(4)	(5)
Urban location	0.011	−0.008	−0.007	−0.007	−0.007
	(0.077)	(0.077)	(0.077)	(0.077)	(0.077)
School size	−0.113*	−0.112*	−0.112*	−0.112*	−0.109*
	(0.051)	(0.051)	(0.051)	(0.051)	(0.051)
School student/teacher ratio	0.026	0.036	0.036	0.036	0.036
	(0.046)	(0.047)	(0.047)	(0.047)	(0.047)
African-American students (percent)	−0.004	−0.004	−0.004	−0.004	−0.004
	(0.002)	(0.002)	(0.002)	(0.002)	(0.002)
Hispanic students (%)	−0.005	−0.005*	−0.005*	−0.005*	−0.005*
	(0.003)	(0.003)	(0.003)	(0.003)	(0.003)
Poor students (%)	0.000	0.000	0.000	0.000	0.000
	(0.002)	(0.002)	(0.002)	(0.002)	(0.002)
Average student SES	−0.162**	−0.168**	−0.168**	−0.167**	−0.167**
	(0.036)	(0.036)	(0.036)	(0.036)	(0.036)
Dropout rate (%)	0.004	0.004	0.004	0.004	0.004
	(0.003)	(0.003)	(0.003)	(0.003)	(0.003)
African-American teachers (%)	0.001	0.002	0.002	0.002	0.002
	(0.003)	(0.003)	(0.003)	(0.003)	(0.003)
Hispanic teachers (%)	0.002	0.002	0.002	0.002	0.002
	(0.005)	(0.005)	(0.005)	(0.005)	(0.005)
Individual characteristics					
Male	−0.918**	−0.917**	−0.917**	−0.917**	−0.913**
	(0.036)	(0.036)	(0.036)	(0.036)	(0.036)
Hispanic	−0.206**	−0.190**	−0.190**	−0.191**	−0.190**
	(0.069)	(0.068)	(0.068)	(0.068)	(0.068)

Table 5.D (continued)

	(1)	(2)	(3)	(4)	(5)
African-American	0.348**	0.352**	0.352**	0.353**	0.351**
	(0.074)	(0.073)	(0.073)	(0.073)	(0.073)
Two-parent family	0.263**	0.248**	0.248**	0.247**	0.248**
	(0.045)	(0.045)	(0.045)	(0.045)	(0.045)
Test score (tenth grade)	0.101**	0.091**	0.091**	0.091**	0.086**
	(0.022)	(0.022)	(0.022)	(0.022)	(0.022)
Academic track	0.741**	0.705**	0.705**	0.705**	0.705**
	(0.045)	(0.045)	(0.045)	(0.045)	(0.045)
Vocational track	0.265**	0.266**	0.266**	0.266**	0.267**
	(0.049)	(0.049)	(0.049)	(0.049)	(0.049)
Siblings	−0.044**	−0.043**	−0.043**	−0.043**	−0.043**
	(0.010)	(0.010)	(0.010)	(0.010)	(0.010)
Student SES	0.016	0.013	0.013	0.012	0.013
	(0.021)	(0.021)	(0.021)	(0.021)	(0.021)
Non-English home	0.058	0.031	0.031	0.032	0.032
	(0.105)	(0.105)	(0.105)	(0.105)	(0.105)

*$p < .05$. **$p < .01$. $N = 23,655$. For details on data, see Tables 5.A and 5.B.

Note: Means substitution for missing data on school and student characteristics; dummy variables for substitution not reported.

Table 5.E Hierarchical linear modeling of student grades on school rules, student perceptions of school discipline, and other variables, 1982 and 1992 pooled data

	(1)	(2)	(3)	(4)	(5)
Intercept	0.626**	0.398**	0.295*	0.481**	0.321**
	(0.112)	(0.114)	(0.119)	(0.121)	(0.115)
Discipline—school level					
School rules	−0.006	−0.014	−0.014	−0.013	−0.014
	(0.010)	(0.010)	(0.010)	(0.010)	(0.010)
Strictness perception (average)	−0.030**	−0.035**	−0.034**	−0.035**	−0.035**
	(0.010)	(0.010)	(0.010)	(0.010)	(0.010)
Fairness perception (average)	0.016	−0.001	−0.001	−0.001	−0.002
	(0.008)	(0.009)	(0.009)	(0.009)	(0.009)
Discipline—student level					
Strictness perception		0.025**	0.117**	−0.007	0.024**
		(0.006)	(0.033)	(0.018)	(0.006)
Fairness perception		0.075**	0.073**	0.038	0.072**
		(0.007)	(0.007)	(0.020)	(0.007)
Strictness perception (squared)			−0.018**		
			(0.006)		
Strictness*fairness perception				0.014*	
				(0.007)	
Safe school (perception)					0.086**
					(0.018)
School characteristics					
Rural location	0.099**	0.097**	0.096**	0.098**	0.097**
	(0.023)	(0.023)	(0.023)	(0.023)	(0.023)

Table 5.E (continued)

	(1)	(2)	(3)	(4)	(5)
Urban location	−0.013	−0.017	−0.018	−0.017	−0.017
	(0.026)	(0.026)	(0.026)	(0.026)	(0.026)
School size	−0.128**	−0.128**	−0.128**	−0.128**	−0.127**
	(0.017)	(0.017)	(0.017)	(0.017)	(0.017)
School student/teacher ratio	0.040*	0.042**	0.043**	0.042**	0.042**
	(0.016)	(0.016)	(0.016)	(0.016)	(0.016)
African-American students (%)	0.001	0.001	0.001	0.001	0.001
	(0.001)	(0.001)	(0.001)	(0.001)	(0.001)
Hispanic students (%)	0.001	0.001	0.001	0.001	0.001
	(0.001)	(0.001)	(0.001)	(0.001)	(0.001)
Poor students (%)	0.001	0.001	0.001	0.001	0.001
	(0.001)	(0.001)	(0.001)	(0.001)	(0.001)
Average Student SES	−0.022	−0.024*	−0.025*	−0.024	−0.024
	(0.012)	(0.012)	(0.012)	(0.012)	(0.012)
Dropout rate (%)	0.001	0.001	0.001	0.001	0.001
	(0.001)	(0.001)	(0.001)	(0.001)	(0.001)
African-American teachers (%)	0.002	0.002	0.002	0.002	0.002
	(0.001)	(0.001)	(0.001)	(0.001)	(0.001)
Hispanic teachers (%)	0.002	0.002	0.002	0.002	0.002
	(0.002)	(0.002)	(0.002)	(0.002)	(0.002)
Individual characteristics					
Male	−0.349**	−0.349**	−0.349**	−0.349**	−0.347**
	(0.010)	(0.010)	(0.010)	(0.010)	(0.010)
Hispanic	−0.069**	−0.066**	−0.066**	−0.066**	−0.066**
	(0.019)	(0.019)	(0.019)	(0.019)	(0.019)

	(1)	(2)	(3)	(4)	(5)
African-American	-0.029	-0.028	-0.028	-0.028	-0.029
	(0.021)	(0.021)	(0.021)	(0.021)	(0.021)
Two-parent family	0.093**	0.090**	0.090**	0.089**	0.089**
	(0.013)	(0.013)	(0.013)	(0.013)	(0.013)
Test score (tenth grade)	0.448**	0.446**	0.446**	0.446**	0.444**
	(0.006)	(0.006)	(0.006)	(0.006)	(0.006)
Academic track	0.408**	0.398**	0.398**	0.398**	0.398**
	(0.013)	(0.013)	(0.013)	(0.013)	(0.013)
Vocational track	0.146**	0.146**	0.146**	0.146**	0.146**
	(0.014)	(0.014)	(0.014)	(0.014)	(0.014)
Siblings	-0.012**	-0.011**	-0.011**	-0.011**	-0.012**
	(0.003)	(0.003)	(0.003)	(0.003)	(0.003)
Student SES	0.059**	0.058**	0.058**	0.058**	0.058**
	(0.006)	(0.006)	(0.006)	(0.006)	(0.006)
Non-English home	0.108**	0.100**	0.100**	0.100**	0.101**
	(0.030)	(0.030)	(0.030)	(0.030)	(0.030)

*$p < .05$. **$p < .01$. $N = 22{,}686$. For details on data, see Tables 5.A and 5.B.

Note: Means substitution for missing data on school and student characteristics; dummy variables for substitution not reported.

Table 5.F Logistic regression of student high school graduation on school rules, student perceptions of school discipline, and other variables, 1982 and 1992 pooled data

	(1)	(2)	(3)	(4)	(5)
Intercept	-5.307**	-5.342**	-5.095**	-6.043**	-5.090**
	(0.700)	(0.721)	(0.830)	(0.855)	(0.737)
Discipline—school level					
School rules	-0.220**	-0.222**	-0.222**	-0.216**	-0.222**
	(0.062)	(0.062)	(0.062)	(0.062)	(0.062)
Strictness perception (average)	-0.046	-0.018	-0.017	-0.019	-0.017
	(0.051)	(0.053)	(0.053)	(0.053)	(0.053)
Fairness perception (average)	0.061	0.032	0.032	0.033	0.030
	(0.046)	(0.049)	(0.049)	(0.049)	(0.049)
Discipline—student level					
Strictness perception		-0.136*	0.075	-0.377*	-0.138*
		(0.060)	(0.363)	(0.170)	(0.060)
Fairness perception		0.112	0.105	-0.185	0.093
		(0.058)	(0.059)	(0.213)	(0.058)
Strictness perception (squared)			-0.039		
			(0.064)		
Strictness*fairness perception				0.104	
				(0.069)	
Safe school (perception)					0.283
					(0.145)
School characteristics					
Rural location	-0.109	-0.103	-0.101	-0.100	-0.104
	(0.118)	(0.118)	(0.118)	(0.118)	(0.118)

	(1)	(2)	(3)	(4)	(5)
Urban location	-0.236	-0.244	-0.244	-0.237	-0.243
	(0.137)	(0.137)	(0.137)	(0.137)	(0.137)
School size	-0.340**	-0.332**	-0.333**	-0.337**	-0.326**
	(0.103)	(0.103)	(0.103)	(0.103)	(0.103)
School student/teacher ratio	0.119	0.119	0.120	0.119	0.116
	(0.070)	(0.070)	(0.070)	(0.070)	(0.070)
African-American students (%)	-1.216**	-1.252**	-1.244**	-1.263**	-1.226**
	(0.367)	(0.367)	(0.368)	(0.369)	(0.369)
Hispanic students (%)	-0.919*	-0.929*	-0.926*	-0.929*	-0.930*
	(0.385)	(0.387)	(0.388)	(0.386)	(0.385)
Poor students (%)	-0.441	-0.440	-0.440	-0.449	-0.426
	(0.290)	(0.290)	(0.291)	(0.289)	(0.292)
Average student SES	0.034	0.038	0.040	0.043	0.039
	(0.079)	(0.079)	(0.079)	(0.079)	(0.080)
Dropout rate (%)	-0.027	-0.044	-0.056	-0.031	-0.050
	(0.564)	(0.559)	(0.560)	(0.560)	(0.560)
African-American teachers (%)	1.720**	1.756**	1.765**	1.761**	1.782**
	(0.579)	(0.580)	(0.582)	(0.582)	(0.580)
Hispanic teachers (%)	1.141	1.174	1.178	1.181	1.194
	(0.616)	(0.618)	(0.618)	(0.618)	(0.625)
Individual characteristics					
Male	-0.228*	-0.221*	-0.219*	-0.219*	-0.214*
	(0.099)	(0.099)	(0.099)	(0.099)	(0.099)

Table 5.F (continued)

	(1)	(2)	(3)	(4)	(5)
Hispanic	0.335*	0.338*	0.339*	0.327	0.340*
	(0.168)	(0.168)	(0.168)	(0.169)	(0.168)
African-American	0.607**	0.616**	0.616**	0.619**	0.602**
	(0.162)	(0.162)	(0.162)	(0.164)	(0.160)
Two-parent family	0.184	0.182	0.181	0.181	0.182
	(0.112)	(0.112)	(0.112)	(0.113)	(0.112)
Test score (tenth grade)	0.552**	0.541**	0.540**	0.541**	0.532**
	(0.066)	(0.067)	(0.067)	(0.067)	(0.067)
Academic track	1.316**	1.312**	1.312**	1.311**	1.314**
	(0.144)	(0.144)	(0.144)	(0.144)	(0.143)
Vocational track	0.868**	0.873**	0.876**	0.874**	0.877**
	(0.119)	(0.119)	(0.120)	(0.120)	(0.120)
Siblings	−0.016	−0.015	−0.015	−0.015	−0.016
	(0.023)	(0.023)	(0.023)	(0.023)	(0.023)
Student SES	0.412**	0.413**	0.412**	0.411**	0.413**
	(0.063)	(0.063)	(0.063)	(0.063)	(0.062)
Non-English home	0.254	0.248	0.246	0.258	0.255
	(0.206)	(0.206)	(0.207)	(0.207)	(0.205)
Pseudo R^2	0.182	0.184	0.184	0.184	0.185

*$p < .05$. **$p < .01$. $N = 14{,}986$. For details on data, see Tables 5.A and 5.B.
Note: Means substitution for missing data on school and student characteristics; dummy variables for substitution not reported. Robust standard errors with clustering at school level.

Table 5.G Hierarchical linear modeling of student twelfth-grade test scores on school rules, student perceptions of school discipline, and other variables, 1982 and 1992 pooled data

	(1)	(2)	(3)	(4)	(5)
Intercept	-0.042 (0.058)	-0.041 (0.060)	-0.127* (0.065)	-0.062 (0.066)	-0.070 (0.061)
Discipline—school level					
School rules	-0.031** (0.005)	-0.031** (0.005)	-0.031** (0.005)	-0.031** (0.005)	-0.031** (0.005)
Strictness perception (average)	0.006 (0.005)	0.009 (0.005)	0.009 (0.005)	0.009 (0.005)	0.009 (0.005)
Fairness perception (average)	-0.002 (0.004)	-0.004 (0.005)	-0.004 (0.005)	-0.004 (0.005)	-0.004 (0.005)
Discipline—student level					
Strictness perception		-0.012** (0.004)	0.065** (0.022)	-0.004 (0.012)	-0.013** (0.004)
Fairness perception		0.011* (0.004)	0.009* (0.004)	0.020 (0.013)	0.009* (0.004)
Strictness perception (squared)			-0.015** (0.004)		
Strictness*fairness perception				-0.004 (0.005)	
Safe school (perception)					0.033** (0.012)
School characteristics					
Rural location	-0.016 (0.012)	-0.016 (0.012)	-0.017 (0.012)	-0.016 (0.012)	-0.016 (0.012)

Table 5.G (continued)

	(1)	(2)	(3)	(4)	(5)
Urban location	−0.008	−0.008	−0.009	−0.008	−0.008
	(0.014)	(0.014)	(0.014)	(0.014)	(0.014)
School size	0.013	0.014	0.014	0.014	0.014
	(0.009)	(0.009)	(0.009)	(0.009)	(0.009)
School student/teacher ratio	−0.006	−0.006	−0.006	−0.006	−0.006
	(0.008)	(0.008)	(0.008)	(0.008)	(0.008)
African-American students (%)	0.001	0.001	0.001	0.001	0.001
	(0.001)	(0.001)	(0.001)	(0.001)	(0.001)
Hispanic students (%)	0.001	0.001	0.001	0.001	0.001
	(0.000)	(0.000)	(0.000)	(0.000)	(0.000)
Poor students (%)	0.001	0.001	−0.001	0.001	0.001
	(0.001)	(0.001)	(0.001)	(0.001)	(0.001)
Average student SES	0.014*	0.014*	0.014*	0.014*	0.014*
	(0.007)	(0.007)	(0.007)	(0.007)	(0.007)
Dropout rate (%)	−0.001	−0.001	−0.001	−0.001	−0.001
	(0.001)	(0.001)	(0.001)	(0.001)	(0.001)
African-American teachers (%)	0.001	0.001	0.001	0.001	0.001
	(0.001)	(0.001)	(0.001)	(0.001)	(0.001)
Hispanic teachers (%)	0.001	0.001	0.001	0.001	0.001
	(0.001)	(0.001)	(0.001)	(0.001)	(0.001)
Individual characteristics					
Male	0.038**	0.038**	0.039**	0.038**	0.039**
	(0.007)	(0.007)	(0.007)	(0.007)	(0.007)

	(1)	(2)	(3)	(4)	(5)
Hispanic	-0.076**	-0.076**	-0.076**	-0.076**	-0.076**
	(0.013)	(0.013)	(0.013)	(0.013)	(0.013)
African-American	-0.115**	-0.115**	-0.114**	-0.115**	-0.115**
	(0.014)	(0.014)	(0.014)	(0.014)	(0.014)
Two-parent family	0.036**	0.035**	0.035**	0.035**	0.035**
	(0.008)	(0.008)	(0.008)	(0.008)	(0.008)
Test score (tenth grade)	0.759**	0.758**	0.758**	0.758**	0.757**
	(0.004)	(0.004)	(0.004)	(0.004)	(0.004)
Academic track	0.203**	0.202**	0.202**	0.202**	0.202**
	(0.008)	(0.008)	(0.008)	(0.008)	(0.008)
Vocational track	-0.052**	-0.052**	-0.052**	-0.052**	-0.052**
	(0.009)	(0.009)	(0.009)	(0.009)	(0.009)
Siblings	0.004*	0.005*	0.005*	0.005*	0.005*
	(0.002)	(0.002)	(0.002)	(0.002)	(0.002)
Student SES	0.038**	0.038**	0.038**	0.038**	0.038**
	(0.004)	(0.004)	(0.004)	(0.004)	(0.004)
Non-English home	0.035	0.034	0.033	0.034	0.034
	(0.020)	(0.020)	(0.020)	(0.020)	(0.020)

$*p < .05.$ $**p < .01.$ $N = 20,866.$ For details on data, see Tables 5.A and 5.B.

Note: Means substitution for missing data on school and student characteristics; dummy variables for substitution not reported.

Table 5.H Ordered logit modeling of student's expressed willingness to disobey rules on school rules, student perceptions of school discipline, and other variables, 1982 and 1992 pooled data

	(1)	(2)	(3)	(4)	(5)
Discipline—school level					
School rules	0.014	0.016	0.015	0.015	0.014
	(0.043)	(0.045)	(0.045)	(0.045)	(0.045)
Strictness perception (average)	0.028	0.000	0.000	0.000	0.000
	(0.040)	(0.043)	(0.044)	(0.043)	(0.043)
Fairness perception (average)	−0.164**	−0.023	−0.023	−0.024	−0.023
	(0.032)	(0.035)	(0.035)	(0.035)	(0.035)
Discipline—student level					
Strictness perception		0.097*	−0.326	0.375**	0.099*
		(0.039)	(0.260)	(0.138)	(0.039)
Fairness perception		−0.709**	−0.696**	−0.387*	−0.697**
		(0.045)	(0.045)	(0.152)	(0.045)
Strictness perception (squared)			0.077		
			(0.047)		
Strictness*fairness perception				−0.111*	
				(0.052)	
Safe school (perception)					−0.259*
					(0.104)
School characteristics					
Rural location	−0.007	−0.019	−0.017	−0.021	−0.019
	(0.071)	(0.073)	(0.073)	(0.073)	(0.073)
Urban location	0.040	0.046	0.047	0.042	0.041
	(0.084)	(0.086)	(0.086)	(0.085)	(0.086)

	(1)	(2)	(3)	(4)	(5)
School size	-0.049	-0.073	-0.070	-0.068	-0.078
	(0.067)	(0.069)	(0.069)	(0.069)	(0.069)
School student/teacher ratio	-0.056	-0.055	-0.056	-0.056	-0.052
	(0.046)	(0.047)	(0.047)	(0.047)	(0.047)
African-American students (%)	-0.440	-0.383	-0.400	-0.383	-0.406
	(0.283)	(0.293)	(0.293)	(0.295)	(0.294)
Hispanic students (%)	-0.078	-0.074	-0.083	-0.070	-0.090
	(0.335)	(0.328)	(0.327)	(0.329)	(0.327)
Poor students (%)	-0.286	-0.293	-0.288	-0.279	-0.311
	(0.188)	(0.196)	(0.197)	(0.197)	(0.196)
Average student SES	0.118**	0.105*	0.104*	0.104*	0.103*
	(0.041)	(0.041)	(0.042)	(0.041)	(0.041)
Dropout rate (%)	-0.074	0.048	0.072	0.031	0.025
	(0.326)	(0.326)	(0.326)	(0.328)	(0.326)
African-American teachers (%)	-0.128	-0.191	-0.224	-0.177	-0.192
	(0.448)	(0.465)	(0.464)	(0.470)	(0.468)
Hispanic teachers (%)	0.352	0.376	0.373	0.364	0.379
	(0.510)	(0.517)	(0.517)	(0.518)	(0.520)
Individual characteristics					
Male	0.688**	0.685**	0.687**	0.686**	0.683**
	(0.053)	(0.055)	(0.055)	(0.055)	(0.055)
African-American	0.071	0.061	0.061	0.067	0.064
	(0.113)	(0.114)	(0.115)	(0.115)	(0.114)
Hispanic	-0.113	-0.169	-0.166	-0.174	-0.166
	(0.116)	(0.116)	(0.117)	(0.117)	(0.115)

Table 5.H (continued)

	(1)	(2)	(3)	(4)	(5)
Two-parent family	−0.043	−0.011	−0.010	−0.011	−0.009
	(0.068)	(0.070)	(0.070)	(0.069)	(0.070)
Test score (tenth grade)	0.026	0.058	0.061	0.058	0.066*
	(0.033)	(0.033)	(0.033)	(0.033)	(0.033)
Academic track	−0.295**	−0.260**	−0.261**	−0.258**	−0.260**
	(0.060)	(0.061)	(0.061)	(0.061)	(0.061)
Vocational track	−0.016	−0.025	−0.027	−0.028	−0.024
	(0.086)	(0.085)	(0.085)	(0.085)	(0.085)
Siblings	0.014	0.013	0.012	0.013	0.014
	(0.014)	(0.014)	(0.014)	(0.014)	(0.014)
Student SES	−0.045	−0.040	−0.039	−0.040	−0.040
	(0.031)	(0.031)	(0.031)	(0.031)	(0.031)
Non-English home	−0.255*	−0.233*	−0.231*	−0.238*	−0.235*
	(0.105)	(0.108)	(0.109)	(0.108)	(0.109)
Adjacent logit cut points					
First cut	−0.232	−1.987	−2.475	−1.143	−2.227
	(0.430)	(0.467)	(0.598)	(0.582)	(0.477)
Second cut	1.614	−0.064	−0.551	0.783	−0.302
	(0.428)	(0.464)	(0.594)	(0.582)	(0.474)
Third cut	3.258	1.624	1.140	2.475	1.389
	(0.441)	(0.478)	(0.606)	(0.595)	(0.488)
Pseudo R²	0.028	0.053	0.053	0.054	0.054

*p < .05. **p < .01. N = 8,810. For details on data, see Tables 5.A and 5.B.
Means substitution for missing data on school and student characteristics; dummy variables for substitution not reported. Robust standard errors with clustering at school level.

Table 5.1 Ordered logit modeling of student reported school disruption on school rules, student perceptions of school discipline, and other variables, 1982 and 1992 pooled data

	(1)	(2)	(3)	(4)	(5)
Discipline—school level					
School rules	−0.014	−0.011	−0.011	−0.010	−0.011
	(0.068)	(0.068)	(0.068)	(0.068)	(0.068)
Strictness perception (average)	0.03	0.018	0.019	0.018	0.019
	(0.059)	(0.060)	(0.060)	(0.060)	(0.060)
Fairness perception (average)	−0.017	0.029	0.029	0.029	0.030
	(0.053)	(0.054)	(0.054)	(0.054)	(0.054)
Discipline—student level					
Strictness perception		0.031	0.147	−0.236	0.032
		(0.049)	(0.348)	(0.176)	(0.049)
Fairness perception		−0.243**	−0.246**	−0.538**	−0.238**
		(0.061)	(0.062)	(0.184)	(0.062)
Strictness perception (squared)			−0.021		
			(0.063)		
Strictness*fairness perception				0.104	
				(0.065)	
Safe school (perception)					−0.141
					(0.190)
School characteristics					
Rural location	0.063	0.057	0.057	0.062	0.058
	(0.112)	(0.112)	(0.112)	(0.112)	(0.112)
Urban location	0.048	0.043	0.044	0.050	0.042
	(0.140)	(0.141)	(0.141)	(0.140)	(0.141)

Table 5.1 (continued)

	(1)	(2)	(3)	(4)	(5)
School size	-0.146	-0.151	-0.152	-0.155	-0.153
	(0.096)	(0.096)	(0.095)	(0.095)	(0.096)
School student/teacher ratio	0.039	0.039	0.040	0.040	0.040
	(0.075)	(0.075)	(0.075)	(0.075)	(0.075)
African-American students (%)	-0.649	-0.663	-0.656	-0.646	-0.673
	(0.348)	(0.347)	(0.347)	(0.347)	(0.346)
Hispanic students (%)	-0.198	-0.181	-0.181	-0.180	-0.182
	(0.377)	(0.379)	(0.379)	(0.380)	(0.379)
Poor students (%)	0.054	0.054	0.053	0.030	0.044
	(0.308)	(0.307)	(0.307)	(0.308)	(0.306)
Average student SES	-0.008	-0.012	-0.012	-0.012	-0.014
	(0.067)	(0.067)	(0.067)	(0.067)	(0.067)
Dropout rate (%)	0.235	0.275	0.274	0.286	0.258
	(0.409)	(0.409)	(0.408)	(0.408)	(0.409)
African-American teachers (%)	0.632	0.647	0.655	0.622	0.664
	(0.465)	(0.464)	(0.462)	(0.464)	(0.462)
Hispanic teachers (%)	-0.612	-0.610	-0.611	-0.624	-0.625
	(0.789)	(0.777)	(0.779)	(0.784)	(0.774)
Individual characteristics					
Male	0.890**	0.889**	0.889**	0.888**	0.889**
	(0.083)	(0.083)	(0.083)	(0.083)	(0.083)
African-American	0.182	0.177	0.179	0.171	0.180
	(0.182)	(0.179)	(0.179)	(0.181)	(0.179)
Hispanic	0.000	-0.021	-0.024	-0.019	-0.024
	(0.169)	(0.170)	(0.171)	(0.170)	(0.171)

	(1)	(2)	(3)	(4)	(5)
Two-parent family	-0.132	-0.124	-0.125	-0.127	-0.125
	(0.099)	(0.100)	(0.100)	(0.100)	(0.100)
Test score (tenth grade)	-0.367**	-0.354**	-0.355**	-0.353**	-0.350**
	(0.049)	(0.049)	(0.049)	(0.049)	(0.050)
Academic track	-0.235*	-0.216*	-0.216*	-0.218*	-0.216*
	(0.096)	(0.097)	(0.096)	(0.097)	(0.097)
Vocational track	0.111	0.119	0.120	0.117	0.116
	(0.147)	(0.146)	(0.146)	(0.146)	(0.147)
Siblings	-0.012	-0.013	-0.013	-0.013	-0.013
	(0.021)	(0.021)	(0.021)	(0.021)	(0.021)
Student SES	0.048	0.045	0.045	0.044	0.044
	(0.049)	(0.050)	(0.050)	(0.050)	(0.050)
Non-English home	-0.085	-0.076	-0.077	-0.070	-0.076
	(0.146)	(0.146)	(0.146)	(0.146)	(0.146)
Adjacent logit cut points					
First cut	0.081	-0.505	-0.377	-1.289	-0.634
	(0.645)	(0.673)	(0.809)	(0.783)	(0.701)
Second cut	1.451	0.870	0.998	0.087	0.741
	(0.645)	(0.672)	(0.810)	(0.779)	(0.700)
Third cut	3.343	2.767	2.895	1.983	2.638
	(0.649)	(0.675)	(0.816)	(0.781)	(0.704)
Fourth cut	5.563	4.989	5.117	4.205	4.861
	(0.714)	(0.736)	(0.861)	(0.844)	(0.759)
Pseudo R^2	0.051	0.054	0.054	0.054	0.054

$*p < .05.$ $**p < .01.$ $N = 4,789.$ For details on data, see Tables 5.A and 5.B.

Note: Means substitution for missing data on school and student characteristics; dummy variables for substitution not reported. Robust standard errors with clustering at school level.

Table 5.J Ordered logit modeling of student reported school fighting on school rules, student perceptions of school discipline, and other variables, 1982 and 1992 pooled data

	(1)	(2)	(3)	(4)	(5)
Discipline—school level					
School rules	−0.118	−0.119	−0.12	−0.123	−0.119
	(0.072)	(0.072)	(0.072)	(0.072)	(0.072)
Strictness perception (average)	0.066	0.055	0.055	0.058	0.056
	(0.057)	(0.059)	(0.059)	(0.059)	(0.059)
Fairness perception (average)	−0.022	0.037	0.037	0.038	0.039
	(0.054)	(0.055)	(0.055)	(0.055)	(0.055)
Discipline—student level					
Strictness perception		0.034	−0.357	0.365*	0.031
		(0.065)	(0.337)	(0.179)	(0.064)
Fairness perception		−0.273**	−0.259**	0.130	−0.255**
		(0.060)	(0.061)	(0.218)	(0.060)
Strictness perception (squared)			0.071		
			(0.060)		
Strictness*fairness perception				−0.136	
				(0.070)	
Safe school (perception)					−0.355*
					(0.175)
School characteristics					
Rural location	−0.078	−0.079	−0.078	−0.082	−0.078
	(0.119)	(0.119)	(0.119)	(0.120)	(0.120)
Urban location	0.041	0.032	0.035	0.020	0.025
	(0.143)	(0.143)	(0.143)	(0.144)	(0.143)

	(1)	(2)	(3)	(4)	(5)
School size	0.003	0.002	0.003	0.005	−0.008
	(0.086)	(0.085)	(0.085)	(0.085)	(0.085)
School student/teacher ratio	0.038	0.036	0.035	0.038	0.044
	(0.067)	(0.067)	(0.067)	(0.067)	(0.068)
African-American students (%)	0.127	0.143	0.128	0.142	0.130
	(0.340)	(0.339)	(0.342)	(0.340)	(0.345)
Hispanic students (%)	0.148	0.154	0.149	0.172	0.177
	(0.392)	(0.391)	(0.388)	(0.388)	(0.387)
Poor students (%)	−0.273	−0.265	−0.270	−0.242	−0.292
	(0.284)	(0.284)	(0.285)	(0.286)	(0.285)
Average student SES	0.033	0.026	0.025	0.027	0.026
	(0.077)	(0.078)	(0.078)	(0.078)	(0.077)
Dropout rate (%)	0.210	0.239	0.268	0.228	0.188
	(0.467)	(0.471)	(0.470)	(0.472)	(0.466)
African-American teachers (%)	−0.478	−0.471	−0.497	−0.448	−0.447
	(0.624)	(0.626)	(0.626)	(0.628)	(0.630)
Hispanic teachers (%)	−0.180	−0.206	−0.199	−0.223	−0.282
	(0.634)	(0.625)	(0.626)	(0.622)	(0.634)
Individual characteristics					
Male	1.318**	1.311**	1.310**	1.315**	1.308**
	(0.097)	(0.098)	(0.098)	(0.098)	(0.098)
African-American	−0.043	−0.039	−0.040	−0.038	−0.046
	(0.186)	(0.187)	(0.187)	(0.188)	(0.188)

Table 5.J (continued)

	(1)	(2)	(3)	(4)	(5)
Hispanic	0.171	0.155	0.157	0.152	0.154
	(0.186)	(0.184)	(0.184)	(0.184)	(0.181)
Two-parent family	−0.093	−0.083	−0.082	−0.079	−0.083
	(0.115)	(0.115)	(0.115)	(0.114)	(0.114)
Test score (tenth grade)	−0.600**	−0.586**	−0.583**	−0.590**	−0.574**
	(0.060)	(0.060)	(0.060)	(0.060)	(0.060)
Academic track	−0.405**	−0.393**	−0.393**	−0.391**	−0.391**
	(0.114)	(0.116)	(0.116)	(0.116)	(0.115)
Vocational track	0.072	0.073	0.072	0.071	0.068
	(0.122)	(0.120)	(0.120)	(0.120)	(0.120)
Siblings	0.035	0.033	0.032	0.032	0.033
	(0.020)	(0.020)	(0.020)	(0.020)	(0.020)
Student SES	−0.069	−0.071	−0.070	−0.071	−0.073
	(0.053)	(0.053)	(0.054)	(0.054)	(0.054)
Non-English home	−0.097	−0.080	−0.078	−0.083	−0.078
	(0.174)	(0.173)	(0.173)	(0.174)	(0.173)
Adjacent logit cut points					
First cut	2.553	1.921	1.451	2.937	1.578
	(0.624)	(0.657)	(0.766)	(0.840)	(0.685)
Second cut	4.369	3.744	3.274	4.761	3.403
	(0.629)	(0.666)	(0.777)	(0.848)	(0.696)
Pseudo R^2	0.112	0.116	0.116	0.117	0.117

*$p < .05$. **$p < .01$. $N = 8,114$. For details on data, see Tables 5.A and 5.B.
Note: Means substitution for missing data on school and student characteristics; dummy variables for substitution not reported. Robust standard errors with clustering at school level.

Table 5.K Logistic regression of student-reported arrest on school rules, student perceptions of school discipline, and other variables, 1982 and 1992 pooled data

	(1)	(2)	(3)	(4)	(5)
Intercept	4.608**	3.639**	3.136**	4.242**	3.313**
	(0.609)	(0.623)	(0.706)	(0.751)	(0.635)
Discipline—school level					
School rules	−0.003	0.027	0.027	0.022	0.028
	(0.052)	(0.052)	(0.053)	(0.052)	(0.052)
Strictness perception (average)	0.042	0.052	0.051	0.056	0.053
	(0.054)	(0.056)	(0.056)	(0.056)	(0.056)
Fairness perception (average)	−0.163**	−0.084	−0.082	−0.083	−0.079
	(0.046)	(0.048)	(0.048)	(0.048)	(0.048)
Discipline—student level					
Strictness perception		−0.084	−0.551*	0.148	−0.079
		(0.052)	(0.269)	(0.131)	(0.052)
Fairness perception		−0.351**	−0.335**	−0.050	−0.328**
		(0.057)	(0.058)	(0.174)	(0.056)
Strictness perception (squared)			0.092		
			(0.050)		
Strictness*fairness perception				−0.115	
				(0.062)	
Safe school (perception)					−0.391**
					(0.121)
School characteristics					
Rural location	0.022	0.034	0.034	0.035	0.034
	(0.118)	(0.118)	(0.118)	(0.118)	(0.119)

Table 5.K (continued)

	(1)	(2)	(3)	(4)	(5)
Urban location	-0.173	-0.145	-0.142	-0.147	-0.145
	(0.147)	(0.147)	(0.148)	(0.147)	(0.147)
School size	0.124	0.126	0.127	0.128	0.122
	(0.094)	(0.094)	(0.094)	(0.094)	(0.094)
School student/teacher ratio	0.048	0.035	0.031	0.034	0.035
	(0.080)	(0.082)	(0.082)	(0.081)	(0.083)
African-American students (%)	0.077	0.051	0.028	0.055	0.027
	(0.420)	(0.424)	(0.423)	(0.426)	(0.425)
Hispanic students (%)	0.344	0.394	0.394	0.403	0.358
	(0.439)	(0.436)	(0.436)	(0.434)	(0.436)
Poor students (%)	-0.571	-0.502	-0.503	-0.500	-0.525
	(0.300)	(0.302)	(0.303)	(0.302)	(0.302)
Average student SES	0.059	0.068	0.067	0.064	0.063
	(0.071)	(0.071)	(0.071)	(0.072)	(0.072)
Dropout rate (%)	-1.378*	-1.373*	-1.373*	-1.379*	-1.363*
	(0.670)	(0.673)	(0.675)	(0.675)	(0.674)
African-American teachers (%)	-0.221	-0.213	-0.215	-0.211	-0.240
	(0.735)	(0.743)	(0.746)	(0.746)	(0.737)
Hispanic teachers (%)	-1.675	-1.585	-1.600	-1.605	-1.628
	(0.937)	(0.906)	(0.908)	(0.905)	(0.923)
Individual characteristics					
Male	1.451**	1.451**	1.447**	1.449**	1.438**
	(0.097)	(0.097)	(0.097)	(0.097)	(0.097)
Hispanic	0.018	-0.019	-0.015	-0.014	-0.020
	(0.147)	(0.146)	(0.147)	(0.146)	(0.146)

	(1)	(2)	(3)	(4)	(5)
African-American	-0.283	-0.268	-0.264	-0.270	-0.261
	(0.179)	(0.178)	(0.179)	(0.178)	(0.176)
Two-parent family	-0.340**	-0.323**	-0.321**	-0.320**	-0.322**
	(0.104)	(0.104)	(0.104)	(0.104)	(0.104)
Test score (tenth grade)	-0.312**	-0.303**	-0.298**	-0.304**	-0.288**
	(0.059)	(0.058)	(0.058)	(0.058)	(0.058)
Academic track	-0.708**	-0.673**	-0.675**	-0.671**	-0.672**
	(0.121)	(0.121)	(0.121)	(0.120)	(0.121)
Vocational track	-0.061	-0.067	-0.070	-0.065	-0.071
	(0.104)	(0.104)	(0.104)	(0.104)	(0.104)
Siblings	0.030	0.027	0.027	0.029	0.028
	(0.023)	(0.023)	(0.023)	(0.023)	(0.023)
Student SES	0.053	0.055	0.055	0.057	0.057
	(0.050)	(0.051)	(0.050)	(0.051)	(0.051)
Non-English home	0.128	0.173	0.178	0.173	0.170
	(0.216)	(0.216)	(0.216)	(0.217)	(0.217)
Pseudo R^2	0.089	0.098	0.099	0.099	0.100

$*p < .05.$ $**p < .01.$ $N = 23,857.$ For details on data, see Tables 5.A and 5.B.

Note: Means substitution for missing data on school and student characteristics; dummy variables for substitution not reported. Robust standard errors with clustering at school level.

Notes

1. Questioning School Authority

1. See U.S. Department of Education, *Digest of Education Statistics, 1995* (Washington, D.C.: Government Printing House, 1995), table 8.
2. David Berliner and Bruce Biddle, *The Manufactured Crisis: Myths, Fraud, and the Attack on America's Public Schools* (New York: Addison Wesley, 1996).
3. Although one would not want to rule out the extent to which the erosion of moral authority in schools may also relate to stagnation in test scores and the tripling of the U.S. prison population in the last three decades.
4. George Gallup, *The Gallup Poll: Public Opinion 1935–1971* (New York: Random House, 1972), 1281, 1587.
5. Jill F. Devoe, et al., *Indicators of School Crime and Safety 2002* (Washington D.C.: U.S. Departments of Education and Justice; NCES 2003–009/NCJ 196753), 48, 78–80, 86.
6. See, for example, Denise Gottfredson, *Schools and Delinquency* (New York: Cambridge University Press, 2001), 21. Also Gary Gottfredson and Denise Gottfredson, *Victimization in Schools* (New York: Plenum Press; 1985).
7. George Gallup, *The Gallup Poll: Public Opinion 2001* (Wilmington, Del.: Scholarly Resources Inc., 2002), 78.
8. George Gallup, *The Gallup Poll: Public Opinion 1993* (Wilmington, Del.: Scholarly Resources Inc., 1994), 184–85.
9. Emile Durkheim, *Moral Education: A Study in the Theory and Application of the Sociology of Education* (New York: Macmillan Publishers, 1973 [1925]), 148, 149.
10. Developmental psychologists such as Erik Erikson and Carol Gilligan have suggested that adolescent development has this moral character.
11. See, for example, Gallup Poll surveys over the past several decades that have listed discipline as a primary educational concern of citizens.
12. For other examples of how social scientists have begun to examine court deci-

sions systematically, see recent work by sociologists examining Equal Employment Opportunity Law, esp. Paul Burstein, "Legal Mobilization as a Social Movement Tactic: The Struggle for Equal Employment Opportunity," *American Journal of Sociology* 96 (1991): 1201–25; and Robert Nelson and William Bridges, *Legalizing Gender Inequality: Courts, Markets and Unequal Pay for Women in America* (New York: Cambridge University Press, 1999).

13. Our analysis has focused on court cases that have reached the appellate level and thus were relevant to defining case law in this area. Cases at the trial level have not been systematically collected. Justification for examining cases at this level was articulated by Paul Burstein in his analysis of similar cases applying to Equal Employment Opportunity Law. Burstein argued that "the justification for studying appellate cases is not in their being a random sample but rather in their great importance; they influence the judgment of employees (and their lawyers) about whether particular disputes are worth pursuing and set the terms within which employees bargain with employers or unions in the hope of settling out of court." Burstein, "Legal Mobilization," 1208. We discuss related issues in Chapter 2.

14. Research by Perry Zirkel has reported the following annual averaged volumes of state and federal case decisions by decade: 1,552 for the 1940s; 2,452 for the 1950s; 3,413 for the 1960s; 6,788 for the 1970s; 6,714 for the 1980s; and 6,053 estimated for the 1990s. See "The 'Explosion' in Educational Litigation: An Update," *Education Law Reporter* 114 (January 1997): 341–51. David Tyack, Tom James, and Aaron Benavot identified a fairly steady increase of litigation up to the mid 1960s, utilizing a methodology based on sampling cases (thus the Zirkel and Tyack, James, and Benavot figures are not directly comparable). See David Tyack, Tom James and Aaron Benavot, *Law and the Shaping of Public Education, 1785–1954* (Madison: University of Wisconsin Press, 1987).

15. See, for example, Gerald Grant and John Briggs, "Today's Children are Different," *Educational Leadership* 40 (March 1983): 4–9.

16. On protest activities at college campuses, see Nella Van Dyke, "Protest Cycles and Party Politics: The Effect of Elite Allies and Antagonists on Student Protest in the United States, 1930–1990," in Jack Goldstone, ed., *Parties, Politics and Movements* (Cambridge: Cambridge University Press, 2002).

17. Hillary Rodham, "Children Under the Law," *Harvard Educational Review* 43 (November 1973): 487–514.

18. We used "NAACP Fund" rather than the more conventionally used "NAACP Fund, Inc." for convenience. Readers should be aware that since 1957 the NAACP Fund has been organizationally distinct from the NAACP, with a separate board, program, staff, office and budget.

19. See Joel Handler, Betsy Ginsberg, and Arthur Snow, "The Public Interest Law Industry," in Burton Weisbrod, Joel Handler, and Neil Komesar, eds., *Public In-*

terest Law: An Economic and Institutional Analysis (Berkeley: University of California Press, 1978), 42–79.

20. Michael Schudson, *The Good Citizen: A History of American Civic Life* (New York: Free Press, 1998), 249. See also Laura Kalman, *The Strange Career of Legal Liberalism* (New Haven: Yale University Press, 1996).

21. David Trubeck, "Back to the Future: The Short, Happy Life of the Law and Society Movement," *Florida State University Law Review* 18 (1990). Cited in Kalman, *The Strange Career of Legal Liberalism*, 43.

22. Joel Handler, Ellen Jane Hollingsworth, and Howard Erlanger, *Lawyers and the Pursuit of Legal Rights* (New York: Academic Press, 1978), 43. See also Handler, Ginsberg, and Snow, "The Public Interest Law Industry," 50, 54. They estimated that 81 percent of the 72 largest public interest law firms in 1976 were established between 1969 and 1974. While their estimates may be somewhat exaggerated as a result of a sampling methodology that did not consider effects of organizational mortality, their results nevertheless suggest a large surge of firm formation during this period. Their Table 4.4 estimated Foundation Grants as comprising between 42 and 45 percent of sources of income for these firms.

23. Handler, Hollingsworth, and Erlanger, *Lawyers and the Pursuit of Legal Rights*, 73.

24. Handler, Ginsberg, and Snow, "The Public Interest Law Industry," 51. The authors analyzed the firms identified in the *National Inventory of the Public Interest Law Programs* (Washington, D.C.: Council for Public Interest Law, 1976).

25. H. P. Stumpf, "Law and Poverty: A Political Perspective," *Wisconsin Law Review* (1968): 711.

26. Earl Johnson, Jr., *Proceedings of the Harvard Conference on Law and Poverty* (March 1967), 1–6.

27. Handler, Hollingsworth, and Erlanger, *Lawyers and the Pursuit of Legal Rights*, 37.

28. Earl Johnson, Jr., "Discussion (on Ellen Jane Hollingsworth, "Ten Years of Legal Services for the Poor")," in Robert Haveman, ed., *A Decade of Federal Antipoverty Programs* (New York: Academic Press, 1979), 316–317.

29. See Center for Law and Education website, "Center for Law and Education— Celebrating 29 Years," <http://www.cleweb.org/aboutcle/timeline.htm>.

30. Handler, Hollingsworth, and Erlanger, *Lawyers and the Pursuit of Legal Rights*, 33.

31. Ibid., 73.

32. Ellen Jane Hollingsworth noted: "Given the dearth of experience in other countries from which to borrow, and the lack of United States precedents, Legal Services as a program felt less pressure for evaluation than many other programs of the Great Society. Even those who pushed for early evaluation of

Legal Services could not agree upon conceptualization or methodology appropriate to apply." Ellen Jane Hollingsworth, "Ten Years of Legal Services for the Poor," in Haveman, ed., *A Decade of Federal Antipoverty Programs,* 287.

33. Johnson Jr., "Discussion" in Haveman, ed., *A Decade of Federal Antipoverty Programs,* 319. Emphasis in original. On Legal Services' relationship to the American Bar Association, see Handler, Hollingsworth, and Erlanger. On support for Legal Services in 1981 from the deans of 143 out of 168 accredited law schools in the country, see Stuart Taylor, "Legal Aid for the Poor Did Work, and That's the Rub," *New York Times,* 15 March 1981, sec. 4, p. 3.

34. *New York Times,* 8 July 1972, p. 17. Cited in Stuart Scheingold, *The Politics of Rights: Lawyers, Public Policy, and Political Change* (New Haven: Yale University Press, 1974), 192.

35. Johnson suggested that Legal Services enjoyed "a firm political base in the U.S. Congress," and noted that Republican Senators Robert Taft, Jacob Javits, Richard Schweiker, and William Stafford joined Democrats Walter Mondale, Ted Kennedy, and Alan Cranston in being vocal defenders of the program. Johnson, "Discussion," 316–319.

36. Walter Mondale, "Justice for Children" (speech delivered to the U.S. Senate on December 9, 1970) (Washington, D.C.: Select Committee on Equal Educational Opportunity, 1972), 29.

37. This compares to about 7 percent of funding that major public interest law firms received from federal sources. See Handler, Ginsberg, and Snow, "The Public Interest Law Industry," 55 and 70.

38. There are, of course, exceptions to this, including federal promotion of vocational education as early as the Smith-Hughes Act of 1917. Even with vocational education, however, federal support for these programs increased dramatically during the 1960s and 1970s; see Richard Arum, "The Effects of Resources on Vocational Student Educational Outcomes: Invested Dollars or Diverted Dreams," *Sociology of Education* 71 (1998): 130–151.

39. See U.S. Department of Education, *Digest of Education Statistics, 2000* (Washington, D.C.: Government Printing House, 2000), Table 158.

40. John Meyer, W. Richard Scott, and David Strang, "Centralization, Fragmentation and School District Complexity," in W. Richard Scott, John Meyer, and Associates, *Institutional Environments and Organizations: Structural Complexity and Individualism* (Thousand Oaks, CA: Sage Publications, 1994), 166.

41. In the neoinstitutional literature this conformity has been termed "institutional isomorphism." Meyer and his colleagues have tended to emphasize normative and mimetic pressures for isomorphism rather than coercive ones. See editors' introduction in Walter Powell and Paul DiMaggio, eds., *The New Institutionalism in Organizational Analysis* (Chicago: University of Chicago Press, 1991).

42. While Jencks saw this increased federal role as inevitable and mostly desirable, he also suggested that the federal government should consider sponsoring expanded school choice through the provision of scholarships (i.e. vouchers). Christopher Jencks, "The Future of Education," in Hans J. Morgenthau, ed., *The Crossroad Papers: A Look into the American Future* (New York: W. W. Norton, 1965), 92–111; Christopher Jencks et al., *Inequality: A Reassessment of the Effect of Family and Schooling in America* (New York: Harper Torch Books, 1972), 148; James Coleman et al., *Equality of Educational Opportunity* (Washington, D.C.: U.S. Department of Health, Education and Welfare, 1966).

43. Hollingsworth, "Ten Years of Legal Services for the Poor," 291. On the fellowships used to attract young legal talent, see details about the REGGIE Fellowship Program in Earl Johnson Jr., *Justice and Reform: The Formative Years of the American Legal Services Program* (New York: Russell Sage, 1974).

44. See Susan Lawrence, *The Poor in Court: The Legal Services Program and Supreme Court Decision Making* (Princeton: Princeton University Press, 1990), esp. 100; and Martha Davis, *Brutal Need: Lawyers and the Welfare Rights Movement, 1960–1973* (New Haven: Yale University Press, 1993), 10–11.

45. Kalman, *The Strange Career of Legal Liberalism*, 43.

46. Handler, Hollingsworth, and Erlanger, *Lawyers and the Pursuit of Legal Rights*, 8. On the elite (as opposed to the grassroots) origins of the Rights Revolution, see John David Skrentny, *The Minority Rights Revolution* (Cambridge, MA: Harvard University Press, 2002).

47. While we have not attempted to conduct the archival work required to document this institutional-level orientation, we have been willing to assume its presence given the insights of social science research and theory on organizations. See, for example, Philip Selznick, *TVA and the Grass Roots* (Berkeley: University of California Press, 1949); Philip Selznick, *Leadership in Administration* (Evanston, IL: Row Peterson, 1957); Jeffrey Pfeffer and Gerlad Salancik, *The External Control of Organizations: A Resource Dependence Perspective* (New York: Harper and Row, 1978).

48. Robert Kagan, "Regulating Business, Regulating Schools," in David Kirp and Donald Jensen, eds., *School Days, Rule Days: the Legalization and Regulation of Education* (Philadelphia: Falmer Press, 1986), 64–90.

49. As Arthur Wise noted in *Legislated Learning*, "once courts insist that due process be granted, 'the logic of that position must be worked out'. Legislatures begin to draft legislation; executives begin to draft guidelines. The schools begin to develop procedures to conform to the court ruling, to the legislation, and to the guidelines. The procedures, if they are to satisfy the legal concept of due process, must mimic the judicial process. If the procedures fail to guarantee due process, appeal is made again to the courts." Arthur Wise, *Legislated Learning* (Berkeley: University of California Press, 1979), 119; see also

Nathan Glazer, "Towards an Imperial Judiciary," *The Public Interest* 41 (Fall 1975): 113.

50. See Lauren Edelman, "Legal Ambiguity and Symbolic Structures: Organizational Mediation of Civil Rights," *American Journal of Sociology* 97 (1992): 1531–76.

51. While Kirp referred here explicitly to the possibilities of court review, the larger social implications were also inescapable. David Kirp and Mark Yudof, *Educational Policy and the Law: Cases and Materials* (Berkeley: McCutchan, 1974), 135.

52. Durkheim, *Moral Education*, 43, 167.

53. Ibid., 165.

54. Robert Putnam, "Bowling Alone: America's Declining Social Capital," *Journal of Democracy* 6 (1995): 65–78.

55. Theda Skocpol, "The Tocqueville Problem," *Social Science History* 21 (1997): 455–479.

56. Mark Schudson, *The Good Citizen: A History of American Civic Life* (New York: Free Press, 1998).

57. See Richard Arum, "Schools and Communities: Ecological and Institutional Dimensions," *Annual Review of Sociology* 26 (2000): 395–418.

58. *Tinker v. Des Moines Independent Community School District*, 393 U.S. 503 [503, 506] (Supreme Court of the United States, 1969).

59. Jane Handler, *Neighborhood Legal Services—New Dimensions in the Law* (Washington, D.C.: U.S. Department of Health, Education and Welfare, 1966), 8.

60. *Ladson v. Board of Education, Union Free School District No. 9*, 67 Misc. 2d 173 [173] (Supreme Court of New York, Special Term, Nassau County, 1974).

61. Ibid., [177]. Emphasis added.

62. Ibid.

63. *Jacobs v. Benedict*, 39 Ohio App. 2d 141 [142–43] (Court of Appeals of Ohio, First Appellate District, Hamilton, 1973). Emphasis added.

64. *The People of the State of New York, Respondent, v. Scott D.*, 34 N.Y. 2d 483 [485, 486, and 490] (Court of Appeals of New York, 1974).

65. See, for example, Sally Riggs Fuller, Lauren Edelman, and Sharon Matusik, "Legal Readings: Employee Interpretations and Mobilization of Law," *Academy of Management Review* 25 (2000): 200–16.

66. *Adams v. City of Dothan Board of Education*, 485 So. 2d 757 [761] (Court of Civil Appeals of Alabama, 1986). For precedent on the last point, the judges cited *Lee v. Macon County Board of Education*, 995 F.2d 184 (U.S. Court Of Appeals, Eleventh Circuit, 1993).

67. *Adams v. City of Dothan Board of Education*, [761]. Emphasis added.

68. *In re Appeal of Huffer*, 47 Ohio St. 3d 12 [15] (Supreme Court of Ohio, 1989).

69. Ibid.

70. Survey data have indicated that adolescent drug and alcohol consumption peaked between 1979 and 1981, and has been in significant decline since. Survey results for senior high school students from the class of 1980 indicated that in the prior thirty days, 72 percent had consumed alcohol, 19 percent had used marijuana, and 18 percent had used illicit drugs other than marijuana. Twelve years later, seniors in the high school class of 1992 reported 51 percent drinking alcohol, 8 percent using marijuana, and 6 percent using illicit drugs other than marijuana. See U.S. Department of Education, *Digest of Education Statistics, 1995* (Washington, D.C.: Government Printing House, 1995), Table 146.

71. *Fishel v. Frederick County School Board,* 11 Va. Cir. 283 [285–86] (Circuit Court of Frederick County, Virginia, 1988).

72. *Lusk v. Triad Community Unit No. 2,* 194 Ill. App. 3d 426 [427–28] (Appellate Court of Illinois, Fifth District, 1990).

73. *Gaspersohn v. Harnett County Board Of Education,* 75 N.C. App. 23 [25] (Court of Appeals of North Carolina, 1985).

74. Ibid. [32, 27].

75. *Guillory v. Ortego,* 449 So. 2d 182 [185] (Court of Appeal Of Louisiana, Third Circuit, 1984).

76. Paul Weckstein, *School Discipline and Student Rights: An Advocate's Manual* (Cambridge, Mass.: Center for Law and Education, 1982), 1.

77. Robert Pressman and Susan Weinstein, *Procedural Due Process Rights in Student Discipline: An Update and Revision of the Procedural Due Process Section of School Discipline and Student Rights by Paul Weckstein* (Cambridge, Mass.: Center for Law and Education, 1990).

78. Seymour Sarason, *Revisiting the Culture of the School and the Problem of Change* (New York: Teachers College Press, 1996 [1971]); Karl Weick, "Educational Organizations as Loosely Coupled Systems," *Administrative Science Quarterly* 21 (1976): 1–19.

79. Gerald Rosenberg, *The Hollow Hope: Can Courts Bring About Social Change?* (Chicago: University of Chicago Press, 1991).

80. See John Meyer and Brian Rowan, "Institutionalized Organizations: Formal Structure as Myth and Ceremony," *American Journal of Sociology* 83 (1977): 340–363; Paul DiMaggio and Walter Powell, "The Iron Cage Revisited: Institutional Isomorphism and Collective Rationality in Organizational Fields," *American Sociological Review* 48 (1983): 147–160; John Chubb and Terry Moe, *Politics, Markets and American Schools* (Washington, D.C.: The Brookings Institute, 1990).

81. "Politics of Paddling," editorial, *San Francisco Chronicle,* 30 January 1996, sec. A, p. 14.

82. Robert Gunnison, "Assemblyman Calls for Paddling," in ibid.

83. Eric Bailey, "Conroy Files Bill to Allow the Paddling of Students Legislation: The Orange County Lawmaker's Proposal Is Designed to Undo a 1986 Ban on Corporal Punishment," *Los Angeles Times,* 10 January 1995, p. 1.

84. Dana Wilkies, "School Spanking Bill Beaten in Assembly," *San Diego Union Tribune,* 31 January 1996, sec. A, p. 1.

85. Ellen Jane Hollingsworth, Henry Luffler, and William Clune, *School Discipline: Order and Autonomy* (New York: Praeger Publishers, 1984), 124.

86. Gerald Grant, *The World We Created at Hamilton High* (Cambridge, Mass.: Harvard University Press, 1988), 147.

87. William Bagley, *Classroom Management* (New York: Macmillan Publishers, 1914), 95–96. Cited in Grant, 147.

88. Robert Ramsey, *Educator's Discipline Handbook* (West Nyack, N.Y.: Parker Publishing, 1981), 129–149.

89. James Coleman and Tom Hoffer, *Public and Private High Schools* (New York: Basic Books, 1987).

90. Tom DiPrete, Chandra Muller, and Nona Shaeffer, *Discipline and Order in American High Schools* (Washington, D.C.: National Center for Education Statistics, 1981).

91. Jackson Toby, "The Schools," in James Wilson and Joan Petersilia, eds., *Crime* (San Francisco: Institute for Contemporary Studies, 1995).

92. John Dewey, *On Democracy and Education: An Introduction to the Philosophy of Education* (New York: Free Press, 1916), 129.

93. John Dewey, "Interest in Relation to Training of the Will," in Reginald D. Archambault, ed., *John Dewey on Education* (Chicago: University of Chicago Press, 1974 [1895]), p. 267.

94. John Dewey, "My Pedagogic Creed," in ibid., 436.

95. Wayne Welsh, Patricia Jenkins, and Jack Greene, *Building a Culture and Climate of Safety in Public Schools in Philadelphia: School-Based Management and Violence Reduction* (Philadelphia: Center for Public Policy, 1997). See also Wayne Welsh, Jack Greene, and Patricia Jenkins, "School Disorder: The Influence of Individual, Institutional, and Community Factors," *Criminology* 37 (1999): 73–115.

96. Paul Willis, *Learning to Labor* (New York: Teachers College Press, 1979).

97. Mary Metz, *Classrooms and Corridors: The Crisis of Authority in Desegregated Secondary Schools* (Berkeley: University of California Press, 1978).

98. Pedro Noguera, "Preventing and Producing Violence: A Critical Analysis of Responses to School Violence," *Harvard Educational Review* 62 (1992): 189–212.

99. The percentage of mothers with children under age 18 active in the labor force increased from 45 percent in 1975 to 70 percent in 1999. U.S. Census

Bureau, *2000 Statistical Abstracts* (Washington, D.C.: Government Printing House, 2000), 409.

2. Student Rights versus School Rules

1. "Racial Strife Hits Schools," editorial, *Columbus Dispatch,* 20 January 1979, sec. 1, p. 19.
2. Frank Kemerer and Kenneth Deutsch, *Constitutional Rights and Student Life: Value Conflict in Law and Education, Cases and Materials* (St. Paul, MN: West Publishing, 1979), 411.
3. Kenneth Curtin (Legal Aid Society of Columbus), personal communication with Irenee Beattie on July 26, 2002; and Kemerer and Deutsch, *Constitutional Rights and Student Life,* 412. Peter Roos has suggested that Denis Murphy was institutionally affiliated with the American Civil Liberties Union (personal communication with Counsel Peter Roos on July 19, 2002).
4. Kenneth Curtain (Legal Aid Society of Columbus), personal communication with Irenee Beattie on July 26, 2002; and Kemerer and Deutsch, *Constitutional Rights and Student Life,* 441.
5. *Lopez v. Williams,* 372 F. Supp. 1279 (United States District Court for the Southern District of Ohio, Eastern Division, 1973).
6. Ibid., [1284–85].
7. Ibid., [1285].
8. Ibid., [1300–02].
9. Based on the Fifth and the Fourteenth Amendments, due process has become a guarantee of civil and criminal rights. Due process in the courts has included a provision for ensuring fair and public trials for accused persons, the right to be present at the trial, and the right to be heard in his or her own defense. The Fourteenth Amendment states that no person "shall be deprived of life, liberty, or property without due process of law."
10. *Goss v. Lopez,* 419 U.S. 565 [565] (Supreme Court of the United States, 1975).
11. Ibid., [580].
12. Ibid., [585].
13. Ibid., [592–93] (dissenting opinion).
14. Emile Durkheim, *Moral Education: A Study in the Theory and Application of the Sociology of Education* (New York: Macmillan, 1973 [1925]).
15. *Columbus Evening Dispatch,* 22 January 1975, sec. A, p. 1.
16. 'Lectric Law Library's Legal Lexicon's Lyceum website, <http://www.lectlaw.com/def.htm>.
17. C. K. Rowland and Robert Carp, *Politics and Judgment in Federal District Courts* (Lawrence: University Press of Kansas, 1996), 6–7.

18. Laura Kalman, *The Strange Career of Legal Liberalism* (New Haven: Yale University Press, 1996), 46.

19. In Chapter 4 we provide evidence from past research on schools that also supports our broader conceptualization of court climates.

20. Jack Peltason, *Federal Courts and the Political Process* (New York: Random House, 1955).

21. Beverly Cook, "Sentencing Behavior of Federal Judges: Draft Cases, 1972," *Cincinnati Law Review* 42 (1973): 597–633; Herbert Kritzer, "Political Correlates of the Behavior of Federal District Judges: A Best Case Analysis," *Journal of Politics* 40 (1978): 25–58.

22. Lettie Wenner and Lee Dutter, "Contextual Influences on Judicial Decision-Making," *Western Political Quarterly* 41 (1988): 115–134.

23. For more on criminal defendants, see C. K. Rowland, Robert Carp, and Donald Songer, "The Effect of Presidential Appointment, Group Identification and Fact-Law Ambiguity on Lower Federal Judges' Policy Judgements," paper presented at the annual meeting of the American Political Science Association (1985). On civil rights claims, see Ronald Stidham and Robert Carp, "Judges, Presidents, and Policy Choices: Exploring the Linkage," *Social Science Quarterly* 68 (1987): 395–404. Both cited in Rowland and Carp, *Politics and Judgment in Federal District Courts,* 13.

24. Massachusetts Secondary School Administrators Association website, May 12, 2000, <http://www.mec.edu/mssaa/mssaa-publications.html>.

25. *National Association of Secondary School Principals Bulletin,* September 1998, vol. 82, no. 599. See also NASSP website, <http://www.nassp.org/publications/bulletin/sep98toc.htm>.

26. Council of School Attorneys website, May 30, 2000, <http://www.nsba.org/cosa/About/>.

27. Cases collected from August 28, 1998, through September 9, 1998, on Lexis-Nexis Academic Universe website, <http://web.lexis-nexis.com/universe> using search string "student w/p discip! or expulsion or expel! or suspen! or punish!" with records searched from January 1, 1945, to January 1, 1992.

28. The means and standard deviations of the variables coded in the court case data are identified in the appendices.

29. We define the relevant court climate by school discipline cases that have been appealed at either the state or federal levels. Cases that did not make it to the appellate level were less important, received less attention in materials related to school discipline, and their outcomes generally affected only the individuals involved in the particular litigation. In addition, currently insurmountable technical obstacles have prevented systematic collection of these lower level court cases, which have not been collected in existing nationally organized computer archives at this time.

30. Black students accounted for the majority of students of color who were disciplined in schools—around 26 percent of corporal punishments and 29 percent of suspensions involved African-American youth.

31. It was difficult to obtain an accurate estimate of the full sample, as judges' decisions did not always indicate the race of students.

32. Joel Handler, Ellen Jane Hollingsworth, and Howard Erlanger, *Lawyers and the Pursuit of Legal Rights* (New York: Academic Press, 1978), 29.

33. On racial wealth disparities see Dalton Conley, *Being Black, Living in the Red: Race, Wealth, and Social Policy in America* (Berkeley: University of California Press, 1999).

34. A technical issue worth discussing is the concept of regression toward the mean. Differences tend to erode over time: there were reasons to suspect that court climates would have such a character, since the decisions to bring cases to court were in part influenced by prior decisions in a jurisdiction. One would anticipate that in pro-school court climates only the most egregious cases of schools violating student rights would be brought in front of the bench. Hence court decisions in such jurisdictions would over time tend to look more politically balanced than was actually the case in our data. For a general discussion of this issue see George Priest, "Selective Characteristics of Litigation," *Journal of Legal Studies* 9 (1980): 399–421; George Priest and Benjamin Klein, "The Selection of Disputes for Litigation," *Journal of Legal Studies* 13 (1984): 1–55; and Paul Burstein, "Legal Mobilization as a Social Movement Tactic: The Struggle for Equal Employment Opportunity," *American Journal of Sociology* 96 (1991): 1213.

35. See, for example, Ivan Illich, *Deschooling Society* (New York: Harper and Row, 1971); Paolo Freire, *Pedagogy of the Oppressed* (New York: Continuum, 1970); Lawrence Kohlberg, "High School Democracy and Educating for a Just Society," in Ralph Mosher, ed., *Moral Education: A First Generation of Research and Development* (New York: Praeger, 1980).

36. In addition, state appellate court cases prior to 1960 were not uniformly included for all jurisdictions in the legal data archives that we utilized.

37. Jethro Lieberman, *The Litigious Society* (New York: Basic Books, 1981).

38. John Sutton, Frank Dobbin, John Meyer and Richard Scott, "The Legalization of the Workplace," *American Journal of Sociology* 99 (1994); 948.

39. We restrict our discussion here to cases that involved public schools at the elementary and secondary level, although our data also contained cases involving private and post-secondary schools.

40. *In re Gault,* 387 U.S. 1 (Supreme Court of the United States, 1967).

41. *Epperson v. Arkansas.* 393 U.S. 97 [97] (Supreme Court of the United States, 1968).

42. *Tinker v. Des Moines,* 393 U.S. 503 [507] (Supreme Court of the United States, 1969). Our emphasis.

43. Ibid., [504]. While the events leading up to this case occurred earlier than the 1969–1975 period, the actual decision—which was what generated court climate—was handed down in 1969.

44. Ibid., [506]. The First Amendment of the U.S. Constitution states: "Congress shall make no law respecting an establishment of religion, or prohibiting the free exercise thereof; or abridging the freedom of speech, or of the press; or the right of the people peaceably to assemble, and to petition the government for a redress of grievances."

45. *Burnside v. Byars,* 363 F.2d 749 [749] (United Court of Appeals, Fifth Circuit, 1966).

46. *Tinker v. Des Moines,* [513]. Footnote excluded.

47. Ibid., [518].

48. Ibid., [524]. Dissenting opinion.

49. *Statistical Abstract of the United States* (1968), Table 578, p. 406. Cited in *Tinker v. Des Moines.*

50. *Tinker v. Des Moines,* [524–25]. Dissenting opinion. Paragraph spacing added.

51. 'Lectric Law Library's Lexicon on 'Amicus Curiae' website, <http://www.lect law.com/def/a048.htm>.

52. *Wood v. Strickland.* 420 U.S. 308 [325] (Supreme Court of the United States, 1975).

53. *Pierson v. Ray,* 386 U.S. 547 [554] (Supreme Court of the United States, 1967). Cited in *Wood v. Strickland.*

54. *Wood v. Strickland,* [319–20]. Footnotes omitted.

55. Ibid., [322].

56. Ibid., [328].

57. Ibid., [329].

58. Quotation from the National School Board Association's Council of School Attorneys website, July 22, 2002, <http://www.nsba.org/cosa/About/mem bership.htm>. Membership information and founding date as reported by Lindsay Andrews, Manager, Council of School Attorneys, conversation with Richard Arum, July 22, 2002.

59. Nathan Glazer, forward to David Kirp and Mark Yudof, *Educational Policy and the Law* (Berkeley: McCutchan, 1974), xxxv.

60. *Ingraham v. Wright,* 430 U.S. 651 [656] (Supreme Court of the United States, 1977). Footnotes omitted.

61. Ibid., [657].

62. The Eighth Amendment of the Constitution states: "Excessive bail shall not be required, nor excessive fines imposed, nor cruel and unusual punishments inflicted." See n9 above for the wording of the Fourteenth Amendment.

63. *Ingraham v. Wright,* [682]. Footnotes omitted.

64. Ibid., [683].

65. Ibid., [684–92].

66. *Carey v. Piphus,* 435 U.S. 247 [247] (Supreme Court of the United States, 1978).

67. Ibid.

68. *Board of Education of Rogers, Arkansas v. McCluskey,* 458 U.S. 966 [972–73] (Supreme Court of the United States, 1982).

69. The Fourth Amendment to the Constitution states: "The right of the people to be secure in their persons, houses, papers, and effects, against unreasonable searches and seizures, shall not be violated, and no Warrants shall issue, but upon probable cause, supported by Oath or affirmation, and particularly describing the place to be searched, and the persons or things to be seized."

70. *New Jersey v. T.L.O.,* 469 U.S. 325 [336–37] (Supreme Court of the United States, 1985). Footnotes omitted.

71. Ibid., [337].

72. Ibid., [339]. Footnotes omitted.

73. Ibid., [340].

74. Ibid.

75. Ibid., [341–42]. Footnotes omitted.

76. Ibid., [354]. Dissenting opinion. Emphasis in original.

77. Ibid., [384]. Dissenting opinion. Footnotes omitted.

78. *West Virginia State Board of Education v. Barnette,* 319 U.S. 624 [638] (Supreme Court of the United States, 1943).

79. *New Jersey v. T.L.O.,* [385–86]. Dissenting opinion.

80. *Bethel School District v. Fraser,* 478 U.S. 675 [677] (Supreme Court of the United States, 1986). See n44 above for wording of the First Amendment.

81. Ibid., [687]. Concurring opinion (Brennan).

82. Ibid., [678].

83. Ibid.

84. Ibid., [678–79].

85. Ibid., [683].

86. Ibid., [682–83]. Footnotes omitted.

87. Ibid., [690]. Dissenting opinion.

88. Ibid., [691–92].

89. Ibid., [694].

90. Ibid., [695].

91. Ibid., [696].

92. "Guardian of Liberty: American Civil Liberties Union," ACLU Briefing Paper, Number 1, American Civil Liberties Union website, <http://www.aclu.org/library/pbp1.html>.

93. "About the NAACP," National Association for the Advancement of Colored People website, <http://www.naacp.org/about.asp>.

94. Melanie Gurley Keeney and Peter Yelkovac, "Selection, Recruitment and Retention of School District Legal Counsel," in *Selecting and Working with a School Attorney: A Guide for School Boards* (Alexandria, VA: National Council of School Boards' Council of School Attorneys, 1997), 3–1.

95. *Stevenson v. Wheeler County Board of Education*, 306 F. Supp. 97 [101] (United States District Court for the Southern District of Georgia, 1969).

96. *Breen v. Kahl*, 419 F.2d 1034 [1038] (United States Court of Appeals, Seventh Circuit, 1969).

97. Suggested by Peter Roos in personal conversation with Richard Arum, July 19, 2002.

98. *State in Interest of T.L.O., Juvenile-Appellant*, 185 N.J. Super. 279 [282] (Superior Court of New Jersey, Appellate Division, 1982). Dissenting opinion.

3. How Judges Rule

1. *Breen v. Kahl*, 419 F.2d 1034 [1037] (United States Court of Appeals, Seventh Circuit, 1969).

2. Jeffrey Segal and Harold Spaeth, *The Supreme Court and the Attitudinal Model* (New York: Cambridge University Press, 1993). Cited in C. K. Rowland and Robert Carp, *Politics and Judgment in Federal District Courts* (Lawrence: University Press of Kansas, 1996).

3. Ibid. For evidence on local environmental effects, see Lettie Wenner and Lee Dutter, "Contextual Influences on Judicial Decision Making," *Western Political Quarterly* 41 (1988): 115–134; and Michael Giles and Thomas Walker, "Judicial Policy Making and Southern School Segregation," *Journal of Politics* 37 (1975): 917–937. For effects of the politics of appointment on decisions, see Steve Alumbaugh and C. K. Rowland, "The Links Between Platform-Based Appointment Criteria and Trial Judges' Abortion Judgments," *Judicature* 74 (1990): 153–62. For evidence supporting an attitudinal model, see Segal and Spaeth, *The Supreme Court and the Attitudinal Model.*

4. Predicted probabilities in Figure 3.1 were derived from logistic regression estimates of the effects of several covariates on pro-student decisions, similar to those in Table 3.A (but with more detailed measurement of time period).

5. Results based on Table 3.B, Model 1.

6. Given the relatively small number of cases relevant to each state from 1960–1968, we could not produce a map for this period. These maps were constructed using the case decisions that have jurisdiction over a given state. Thus, Supreme Court decisions were relevant to all states, while district court decisions applied only to the states in a particular district.

7. This was the actual percentage of cases decided in favor of students. It differed from the predicted probabilities that we presented because those were estimates based on logistic regression models including independent variables

measuring factors which influenced case outcomes such as time period, region, court level, student and school characteristics, form of school discipline, and type of student misbehavior.

8. Table 3.C presents results from logistic regressions performed on a sample including both public and private schools. Model 2 illustrates that courts were significantly less likely to decide in favor of students in private than public schools, with controls for type of student infraction included in the model.

9. *Geraci v. St. Xavier High School,* 13 Ohio Op. 3d 146; 1978 Ohio App. LEXIS 7764 [7–8] (Court of Appeals of Ohio, First Appellate District, Hamilton County, 1978).

10. Ibid., [7–9].

11. *Flint v. St. Augustine High School,* 323 So.2d 229 [230] (Court of Appeals of Louisiana, 1975). Emphasis in original.

12. Ibid., [235].

13. James Coleman and Thomas Hoffer, *Public and Private High Schools* (New York: Basic Books, 1987), 211–243; James Coleman, Thomas Hoffer, and Sally Kilgore, *High School Achievement: Public, Catholic, and Private Schools Compared* (New York: Basic Books, 1982).

14. Coleman and Hoffer, *Public and Private High Schools,* 219.

15. *Fielder v. Marumsco Christian School,* 631 F.2d 1144 [1147] (United States Court of Appeals, Fourth Circuit, 1980). Bostic was not involved in the suit because he voluntarily left the school without being expelled.

16. *Fielder v. Marumsco Baptist Church,* 486 F. Supp. 960 [962] (United States District Court, Eastern District of Virginia, 1979).

17. *Fiedler v. Marumsco Christian School,* 631 F.2d 1144 [1153–54] (United States Court of Appeals, Fourth Circuit, 1980).

18. We also coded for whether or not students were identified explicitly as disabled or handicapped in the case. These case outcomes did not significantly differ from other types of cases.

19. *Woods v. Wright,* 334 F.2d 369 [370–71] (United States Court of Appeals, Fifth Circuit, 1964).

20. Ibid., [375].

21. Ibid., [374–75].

22. *Jordan v. School District of the City of Erie, Pennsylvania,* 548 F.2d 117 (United States Court of Appeals, Third Circuit, 1977).

23. *Tate v. Board of Education,* 453 F.2d 975 [977] (United States Court of Appeals, Eighth Circuit, 1972).

24. Ibid., [982].

25. Refer back to Figure 3.2 for graphical illustration of this relationship. Also, see Table 3.B, logistic regression analyses of our sample, for coefficients upon which we have based these estimates.

26. *Leonard v. School Committee of Attleboro,* 349 Mass. 704 [704–10] (Supreme Judicial Court of Massachusetts, 1965).

27. *Ferrell v. Dallas Independent School District,* 261 F. Supp. 545 [546–47] (United States District Court for the Northern District of Texas, Dallas Division, 1966).

28. Ibid., [549].

29. Ibid., [547].

30. Ibid., [547–48].

31. *Ferrell v. Dallas Independent School District,* 392 F.2d 697 [700–01] (United States Court of Appeals, 1968).

32. Ibid., [703].

33. Ibid., [706].

34. *Davis v. Firment,* 269 F. Supp. 524 [528] (United States District Court for the Eastern District of Louisiana, 1967).

35. *Breen v. Kahl,* 296 F. Supp. 702 [705–09] (United States District Court for the Western District of Wisconsin, 1969). Footnotes omitted.

36. *Breen v. Kahl,* 419 F.2d. 1034 [1037–38] (United States Court of Appeals, Seventh Circuit, 1969).

37. Ibid., [1039–40].

38. *Brick v. Board of Education,* 305 F. Supp. 1316 [1318–19] (United States District Court, Colorado, 1969).

39. *Montalvo v. Madera Unified School District Board of Education et al.,* 21 Cal. App. 3d 323 [336] (Court of Appeals of California, Fifth Appellate District, 1971).

40. *Stevenson v. Wheeler County Board of Education,* 306 F. Supp. 97 [98] (United States District Court for the Southern District of Georgia, Dublin Division, 1969).

41. Ibid., [99], [101].

42. *Stevenson v. Board of Education of Wheeler County,* 426 F.2d 1154 [1156] (United States Court of Appeals, Fifth Circuit, 1970).

43. *Scott v. Board of Education, Union Free School District,* 61 Misc. 2d 333 [337–38] (Supreme Court of New York, Special Term, Nassau County, 1969).

44. This was evidence of one of the ways a court climate could influence school practices: in reaction to what was going on in courtrooms around the nation, many schools rewrote rules to avoid future legal action.

45. *Thomas et al. v. Board of Education, Granville Central School District et al.,* 607 F.2d 1043 [1045] (United States Court of Appeals, Second Circuit, 1979).

46. Ibid.

47. Ibid., [1046].

48. Ibid.

49. Ibid., [1051–52]. Footnotes omitted.

50. Refer to Figure 3.4.

51. *Dodd v. Rambis,* 535 F. Supp. 23 [25] (United States District Court, Southern District of Indiana, 1981).

52. Ibid., [30–31].

53. *Schaill v. Tippecanoe County School Corporation,* 864 F.2d 1309 [1324] (United States Court of Appeals, Seventh Circuit, 1988).

54. *Scott L. v. State of Nevada,* 104 Nev. 419 [421–22] (Supreme Court of Nevada, 1988).

55. *Consolidated School District Number 2 v. Art King,* 786 S.W.2d 217 [220] (Court of Appeals of Missouri, Western District, 1990).

56. *In the Matter of Ronald B. (Anonymous),* 61 A.D.2d 204 [207] (Supreme Court of New York, Appellate Division, 1978).

57. Ibid., [210].

58. Hamilton County Circuit Court (Juvenile Division), 1969, Edward F. New Jr., Judge. Cited in *Warner v. State of Indiana,* 254 Ind. 209 [216–17] (Supreme Court of Indiana, 1970).

59. *Warner v. State of Indiana,* [217].

60. Ibid., [215].

61. *C.J. v. School Board of Broward County,* 438 So.2d 87 [88] (Court of Appeals of Florida, Fourth District, 1983).

62. Ibid.

63. *Manico v. South Colonie Central School District,* 153 Misc.2d 1008 [1009] (Supreme Court of New York, Albany County, 1992).

64. Ibid., [1015–16].

65. Courts generally defined long-term exclusion as any removal involving more than ten days.

66. *Lee v. Macon County Board of Education,* 490 F.2d 458 [460] (United States Court of Appeals, Fifth Circuit, 1974).

67. *C.L.S. v. Hoover Board of Education,* 594 So.2d 138 [139] (Court of Civil Appeals of Alabama, 1991).

68. Ibid.

69. *Dillon v Pulaski County Special School District et al.,* 468 F. Supp. 54 [55–56] (United States District Court, Eastern District of Arkansas, 1978).

70. Ibid., [58].

71. *Gonzales v. McEuen,* 435 F. Supp. 460 [467] (United States District Court for the Central District of California, 1977).

72. *Kelly v. Martin,* 490 P.2d 836 [840] (Court of Appeals, Arizona, 1971).

73. *Petrey vs. Flaugher,* 505 F. Supp. 1087 [1091–92] (United States District Court, Eastern Division of Kentucky, 1981). Footnotes omitted.

74. Refer to Figure 2.2c.

75. See Paul Weckstein, *School Discipline and Student Rights: An Advocate's Manual* (Cambridge, MA: Center for Law and Education, 1982); and Robert Pressman

and Susan Weinstein, *Procedural Due Process Rights in Student Discipline: An Update and Revision of the Procedural Due Process Section of School Discipline and Student Rights by Paul Weckstein* (Cambridge, MA: Center for Law and Education, 1990).

76. *Hamer v. Board of Education of Township High School,* 66 Ill. App. 3d 7 [9] (Appellate Court of Illinois, 1978).

77. Ibid., [11].

78. Ibid.

79. *Rhodus v. Dumiller,* 552 F. Supp. 425 [425] (United States District Court for the Middle District of Louisiana, 1982).

4. From the Bench to the Paddle

1. See, for example, Seymour Sarason, *Revisiting "The Culture of the School and the Problem of Social Change"* (New York: Teachers College Press, 1996); and Karl Weick, "Educational Organizations as Loosely Coupled Systems," *Administrative Science Quarterly* 21 (1976): 1–19.

2. Ellen Jane Hollingsworth, Henry Lufler, and William Clune, *School Discipline: Order and Autonomy* (New York: Praeger, 1984), 124–126.

3. Ibid., 62–64.

4. Gerald Grant, *The World We Created at Hamilton High* (Cambridge, MA: Harvard University Press, 1988), 56.

5. Hollingsworth, Lufler, and Clune, *School Discipline,* 126.

6. "Keep Your School Out of Trouble," solicitation to one-year subscription of *School Discipline Law Bulletin,* Fall 2000 (Boston: Quinlan Publishing Group, 2000).

7. August 2000 solicitation for the *Trust for Insuring Educators,* Forrest T. Jones and Company, Group Insurance Administrator; and additional information found on their website, <www.ftj.com/2000/probabilityplans.asp>.

8. Henry Lufler, "Discipline: A New Look at an Old Problem," *Phi Delta Kappan* 6 (1978): 18.

9. Michael Sedlak et al., *Selling Students Short: Classroom Bargains and Academic Reform in the American Highschool* (New York: Teacher's College Press, 1986), 89.

10. See Henry Lufler "Courts and School Discipline Policies" in Oliver Moles, ed., *Student Discipline Strategies* (New York: State University of New York Press, 1990), 197–212.

11. It is for this reason—to stimulate future social scientific research—that we have provided such detailed methodological tables on our data and analyses.

12. Richard Arum is currently collaborating with Lauren Edelman, Calvin Morrill, and Karolyn Tyson on organizing a multisite school study that will attempt to address this data limitation.

13. These sources included the Department of Education's Common Core of Data, U.S. Census reports, and information on religious membership affiliations from Mary Bernstein, "Sexual Orientation Policy, Protest, and the State" (Ph.D. diss., New York University, 1997).

14. Only student expulsion was particularly likely to receive court sanction, and this outcome was tied to the expansion of federal case law in the *Goss v. Lopez* Supreme Court case. Expulsions were often overturned, whereas corporal punishment was usually not, as a result of the particularities of case law.

15. John Sutton, Frank Dobbin, John Meyer, and Richard Scott, "The Legalization of the Workplace," *American Journal of Sociology* 99 (1994): 944–971.

16. Gerald Rosenberg, *The Hollow Hope: Can Courts Bring About Social Change?* (Chicago: University of Chicago Press), 338.

17. Since the number of possible factors is infinite, one is never able to respond fully to an "omitted variable bias" critique. Thus, in assessing the merits of social scientific work relying on observational data, one must consider whether a *plausible* set of alternative factors has been examined. We believe our research employs such a set of controls throughout.

18. We formulated this influence following the methods prescribed by Mary Bernstein; see "Sexual Orientation Policy, Protest and the State."

19. When possible, we have attempted to employ our controls at the individual, school, or neighborhood level rather than at the state level, because such a methodology typically has a greater ability to explain observed variance.

20. District of Columbia Public Schools Board of Education, *Rules of the Board of Education;* chapter 4, section 423.

21. Michel Foucault, *Discipline and Punish: The Birth of the Prison* (New York: Random House, 1995 [1977]).

22. Pierre Bourdieu, *Distinctions: A Social Critique of the Judgment of Taste* (Cambridge, MA: Harvard University Press, 1979).

23. In the final two chapters we will discuss the negative effects on students of the use of "authoritarian discipline" and disciplinary practices that were considered by students as particularly "strict." One can speculate that corporal punishment potentially fits this definition.

24. *Ingraham v. Wright,* 430 U.S. 651 (Supreme Court of the United States, 1977).

25. Nevada Revised Statutes 392–465.

26. Corporal punishment should be distinguished from another practice referred to as "corporal restraint." Corporal restraint is the use of force aimed at preventing either damage to property or some kind of physical injury to oneself or others in their care. Even those states that have forbidden the use of corporal punishment include a clause in their disciplinary statutes explaining the right of school personnel to defend themselves if they (or someone else) is attacked by a student. New Jersey, one of the earliest states to abandon corporal punishment, was explicit in spelling out the difference between punishment

and restraint. Corporal restraint included using necessary amounts of force to "quell a disturbance," "to gain possession of weapons or other dangerous objects held by a pupil," "for the purpose of self defense," and "for the protection of persons or property."

27. American Academy of Pediatrics website, <http://www.aap.org/advocacy/corpchrt.html>.
28. Office of Civil Rights, 1994 data.
29. Cave City Public Schools website, <http://www.cavecityschools.com/ccps/high/handbook.html>.
30. Jackson County School District website, <http://www.datasync.com/sme.toc.html>.
31. Mobile County Public School System website, <http://www.mcpss.com/conduct/conspe.html>.
32. Ibid.
33. Ibid.
34. Aztec Municipal Schools website, <http://www.aztecschools.com/student/sect_06.html>.
35. Mobile County Public School System website.
36. Indianapolis Public Schools website, <http://www.ips.k12.in.us/policies/corporalpunishment.html>.
37. Cave City Public Schools website.
38. Aztec Municipal Schools website.
39. Connecticut General Statutes 53A-18.
40. Pennsylvania Regulations and Guidelines on Student Rights and Responsibilities, Section 12.5.
41. Cave City Public Schools website.
42. Ashland City School District website, <http://www.ashland-city.k12.oh.us/ahs/docs/handbook.html>.
43. See Table 4.D for results.
44. The values on the percentage of pro-school court decisions discussed in the text are at +2 and −2 standard deviations (roughly 68 percent of the observations in a distribution tend to fall between +1 and −1 standard deviations; roughly 96 percent of observations in a distribution typically occur between +2 and −2 standard deviations). The actual incidence of corporal punishment in state elementary schools was probably double these figures, since corporal punishment was practiced largely in elementary schools, but the rates used for this analysis consider both elementary and secondary students in a state in the denominator.
45. See Table 4.D.
46. See Table 4.E for results.
47. See Table 4.E.

48. See Table 4.F.

49. On isomorphic pressures in organizations see Paul DiMaggio and Walter Powell, "The Iron Cage Revisited: Institutional Isomorphism and Collective Rationality in Organizational Fields," *American Sociological Review* 48 (1983): 147–160. Application of this approach to educational research was discussed in the review essay by Richard Arum, "Schools and Communities: Ecological and Institutional Dimensions," *Annual Review of Sociology* 26 (2000): 395–418.

50. We also modeled the rate of corporal punishment in school districts that were surveyed by the Office of Civil Rights in 1992 (see Table 4.D). The districts were not randomly selected, and thus the relevant test for statistical significance is unidentifiable. The results, however, suggested that pro-school court climates were related to rates of corporal punishment in the 1992 public school districts that appeared in the data.

51. Governing Magazine, "Illinois Part of Trend Against Spanking Pupils," *St. Louis Post-Dispatch*, 19 September 1993, sec. C, p. 5.

52. Carol Kreck, "Spare the Rod," *Denver Post*, 28 April 1994, sec. E, p. 1.

53. Mary Jordan, "Instead of a Hit, Sinatra; Teachers Try 'Creative Detention'" as Discipline," *Washington Post*, February 7, 1993, sec. A, p. 1.

54. Mark Acosta, "School Changes Disciplinary Step after Complaint," *Press-Enterprise* (Riverside, CA), 27 July 1996, sec. B, p. 1.

55. Nannette Asimov, "Spanking Debate Hits Assembly GOP-Backed Bill on Student Discipline to Be Considered Today," *San Francisco Chronicle*, 30 January 1996, sec. A, p. 1.

56. Karina Bland, "Becoming Thing of Past; Many Districts, Private Schools Ban Such Punishment," *Phoenix Gazette*, 31 March 1995, sec. A, p. 16.

57. See, for example, John Meyer, "The Effects of Education as an Institution," *American Journal of Sociology*, 83 (July 1977): 55–77; and DiMaggio and Powell, "The Iron Cage Revisited."

58. Asimov, "Spanking Debate," A1; Examiner News Services, "Bill to Allow Spanking in Schools Loses in Assembly," *San Francisco Examiner*, 31 January 1996, sec. A, p. 10.

59. Examiner News Services, "Bill to Allow Spanking," A10.

60. Ibid.

61. "Politics of Paddling," editorial, *San Francisco Chronicle*, 30 January 1996, sec. A, p. 14.

62. Eric Bailey, "Conroy Files Bill to Allow the Paddling of Students Legislation: The Orange County Lawmaker's Proposal is Designed to Undo a 1986 Ban on Corporal Punishment," *Los Angeles Times*, Orange Country Edition, 10 January 1995, p. 1.

63. Robert Gunnison, "Assemblyman Calls for Paddling," *San Francisco Chronicle*, 10 January 1996, sec. A, p. 14.

64. Dana Wilkies, "School Spanking Bill Beaten in Assembly," *San Diego Union Tribune*, 31 January 1996, sec. A, p. 1.

65. American Academy of Pediatrics website, <http://www.aap.org/advocacy/corpchrt.html>.

66. Doug Finke, "House Denies Three Controversial Waiver Requests," *State Journal-Register* (Illinois), 15 November 1995, sec. A, p. 20.

67. Jeffrey Solochek, "Merits of Paddling Thrashed Out by a 3-to-1 Margin: Concerned Residents Tell the School Board Don't Touch the Children," *Sarasota Herald-Tribune*, 18 February 1998, sec. B, p. 1. Emphasis in original.

68. See Table 4.H, Column 1.

69. North Dakota is an exception here, but this is most likely a statistical artifact produced by the low number of school administrators surveyed in that state.

70. Grant, *Hamilton High*, 54–55.

71. Hollingsworth, Lufler, and Clune, *School Discipline*, 93–94.

72. Actual response options are "strongly agree," "agree," "disagree," "strongly disagree."

73. See Table 4.H, Columns 2 and 3.

74. See Table 4.J for results.

75. Grant, *Hamilton High*, 53.

76. Sara Lawrence Lightfoot, *The Good High School: Portraits of Character and Culture* (New York: Basic Books, 1983), 345.

77. As reported in Grant, *Hamilton High*, 59. Peter Clark spent a year of participant observation at Hamilton High in 1971–72, and kept in touch with developments at the school until he completed his work in 1977.

78. The 1990 strictness prompt's possible response categories were "strongly agree," "agree," "disagree," "strongly disagree." The 1980 categories were that strictness of discipline was "poor," "fair," "good," or "excellent."

79. See Table 4.H, Column 4.

80. Defined as the top two response categories.

81. Hollingsworth, Lufler, and Clune, *School Discipline*, 56.

82. The 1990 fairness prompt was similar to the 1990 strictness prompt in that possible responses were "strongly agree," "agree," "disagree," "strongly disagree." The 1980 fairness prompt was similar to the 1980 strictness prompt ("poor," "fair," "good," "excellent").

83. Mary Metz, *Classrooms and Corridors: The Crisis of Authority in Desegregated Secondary Schools* (Berkeley: University of California Press, 1978), 140.

84. Karolyn Tyson, *Framing Difference: Deviance vs. Diversity and the Consequences and Implications for Black Students* (unpublished manuscript, 1997), 39.

85. Grant, *Hamilton High*, 39. Research cited from James Coleman, Thomas Hoffer, and Sally Kilgore, *Public and Private High Schools* (Chicago: National Opinion Research Center, 1981), 119–121.

86. See Appendices 4.K and 4.L.

87. See Table 4.H, Columns 5 and 6.

88. We do not believe this to be a statistical artifact produced by using different data sets, since we do not find this same pattern with regards to strictness (the South was the strictest region during both time periods).

89. Evidence of this is suggested in examining the student data more closely by region. Twelve percent of students in New England public schools in 1980 used the lowest category available to describe the strictness of school discipline as compared to only 3 percent in 1990 (8 percent of students from Southern public schools in 1980 and 4 percent in 1990 chose the lowest category). Students adopting this low strictness category were also the most likely to report the lowest category of fairness. Examining the highest category for strictness also demonstrates the regional character of this pattern. Eighteen percent of students in Southern public schools in 1980 reported the highest category for strictness as compared to 23 percent by 1990 (9 percent of students in New England public schools adopted this category in 1980 and 12 percent in 1990). For African-American students in the Deep South, reports of strictness were even higher. In 1980, 25 percent reported the highest category of strictness; by 1990, 29 percent did.

90. For expansion of employee rights see Sutton et al., "The Legalization of the Workplace"; Frank Dobbin and John Sutton, "The Strength of a Weak State: The Rights Revolution and the Rise of Human Resources Management Divisions," *American Journal of Sociology* 104 (1998): 441–76; Lauren Edelman, "Legal Environments and Organizational Governance: The Expansion of Due Process Rights in the American Workplace," *American Journal of Sociology* 95 (1990): 1401–40; Lauren Edelman, "Legal Ambiguity and Symbolic Structures: Organizational Mediation of Civil Rights Law," *American Journal of Sociology* 97 (1992): 1531–76; and Robert Nelson and William Bridges, *Legalizing Gender Inequality: Courts, Markets and Unequal Pay for Women in America* (New York: Cambridge University Press, 1999). On the expansion of legalization in schools see Grant, *Hamilton High;* Hollingsworth, Luffler, and Clune, *School Discipline;* and David Kirp and Donald Jenson, eds., *School Days, Rule Days: The Legalization and Regulation of Education* (Philadelphia: Falmer Press, 1986). An interesting intellectual bridge between these two literatures is John Meyer and Brian Rowan, "Institutionalized Organizations: Formal Structure as Myth and Ceremony," *American Journal of Sociology* 83 (1977): 340–363.

91. Exceptions to this are Erin Kelly and Frank Dobbin, "Civil Rights Law at Work: Sex Discrimination and the Rise of Maternity Leave Policies," *American Journal of Sociology* 105 (1999): 455–492; and Doug Guthrie and Louise Marie Roth, "The State, Courts, and Maternity Leave Policies in U.S. Organizations:

Specifying Institutional Mechanisms," *American Sociological Review* 64 (1999): 41–63.

5. School Discipline and Youth Socialization

1. Tom DiPrete, Chandra Muller, and Nona Shaeffer, *Discipline and Order in American High Schools* (Washington, D.C.: National Center for Education Statistics, 1981).
2. Coleman argued that better behavior in private schools was the result of higher rates of intergenerational connections and closures in private school communities (social capital). From our perspective, the difference in disciplinary climates was more likely the result of the difference in the legal environment that public and private schools face. Private schools were more easily able to expel unruly students and in general enforce stricter disciplinary practices with fewer threats to the legitimacy of their actions. See James Coleman and Thomas Hoffer, *Public and Private High Schools: The Impact of Communities* (New York: Basic Books, 1987). For a critique of their findings, see Karl Alexander and Aaron Pallas, "School Sector and Cognitive Performance: When Is a Little a Little?," *Sociology of Education* 58 (1985): 115–128.
3. David Myers, Ann Milne, Keith Baker, and Alan Ginsburg, "Student Discipline and High School Performance," *Sociology of Education* 60 (1987): 18–33.
4. Paul Barton, Richard Coley, and Harold Wenglinsky, *Order in the Classroom* (Princeton: Educational Testing Service, 1998).
5. Wayne Welsh, Patricia Jenkins, and Jack Greene, *Building a Culture and Climate of Safety in Public Schools in Philadelphia: School-Based Management and Violence Reduction* (Philadelphia: Center for Public Policy, 1997), 105. See also Wayne Welsh, Jack Greene, and Patricia Jenkins, "School Disorder: The Influence of Individual, Institutional, and Community Factors," *Criminology* 37 (1999): 73–115.
6. See, for example, Pedro Noguera, "Listen First: How Student Perspectives on Violence Can Be Used to Create Safer Schools," in Valerie Polakow, ed., *The Public Assault on America's Children: Poverty, Violence, and Juvenile Injustice* (New York: Teachers College Press, 2000); and Pedro Noguera, "Preventing and Producing Violence: A Critical Analysis of Responses to School Violence," *Harvard Educational Review* 62 (1992).
7. James Davison Hunter, *The Death of Character: Moral Education in an Age Without Good or Evil* (New York: Basic Books, 2000), 177. On the ascent of a therapeutic professional class and ideology, see also Pierre Bourdieu, *Distinctions: A Social Critique of the Judgment of Taste* (New York: Routledge, 1984), ch. 6.

8. B. F. Skinner, *The Technology of Teaching* (New York: Appleton Century-Croft, 1968), 187.

9. Ibid., 188.

10. Dreikurs and many classroom management theorists would disavow any direct influence of Skinner and behavior modification in their work. Nevertheless, the influence, if not directly acknowledged, was still usually quite pronounced. See Rudolf Dreikurs and L. A. Gray, *A New Approach to Classroom Management, Logical Consequences* (New York: Harper and Row, 1968).

11. John Dewey, *Lectures in the Philosophy of Education: 1899,* ed. Reginald Archambault (New York: Random House, 1966), 123–124.

12. John Dewey, *Democracy and Education: An Introduction to the Philosophy of Education* (New York: Free Press, 1944 [1916]), 87.

13. John Dewey, "My Pedagogic Creed," in Reginald Archambault, ed., *John Dewey on Education* (Chicago: University of Chicago Press, 1964), 432.

14. Jean Piaget, *The Moral Judgment of the Child* (New York: Free Press, 1997), 356.

15. Ibid., 362.

16. Dewey maintained an appreciation for the extent to which discipline might still be required. See the following passage from *Democracy and Education* (p. 27): "In some cases it is well to permit him to experiment, and to discover the consequences for himself in order that he may act intelligently next time under similar circumstances. But some courses or action are too discommoding and obnoxious to others to allow of this course being pursued. Direct disapproval is now resorted to. Shaming, ridicule, disfavor, rebuke, and punishment are used. Or contrary tendencies in the child are appealed to divert him from his troublesome line of behavior. His sensitivities to approbation, his hope of winning favor by an agreeable act, are made use of to induce action in another direction."

17. Piaget, *The Moral Judgment,* 364–366.

18. Carl Rodgers, *On Becoming a Person* (Boston: Houghton Mifflin, 1961).

19. Lawrence Kohlberg, "Stages of Moral Development," in Clive Beck, Brian Crittenden, and Edmund Sullivan, eds., *Moral Education: Interdisciplinary Approaches* (Toronto: University of Toronto Press, 1971), 27.

20. Lawrence Kohlberg, foreword to Joseph Reimer, Diana Pritchard Paolito, and Richerd Hersh, eds., *Promoting Moral Growth: From Piaget to Kohlberg* (New York: Longman, 1983), xiv–xv.

21. Lawrence Kohlberg, "High School Democracy and Educating for a Just Society," in Ralph Mosher, ed., *Moral Education: A First Generation of Research and Development* (New York: Praeger, 1980), 35.

22. Ibid., 47–48.

23. Ibid.

24. See Hunter, *Death of Character.*

25. Michael Schudson, *The Good Citizen: A History of American Civic Life* (New York: Free Press, 1998).

26. Christopher Hurn, "Changes in Authority Relationships in Schools," *Research in Sociology of Education and Socialization* 5 (1985): 31–57; 49.

27. See Tom R. Tyler, *Why People Obey the Law* (New Haven: Yale University Press, 1990).

28. Ellen Jane Hollingsworth, Henry Lufler, and William Clune, *School Discipline: Order and Autonomy* (New York: Praeger, 1984), 59–60.

29. Emile Durkheim, *Moral Education: A Study in the Theory and Application of the Sociology of Education* (New York: Macmillan, 1973 [1925]), 168.

30. Philip Jackson, *Life in Classrooms* (New York: Teachers College Press, 1980), 29.

31. Durkheim, *Moral Education,* 175.

32. See Richard Arum and Irenee Beattie, "High School Experience and the Risk of Incarceration," *Criminology* 37 (1999): 515–539; and Richard Arum, "Education and Crime," in Joshua Dressler, ed., *Encyclopedia of Crime and Justice* (New York: Macmillan Publishers, 2002).

33. More intimately structured settings would allow for greater opportunities for social integration. Participation in school life would lead to the emergence of collectively shared representations and sentiments that would facilitate collective social bonding and the development of mechanistic solidarity. This, of course, is not to suggest that larger organizational units might not be capable of generating sentiments related to organic forms of solidarity if curricular offerings and social roles were better differentiated.

34. Philip Jackson, Robert Boostrom, and David Hansen, *The Moral Life of Schools* (San Francisco: Jossey Bass, 1993), xii.

35. See, for example, the work of Henry Giroux, Stanley Arronowitz, and Michael Apple.

36. One indicator of how liberal pedagogical orientations and working-class parental aspirations were often at odds was suggested by public opinion survey results identifying support for the use of corporal punishment in the schools. Working-class and African-American citizens were more likely than their counterparts to support such practices, net of religious affiliation; see Harold Grasmick, Carolyn Stout Morgan, and Mary Baldwin Kennedy, "Support for Corporal Punishment in Schools: A Comparison of the Effects of Socioeconomic Status and Religion," *Social Science Quarterly* 73 (1992): 177–187.

37. The survey questions ask students to evaluate the strictness of the school rules and the fairness of school discipline. The mean response for perception of strictness was 2.63. On a scale of 1 to 4, these results indicate a tendency toward strictness.

38. We are generally more comfortable relying on less subjective reports than the

type of measures used here (i.e. individual perceptions of school disciplinary climates. Current data limitations in attempting to examine our research subject require such reliance at present; we are hoping in the future to organize and stimulate more social scientific measurement of the phenomena examined inadequately here.

39. Lyric Wallwork Winik, "Students Want More Discipline, Disruptive Students Out," *American Educator* 20 (Fall 1996): 12–14.

40. Administrators were asked whether their schools regulated student dress, required hall passes, closed school grounds, and prohibited smoking. Each affirmative response was counted as one rule for a possible range of zero to four school rules. The majority of schools in the sample, 64%, had at least three of the four rules; only 7% of the schools had one or less.

41. Broadly construed, school climates have been shown to influence school disorder (Welsh). We were interested in how school climates might have an effect on individual student outcomes. By aggregating individual perceptions within the same school, we identified school-level fairness and strictness variables.

42. The number of school rules had a significant impact on only two student outcomes examined: test scores and high school graduation. Effects were opposite of what strict discipline advocates would anticipate. Students from schools with higher number of rules tended to have lower test scores and were actually less likely to graduate from high school. The predicted chance of graduation for students who went to schools with no rules (student dress, smoking, hall passes, and closed campus) was 91%, while for students who attended schools who had rules in all of these areas it was 79%. Student test scores decreased .03 of a standard deviation for every extra school rule. We considered earlier the possibility that increasing the number of school rules might have a positive effect up to a certain level; subsequent additions would have a negative influence on student outcomes. There was no evidence of such a curvilinear relationship. The results suggested that the implementation of school rules did not have much of an effect on student outcomes, and when we did find an effect, such as in the case of test scores and likelihood of graduation, it was a harmful one.

43. Our results suggest that feeling safe in school has a positive influence on all behavior and academic achievement outcomes with the exception of classroom disruption (and perhaps high school graduation, where the results were only marginally significant). We found variation in the effects of safety by gender. Feeling safe was more important for female students' academic achievement, and more important for male students' behavior. Feeling safe had a significant influence on both test scores and grades for female students, and had a significant influence, although not as strong as the effect for females, on male students' grades. Feeling safe also had a significant effect on arrests for male stu-

dents, and a larger significant effect on in school fighting for male students than for female students.

44. Eleven percent of the students in our sample did not feel safe in their schools.

45. There has been some disagreement as to the nature of the relationship between achievement and misbehavior. While research shows a clear relationship between the two, the direction of causation has been ambiguous. Some scholars have argued that it is misbehavior that causes students to perform poorly in school. Others have argued that it is school failure that leads to misbehavior. Our analysis does not directly speak to this debate. Instead we are interested in something that can theoretically precede both misbehavior and academic achievement: school disciplinary practices. Therefore, we have included both behavior and achievement as possible outcomes dependent on prior school rules and student perceptions of school discipline.

46. This time lag also reduces the possibility that reverse-causation is a serious problem in our analysis.

47. At the individual level, we controlled for gender, race (African-American and Hispanic), two-parent family, tenth-grade test score, academic track, siblings, socioeconomic status (a composite measure of mother's education, father's education, family income, father's occupational status (Duncan S.E.I score), and non-English language home.

48. The inclusion of tenth-grade test scores helps to establish that it was not earlier academic experiences that fueled later academic outcomes, and in effect changes the interpretation of the regression on twelfth-grade test scores to a modeling of change in test scores between tenth and twelfth grade. Prior research has also shown that poor academic achievement may precede delinquent behavior and negative attitudes toward school. Including tenth-grade test scores also helped to reduce the possibility that it was earlier academic performance that was generating our results and not school disciplinary practices. As expected, tenth-grade test scores had a strong and significant influence on most of the outcome variables. Only for attitudes about disobeying rules was there no significant effect. Not surprisingly, the strongest effects were for academic achievement outcomes. Many of the same reasons why students performed the way they did on tenth-grade tests were still present and influenced their academic performance two or more years down the line.

49. At the school level, we controlled for rural/urban/suburban location, school size, student-teacher ratio, racial composition of students (percent African-American and percent Hispanic), percent of students in poverty, average of surveyed students socioeconomic status score, dropout rate, and racial composition of teachers (percent African-American and percent Hispanic). School characteristics also influenced student outcomes. The racial and economic composition of the student population in the school also mattered for student

outcomes. Attending schools with higher percentages of ethnic minorities reduced the odds of graduating.

50. Individual background effects were in the expected direction. A two-parent family, higher socioeconomic status, and fewer siblings were associated with higher academic achievement. Parental ability to provide social and economic resources facilitated educational achievement. Family background also influenced some behavioral outcomes. Having fewer siblings was associated with higher educational commitment. Also, being in a two-parent family reduced the probability of arrest, which may be linked to higher levels of supervision.

51. Our findings related to race were generally consistent with previous work that has suggested African-American students have more positive attitudes toward school. When compared to whites, African-American respondents have higher educational commitment. Also supported in the education literature, race was associated with lower test scores but higher likelihood of graduation, net of other background and school factors. Latinos, however, did not fare as well when compared to whites; although they had a higher likelihood of high school graduation, they performed worse on test scores and grades and lower on educational commitment. This was after taking into consideration whether English was usually spoken in the home as well as other differences in social background and school settings. Interestingly, while conventional accounts of immigrant disadvantage have often suggested that children who speak English as a second language have been handicapped in school, our analysis suggests that living in a household in which another language was usually spoken was at times an asset, net of confounding influences. Speaking another language in the home was associated with higher grades and a lower likelihood of expressing a willingness to disobey school rules. We speculate that this academic advantage may be due in part to a more traditional approach to authority.

52. Our results were also consistent with previous research on gender. Males were more likely to engage in antisocial behaviors and attitudes and have lower grades and graduation rates. Male students performed better on standardized tests, especially ones that include significant components assessing mathematical skills (as the ones here).

53. Unfortunately, not all of these variables were included on the *High School and Beyond Survey*. Questions about fighting, disruptive behavior, and attitudes about disobeying rules were asked only on the *National Educational Longitudinal Survey*. Consequently, the analyses for these outcome variables are only performed on the student sample experiencing high school in the early 1990s.

54. Figures in this chapter present results for illustrative purposes based on several assumptions: 1) all variables other than strictness and fairness are held at their mean-level; 2) as individual level strictness and fairness move from one to four, aggregate school level strictness and fairness move in a generally similar

manner from −0.38 to 0.31 standard deviations on strictness and −0.48 to 0.65 standard deviations on fairness (the average level of school discipline reported by students with these perceptions); and 3) covariation in strictness and fairness does not affect results other than with respect to an explicit interaction modeled.

55. John Devine, *Maximum Security: The Culture of Violence in Inner-City Schools* (Chicago: University of Chicago Press, 1996), 42.

56. The description of the event also suggests the degree to which perceptions of general court climates have a much greater influence on the behavior of school actors than actual case law. It would be difficult to find any statutory or case law that would support the specific apprehensions of the security guards.

57. See Table 5.C.

58. See Table 5.D.

59. See Table 5.E.

60. Bruce Wilson and H. Dickson Corbett, *Listening to Urban Kids: School Reform and the Teachers They Want* (New York: State University of New York Press, 2001), 36–37.

61. See Table 5.E.

62. See Table 5.F. The effects of track placement are particularly high, given track mobility and measurement in tenth grade of this concept. For better estimates of how high school vocational coursework affects likelihood of graduation, see Richard Arum, "The Effects of Resources on Vocational Student Educational Outcomes: Invested Dollars or Diverted Dreams," *Sociology of Education* 71 (1998): 130–151.

63. See, for example, Christopher Jencks and Meredith Phillips, eds., *The Black-White Test Score Gap* (Washington, D.C.: Brookings Institution Press, 1998).

64. 26.5% of African-Americans compared to 19.4% of whites report being in these types of school settings.

65. Models were run separately for students based on the strictness*fairness perception interaction. Models included all covariates reported in Table 5.G with the exception of other school and student level disciplinary measures. Results in these models for the African-American coefficient (standard deviation) and N of model were as follows: strict*fair-1, −0.171 (0.102), N=515; strict*fair-2, −0.169 (0.051), N=1,663; strict*fair-3, −0.194 (0.054), N= 1,416; strict*fair-4, −0.196 (0.036), N=1,449; strict*fair-6, −0.054 (0.024), N=6,920; strict*fair-8, −0.118 (0.053), N=1,179; strict*fair-9, −0.070 (0.028), N=5,068; strict*fair-12, -0.109 (0.043), N=1,708; strict*fair-16, 0.046 (0.108), N=269. Figure 5.6 represents these coefficients with a scatter-plot of data points; the line in the figure is fitted with a third-order polynomial function.

66. Mary Metz, *Classrooms and Corridors: The Crisis of Authority in Desegregated Secondary Schools* (Berkeley: University of California Press, 1978), 136.

67. For ethnographic examples of this research, see work by Paul Willis or John Ogbu. For related survey research, see Arthur Stinchombe, *Rebellion in a High School* (Chicago: Quadrangle Books, 1965) or Travis Hirschi, *Causes of Delinquency* (Berkeley: University of California Press, 1969).

68. See Table 5.I.

69. Devine, *Maximum Security,* 110. For similar findings related to acculturation of Asian immigrants in California, see the work of Min Zhou.

70. Noguera, "Listen First," 145.

71. Durkheim, *Moral Education,* 152–154.

6. Restoring Moral Authority

1. Ernest Boyer, *High School: A Report on Secondary Education in America* (New York: Harper and Row, 1983), 160.

2. John Devine, *Maximum Security: The Culture of Violence in Inner-City Schools* (Chicago: University of Chicago Press, 1996), 109.

3. See, for example, Patricia Graham, *SOS: Sustain Our Schools* (New York: Hill and Wang, 1992); and Barry O'Neill, "The History of a Hoax," *New York Times Magazine,* 6 March 1994, 46–50.

4. National Educational Association, "Teacher Opinion on Pupil Behavior, 1955–1956," *Research Bulletin of the National Educational Association* 34 (1956). Cited in Robert Rubel, *The Unruly School* (New York: D.C. Heath, 1977).

5. Paul Barton, Richard Coley, and Harold Wenglinsky, *Order in the Classroom: Violence, Discipline and Student Achievement* (Princeton: Educational Testing Service, 1998); and National Center of Educational Statistics, *Indicators of School Crime and Safety, 2000* (Washington, D.C.: Government Printing Office, 2000).

6. National Center of Educational Statistics, *Indicators 2000.*

7. Devine, *Maximum Security,* 40.

8. Eric Hartwig and Gary Ruesch, *Discipline in the School* (Horsham, PA: LRP Publications, 1994), vi–x.

9. Lawrence Friedman notes: "'Student rights cases in the nineteenth century usually had little to do with the feelings of students. Overwhelmingly the rights of *parents* were at issue." Lawrence Friedman, "Limited Monarchy: The Rise and Fall of Student Rights," in David Kirp and Donald Jenson, eds., *School Days, Rule Days: The Legalization and Regulation of Education* (Philadelphia: Falmer Press, 1986), 239. Emphasis in original.

10. James Coleman, Sally Kilgore, and Tom Hoffer, *High School Achievement: Public, Catholic and Private Schools Compared* (New York: Basic Books, 1982), 189.

11. Peter Cookson, "Reformers and Revolutionaries: The Drama of Deregulation," in Peter Cookson, *School Choice: The Struggle for the Soul of American Education* (New Haven: Yale University Press; 1994).

12. John Chubb and Terry Moe, *Politics, Markets, and America's Schools* (Washington, D.C.: Brookings Institution, 1990), 66.

13. This distinction, of course, is not meant to ignore the extent to which the judicial system is political, and that legislative and executive braches of government make and enforce law.

14. Chubb and Moe, *Politics, Markets, and America's Schools,* 38.

15. James Davison Hunter, *The Death of Character: Moral Education in an Age Without Good or Evil* (New York: Basic Books, 2000), 210.

16. Ibid., 118.

17. On the ineffectiveness of approaches similar to these, see review of the empirical research found in ibid., 152 and notes.

18. Toby Jackson, "Getting Serious about School Discipline," *The Public Interest* 133 (Fall 1998): 78–79.

19. Advancement Project and Civil Rights Project at Harvard University, *Opportunities Suspended: The Devastating Consequences of Zero Tolerance and School Discipline* (Washington, D.C.: Advancement Project, 2000), 14.

20. Travis Hirschi, *Causes of Delinquency* (Berkeley: University of California Press, 1969), 110.

21. See Richard Arum and Irenee Beattie, "High School Experience and the Risk of Incarceration," *Criminology* 37 (1999): 515–539; and Richard Arum, "Education and Crime," in Joshua Dressler, ed., *Encyclopedia of Crime and Justice* (New York: Macmillan, forthcoming).

22. See Gary Gottfredson and Denise Gottfredson, *Victimization in Schools* (New York: Plenum Press, 1985).

23. Pedro Noguera, "Finding Safety Where We Least Expect It: The Role of Social Capital in Preventing School Violence," in William Ayers, Bernadine Dohrn, and Rick Ayers, eds., *Zero Tolerance: Resisting the Drive for Punishment in Our Schools* (New York: New Press, 2001), 209.

24. See, in particular, Emile Durkheim, *Suicide* (New York: Free Press, 1951); Hirschi, *Causes of Delinquency;* and James Coleman and Thomas Hoffer, *Public and Private High Schools: The Impact of Communities* (New York: Basic Books, 1987).

25. James Wilson and George Kelling, "The Police and Neighborhood Safety: Broken Windows," *The Atlantic Monthly* 249 (March 1982): 31.

26. Pedro Noguera, "Finding Safety."

27. Emile Durkheim, *Moral Education: A Study in the Theory and Application of the Sociology of Education* (New York: Macmillan, 1973 [1925]), 167.

28. Bernard Harcourt, *Illusion of Order: The False Promise of Broken Windows Policing* (Cambridge: Harvard University Press, 2001), 140.

29. See, for example, Pierre Bourdieu, *The Logic of Practice* (Palo Alto, CA: Stanford University Press, 1990 [1980]); Michel Foucault, *Discipline and Punish: The Birth of the Prison* (New York: Vintage Books, 1979 [1975]); and David

Garland, *Punishment and Modern Society* (Chicago: University of Chicago Press, 1990).

30. Harcourt, *Illusion of Order,* 243.

31. See, for example, Jon Saphier and Robert Gower, *The Skillful Teacher* (Carlisle, MA: Research for Better Teaching, 1987 [1979]), 77–168.

32. See, for example, James Rosenbaum, *Beyond College for All: Career Paths for the Forgotten Half* (New York: Russell Sage Foundation, 2001).

33. Reported to Richard Arum by a student observer of a Tucson Unified Public School classroom.

34. Jay Heubert and Robert Hauser, eds., *High Stakes: Testing for Tracking, Promotion and Graduation* (Washington, D.C.: National Academy Press, 1999).

35. For discussion of the criminological concept of "drift," see David Matza, *Delinquency and Drift* (New York: Wiley, 1964).

36. Boyer, *High School,* 121–22.

37. John Dewey, "The School and Society," in Reginald Archambault, ed., *John Dewey on Education* (Chicago: University of Chicago Press, 1964 [1899]), 302.

38. See, for example, Richard Arum and Irenee Beattie, "High School Experience and the Risk of Incarceration," *Criminology* 37 (1999): 515–539; and Richard Arum, "The Effects of Resources on Vocational Student Educational Outcomes: Invested Dollars or Diverted Dreams," *Sociology of Education* 71 (1998): 130–151.

39. See David Kirp, "Proceduralism and Bureacracy: Due Process in the School Setting," *Stanford Law Review* 28 (1976): 838–876. After serving as founding director of the Center for Law and Education responsible for the precedent setting *Goss v. Lopez* case, Kirp had by then moved to the School of Public Policy at Berkeley. The article provides quite early, sophisticated treatment of the limitations and potential pitfalls of the litigation.

40. This is not to argue that lower aggregate spending is inevitably associated with these reforms; rather, the effects are related to complex political processes. For examination of this complex issue see Douglas Reed, *On Equal Terms: The Constitutional Politics of Educational Opportunity* (Princeton: University of Princeton Press, 2001); Molly McUsic, "The Law's Role in the Distribution of Education: The Promises and Pitfalls of School Finance Litigation," in Jay Heubert, ed., *Law and School Reform* (New Haven: Yale University Press, 1999), 88–159; W. N. Evans, S. E. Murray and R. M. Schwab, "Schoolhouses, Courthouses, and Statehouses after *Serrano,*" *Journal of Policy Analysis and Management* 16 (1997): 10–31; Caroline Hoxby, "Are Efficiency and Equity on School Finance Substitutes or Complements," *Journal of Economic Perspectives* 10 (1996): 51–72; and S. E. Murray, W. E. Evans, and R. M. Schwab, "Education-Finance Reform and the Distribution of Education Resources," *American Economics Review* 88 (1998): 789–812.

41. See, for example, Gerald Rosenberg, *The Hollow Hope: Can Courts Bring About*

Social Change? (Chicago: University of Chicago Press, 1991); Gary Orfield, Susan Eaton, and the Harvard Project on School Desegregation, *Dismantling Desegregation: The Quiet Reversal of Brown v. Board of Education* (New York: New Press, 1996); Gary Orfield, "Conservative Activists and the Rush Towards Resegregation," in Heubert, ed., *Law and School Reform,* 39–87; Jennifer Hochschild, *The New American Dilemma: Liberal Democracy and School Desegregation* (New Haven: Yale University Press, 1984).

42. Eric Hanushek and Steven Rivkin, "Understanding the Twentieth-Century Growth in U.S. School Spending," *Journal of Human Resources* 32 (1996): 35–68; David Neal and David Kirp, "The Allure of Legalization Reconsidered: The Case of Special Education," in Kirp and Jensen, eds., *School Days, Rule Days,* 343–367; Thomas Hehir and Sue Gamm, "Special Education: From Legalism to Collaboration," in Heubert, ed., *Law and School Reform,* 205–243.

43. See, for example, *Dixon v. Alabama State Board of Education,* 294 F.2d 150 (United State Court of Appeals, Fifth Circuit, 1961); *Voight v. Van Buren Public Schools,* 306 F. Supp. 1388 [1394–1396] (United States District Court for the Eastern District of Michigan, Southern Division, 1969); *Williams v. Dade County School Board,* 441 F.2d 299 (United States Court of Appeals, Fifth Circuit, 1971).

44. *In re Gault,* 387 U.S. 1 (Supreme Court of the United States, 1967).

45. *Goss v. Lopez,* 419 U.S. 565 (Supreme Court of the United States, 1975).

46. *Ingraham v. Wright,* 430 U.S. 651 (Supreme Court of the United States, 1977).

47. "Rudimentary" due process rights in *Goss v. Lopez* (as in many of the early case law decisions affecting educational law in this area) were in fact extended to a case that involved First Amendment rights.

48. See Paul Barton, "Unequal Learning Environments: Discipline That Works," in Richard Kahlenberg, ed., *A Notion at Risk: Preserving Public Education as an Engine for Social Mobility* (New York: Century Foundation Press, 2000), 223–250; and Barton, Coley, and Wenglinsky, *Order in the Classroom.*

49. Legal advocacy groups may at times contribute to promoting these widespread understandings. See, for example, the ACLU website, "Have Questions about Your Rights in School? Ask Sybil Liberty," <http://www.aclu.org/students/sybil.html>. Information on the site includes such statements as: "Students of color have been suspended at much higher rates than white students, according to the Federal Office of Civil Rights statistics, and students have been discriminated against based on their religion, national origins, gender and other factors. THIS IS ILLEGAL." Conflating racially disproportionate outcomes with racially discriminatory practices does not help to provide greater legal clarity and inform the citizenry in these matters.

50. *Goss v. Lopez.*

51. DiMaggio and Powell have discussed this process by reference to coercive,

normative, and mimetic pressures producing institutional isomorphism. John Meyer has discussed the cultural and normative dimensions related to the spread of legalization in our society.

52. U.S. Department of Education, *Digest of Education Statistics, 2000* (Washington, D.C.: Government Printing Office, 2000), Table 68: Teachers in public and private elementary and secondary schools, by selected characteristics: 1993–94, and Table 85: Principals in public and private elementary and secondary schools, by selected characteristics: 1993–94.

53. John Meyer, "Organizational Factors Affecting Legalization in Education," in Kirp and Jenson, eds., *School Days, Rule Days.*

54. Gary Orfield and John Yun, *Resegregation in American Schools* (Cambridge, MA: Harvard Civil Rights Project, 1999).

55. Eric Slater, "Illinois Students' Expulsions Are Upheld By Federal Judge," *Los Angeles Times,* 12 January 2000, sec. A, p. 5. Jesse Jackson also suggested that it was "very apparent" that the students were given harsher penalties because of their race. Dirk Johnson, "Judge Set to Rule on Youths Expelled Over Illinois Fight," *New York Times,* 3 January 2000, sec. A, p. 12. Legal representation for the students noted that the six expelled students were African-American as were twelve out of thirteen students expelled the previous year by the district. John Dixon, "Decatur's school chief defends decision in court; Students expelled for safety, he says," *Chicago Sun Times,* 28 December 1999, p. 24.

56. "Police say gang dispute led to student brawl," *Milwaukee Journal Sentinel,* 3 December 1999, p. 10. William Clairborne, "In Decatur, Jackson Finds Latest Crusade; Some See Activism, Others Opportunism in Battle at School," *Washington Post,* 21 November 1999, sec. A, p. 3. Dirk Johnson, "Seven Students Charged in a Brawl That Divides Decatur, Illinois," *New York Times,* 10 November 1999, sec. A, p. 19.

57. Eric Slater, "Illinois Students' Expulsions."

58. Dirk Johnson, "Court Upholds Suspensions." The Decatur public schools also reportedly faced a thirty million dollar student suit for revealing confidential information from the students' records to the press. John Leo, "Instigator in Decatur," *U.S. News and World Report,* 29 November 1999, 15.

59. Dirk Johnson, "Court Upholds Suspensions."

60. Durkheim, *Moral Education,* 154.

Index

Achievement, 1–2, 33–34, 126, 160, 170, 172, 187
Adams v. City of Dothan Board of Education (1986), 23–24
Administrators, 5, 13–14, 24, 46–47, 64, 72, 74, 83–84, 87, 127, 132, 144, 148–49, 163, 167, 170, 189, 194–95, 198, 207, 209, 212
Adversarial legalism, 5–7, 12–14, 67, 201–02
Age, 232, 241
Alabama, 23, 24, 97, 120, 139, 142
Alaska, 136
Alcohol, 22–24, 57–59, 113–14, 123, 165–66, 218, 220, 222, 224, 226
American Civil Liberties Union (ACLU), 7, 19, 50, 63–64, 80, 97, 126
American Friends Service Committee, 18
Amici curiae, 19, 63, 206
Appellate court cases, 87, 91, 94–126, 203, 210, 217, 221, 247
Arizona, 122, 136, 145
Arkansas, 60, 64, 99, 121, 138, 140–42
Arrest, 3, 33–35, 184–85, 248, 250, 275–77
Authoritarian discipline, 132–33, 156, 159–63, 187, 192, 195, 207–09

Bamberger, Clinton, 8
Bennett, William, 193
Berliner, David, 1–2
Bethel School District v. Fraser (1986), 75
Biddle, Bruce, 1–2
Bill of Rights, 80; First Amendment, 18–22, 51, 57–61, 72, 75–79, 89, 100–13, 185, 203–07, 212–13; Fourth Amendment

(search and seizure), 21, 72–74, 79, 115; Eighth Amendment (cruel and unusual punishment), 69–70, 79, 136, 139, 147
Black-white test gap, 179–81, 210
Board of Education of Rogers, Arkansas v. McCluskey (1982), 71
Boland, Paula, 146
Bourdieu, Pierre, 135, 198
Breen v. Kahl (1969), 81–82, 86, 104–07
Brick v. Board of Education (1969), 107
Broken Windows approach, 196–97
Brown v. Board of Education (1954), 7, 10, 27, 96

C. J. v. School Board of Broward County (1983), 117–18
C. L. S. v. Hoover Board of Education (1991), 120
California, 26, 29, 47, 91, 136, 144–47, 182, 197
Carey v. Piphus (1978), 70–71
Carnegie Corporation, 7
Case law, 45–46, 127–28, 135–36, 193, 202, 212–13
Center for Law and Education (Harvard University), 9–10, 14, 18, 26, 39, 67, 79, 124
Child-centered approaches, 163–67
Children's Defense Fund, 8, 19, 63, 80, 126
Chubb, John, 28, 192–93
Civil Rights Act (1964), 11, 27
Civil Rights Movement, 6, 57
Clark, Peter, 152

315

Virginia, 24, 136
Vocational training, 34–35, 199–200
Vouchers, 92, 192
Vulnerability of school community, 23–25

Waller, Willard, 188
Warner v. State of Indiana (1970), 116–17
War on Poverty, 8, 10–11, 50
Washington (state), 75, 136
Washington, D.C., 144
Weapons, 3, 22, 25, 58–59, 109, 114–18,
    120, 190, 206, 218, 220, 222, 224, 226
Weber, Max, 167
Weckstein, Paul, 26
Western states, 89–91, 148, 217, 219, 221,
    223, 225

West Virginia, 136, 206–07
White flight, 201, 211
Wilson, Bruce, 177
Wisconsin, 30, 104–07, 127, 136, 150, 167,
    191
Wood v. Strickland (1975), 64–67, 70
Woods v. Wright (1964), 97–98

Youth culture, 4, 6, 125, 194
Youth rights. *See* Student rights
Yudof, Mark, 67

Zero-tolerance, 161, 186, 192, 194–95, 206–
    07, 209, 211–12, 214